America's Natural Treasures

America's Natural Treasures

NATIONAL NATURE MONUMENTS AND SEASHORES

Stewart L. Udall

Published by

COUNTRY BEAUTIFUL CORPORATION

Waukesha, Wisconsin

COUNTRY BEAUTIFUL: *Publisher and Editorial Director:* Michael P. Dineen; *Executive Editor:* Robert L. Polley; *Senior Editors:* Kenneth L. Schmitz, James H. Robb; *Art Director:* Hugh Boettcher; *Associate Editors:* John M. Nuhn, D'Arlyn Marks, Dorothy Deer; *Contributing Editor:* Jerry Fetterolf; *Production Manager:* Donna Griesemer; *Circulation Manager:* Trudy Schnittka; *Editorial Secretary:* Darcy Davies; *Production:* Sally Maahs.

Country Beautiful Corporation is a wholly owned subsidary of Flick-Reedy Corporation:*President:* Frank Flick;*Vice President and General Manager:* Michael P. Dineen;*Treasurer and Secretary:* August Caamano.

ACKNOWLEDGMENTS

The Author and Editors wish to express gratitude to the following for helping make this book possible: to all the National Park Service superintendents and personnel, the National Wildlife Refuge managers, and the U. S. Forest Service personnel; to Edwin N. Winge, John Vosburgh, Fred Bell, Mrs. Rose Hubers, Bruce Miller, Robert L. Burns and Roger J. Rogers of the National Park Service; to Luther Goldman and Mrs. Beatrice Boone of the Bureau of Sport Fisheries and Wildlife; and to M. James Stevens.

Frontispiece: The rocky ground and colorful wildflowers of Capitol Reef National Monument are typical of the natural wonders preserved within America's parklands. (Photo by James Fain)

CONTENTS

Arches

Utah

The Colorado Plateau contains the most colorful, varied, sculptured land on the face of the earth, and Arches is one of its masterpieces. In this 137-square-mile national monument in southeastern Utah, sedimentary rock, formed in lakes and floods before the memory of man, has been shaped gloriously by the carving tools of wind-blown sand, frost and moisture. The result is a superb display of eroded formations that together form a collection of stone arches, windows, spires and pinnacles unequalled in this country.

Established in 1929, the size of Arches National Monument doubled in 1969 when President Lyndon B. Johnson signed an enlargement proclamation. Inside the monument are eighty-eight natural arches carved from Entrada sandstone, layered above the hues of Navajo and Carmel sandstone formations.

These huge sandstone masterpieces, formed near the confluence of the Green and Colorado rivers, are surrounded by picturesque canyons, tall, snow-capped mountains in the distance, and an azure desert sky floating above the red, yellow, buff and brown layers of time-worn rock. Elemental forces have produced beautiful land forms in a surprising number of ways. Giant monoliths tower above all else. Balanced rocks teeter unbraced on fragile pedestals and daring arches symmetrically connect the cliffsides.

Perhaps the most fascinating of these arches is Landscape Arch. Thought to be the longest natural span in the world, it is 291 feet across and towers to a height of 120 feet, with the smallest point in the arch now eroded to less than six feet in diameter. Another spectacular accident of erosion produced Twin Arch, composed of two identical holes drilled through the sheer faces of a cliff.

Other splendid natural arches in all stages of erosion may be seen in the monument with rock strata standing out in bold colors. These Jurassic Age formations begin near the valley floors with the Navajo Formation

Perhaps the world's longest erosion-sculpted span is Landscape Arch (above), drawn out 291 feet across Utah's red-rock country in Arches National Monument. **Opposite:** *"Park Avenue," as the mile-long Entrada sandstone walls are named, is a series of thin, vertical fins weathered to appear like a great city skyline.*

A red monolith (above) towers about 100 feet
above a plain of stunted Utah or desert juniper and
pinyon pines which together form a pygmy forest.

Right: Double Arch displays twin bows, a perfor-
ated fin and a pothole formation, and is located
in the Windows section, an area ideal for studying the rock strata which stand out in bold relief,
showing a general rock matrix 40 million years old.

11

The famous Balanced Rock rises from a sandstone region which began as a vast coastal desert that hardened into rock, was uplifted and twisted, then slowly eroded to its current state.

sweeping upward in a rounded, sloping mass of light-colored sandstone. In this area, the Navajo Formation has become pock-marked allowing enough silt to accumulate for rooting juniper trees, which seem to grow from solid rock.

Above the Navajo is the Carmel Formation, identified by its thin strata of red and bands of wavy sedimentation. The Carmel Formation wears away easily and this erosion is responsible for some of the spectacular features within the monument. Above the Carmel is the layer of Entrada sandstone where most of the arches have been formed. The dominant Entrada is a massive three-hundred-foot-thick, orange-red sandstone that originated as wind-deposited sand.

The basic shapes of these rocks are created naturally through the freezing and thawing of moisture which has seeped into vertical cracks in the sandstone formations. Pressure of freezing water causes slabs to fall from the sheer sides of the cliffs until eventually a single vertical slab of resistant rock remains -- a formation known as a fin. These slabs, in turn, are carved into windows, arches, monoliths, coves, caves and towers in constantly changing patterns.

A length of these eroded vertical slabs near the south end of the monument, looking like rugged spires, reminded early visitors of a city skyline -- hence the name for the mile-long series of towers called Park Avenue. Other resistant patches of rock in the Courthouse Towers area, called monoliths, have assumed recognizable shapes and are named the Three Gossips, Sheep Rock and Organ Rock. One striking outcrop is called the Tower of Babel.

The prodigious power of nature is evident at Balanced Rock where a magnificent Entrada boulder caps a puny pedestal of Carmel Formation, apparently in defiance of the laws of gravity. This, the most famous balanced rock in the monument, is 128 feet high and weighs as much as 1,600 automobiles.

The full splendor of Arches National Monument is best appreciated by hiking. Delicate Arch, for example, which has become the principal symbol of the monument, can be seen in the distance from a turnout near Garden of Eden. But a drive up an unimproved road to Turnbow Cabin, followed by a mile hike to the arch itself, provides a magnificent close-up view of this splendid work of erosion and a series of "slickrock" shapes beyond.

Late afternoon is the best time for a look at the Fiery Furnace area, just north of Salt Valley. A westering sun turns this entire area into a red, glowing mass of odd-shaped slabs etched from the age-old layers of sandstone from a forgotten era. This section, only recently explored, is near Devil's Garden where a jumble of fantastic shapes in sheer cliffs justifies the name.

The shifting angles of sunlight through the day cause

On top of a queerly eroded mesa, the remote Delicate Arch is unsurpassed in the monument for its color, gracefulness and its setting among cliffs and huge domes.

Young

*To the northwest is Tunnel Arch in Devil's
Garden, a section also containing Landscape Arch
as well as parts so rugged they are yet unexplored.*

Fain

A morning sun brightens sandstone pinnacles towering into a dark sky.

captivating changes in the appearance of some of the monoliths as light and shadow play across the texture of the rock faces. Erosion still causes a constant change in the cliff walls and sandstone facings. Occasional rockfalls occur when a formation splits under the forces of freezing, thawing and gravity, and add variety to the appearance of the valley floor. A spectacular rockfall that took place in 1962 in the Windows section provides a special point of interest.

Lovely lakes and aspen glades in the northern portions of the La Sal Mountains outside the monument provide contrast with the red rocks of the valley. On the stark escarpments in the monument, stunted Utah juniper and pinyon-pine forest communities furnish most of the larger vegetation. Indians used these trees to make medicinal preparations and rope and used the bark for making sandals and matting. A special variety of plants, including ferns, columbine and orchids, are found around springs and areas of seepage. This lack of vegetation means there are few birds; yet mammals and reptiles do survive. Deer, foxes, coyotes and snakes are rarely seen, but white-tailed kangaroo rats, ground squirrels, rabbits and lizards are relatively common.

A visitor center at the southern entrance, not far from Moab, Utah -- the gateway city of this monument -- provides maps and descriptions of the formations as well as biological information on wildlife and plants. A picnic and campground area is located within the monument.

The profusion of massive erosion sculptures varies with time of day and season, but Arches National Monument from end to end and beyond offers a lesson in humility as one contrasts the ephemeral works of man with the works of nature.

15

Badlands

South Dakota

The erosion-scarred landscape of Badlands National Monument has the eerie look of a city that was designed, and later deserted, by a mad architect. The land between the Cheyenne and White rivers in southwestern South Dakota is austere and harsh. Sheer cliffs and jagged peaks form skylines of fantastic shapes.

The Dakota Indians and neighboring tribes called this barren land *mako sica,* meaning "land bad," because it was an area of hardship for travelers. Early French-Canadian trappers appropriately termed it *les mauvaises terres a traverser,* "bad lands to travel across." Settlers later called it simply the Badlands, a name applied later to similar eroded areas in many sections of the country.

Jedediah Smith, perhaps the first white man to visit the area, led a party across the Badlands in 1823. His group noted the absence of potable water, for the few streams are thick with white mud.

Explorers and pioneers ignored the inhospitable Badlands region from the time of Smith's journey until 1846 when Dr. Hiram A. Prout of St. Louis published an account of a fossilized jawbone of a Titanothere found in the Badlands, followed a year later by a report of a fossilized camel described by Dr. Joseph Leidy. Dr. Leidy became an authority on Badlands fossils and by 1869 had inspected fossilized remains of more than five hundred ruminating pigs, called Oreodonts, as well as many other now extinct animals that lived twenty-five to forty million years ago.

Early fossil hunters carried away petrified remains by the wagonload. Scientists feared the supply would soon be exhausted, but each new rain unearths new fossils and geologists now believe that as long as the Badlands remain, erosion will continue to uncover them. By far the most common mammalian fossil specimens found are those of the Oreodonts, which chewed cud although they had skeletons similar to a pig. One of the most famous fossils in the world, that of a mother Oreodont and her unborn twins, has been on display in the South Dakota School of Mines and Technology in Rapid City since 1928.

NPS

16

Constant flux is the only certainty in the Badlands of South Dakota where erosion repatterns the land each generation.

Tributaries of the White River and occasional torrential storms tear at the soft, sedimentary layers of siltstone, leaving sawtoothed ridges (above) rising on a plain of whitish mudflats.

The black-footed ferret (below), one of the rarest mammals in the Western Hemisphere, if not the world, has been sighted in the prairie dog towns of the Badlands. A true weasel in habit and appearance, this bold, nocturnal hunter's existence depends now on the diminishing food supply of prairie dogs.

The largest fossils unearthed are those of the Titanothere, a rhinoceros-like animal slightly smaller than today's elephants. These creatures have been extinct for more than thirty million years. Turtle shells, the most common fossil, show that turtles have remained largely unchanged for perhaps 200 million years. Fossilized remains of prehistoric horses, camels, giant pigs, saber-toothed tigers and other members of the ancient cat family have also been found here.

A unique method for preserving and displaying fossils is utilized by the monument's scientists. They carefully brush the soil from around a fossil and cover it with a transparent domelike shield, thus protecting the fossil and allowing it to be viewed in its natural setting.

Bison, bear, elk, white-tailed and mule deer, pronghorns, Audubon bighorn sheep, gray wolves and beaver were originally native to the area and once plentiful. But the invasion of settlers, hunters and trappers in the late nineteenth century caused a serious reduction of wildlife populations. In 1919 a game investigator reported that inquiries at farms and ranches of the area revealed the fact that not even a coyote had been seen or heard in the Badlands for more than a year.

In an effort to help restore wildlife patterns, the National Park Service reintroduced bighorn and bison into the monument in the early 1960's. Rocky Mountain bighorn sheep were settled there, but difficulties were such that five years later the flock numbered only ten. Bison, on the other hand, adapted readily to their old haunts after being brought back in 1963. The original herd of fifty-three tripled in number in just five years. The bison often can be seen from Sage Creek Rim Road and other places in the grassland areas of the monument.

Because of wildlife preservation, chipmunks, prairie dogs, porcupines, and other rodents are now present, as well as rabbits, skunks, raccoons, badgers, pronghorns, deer and bobcats. On rare occasions red foxes, minks, elk and mountain lions are seen. There are also a few black-footed ferrets, a beautiful small animal now on the national list of rare and endangered species. Ferrets are attractive creatures about the size and shape of minks with a white face and black "mask" across their eyes. They are elusive and during the day they usually stay below ground in prairie dog holes, occasionally coming out to sun themselves. At night they are quite active hunting prairie dogs, their principal source of food. It is the severe decline of this food source, primarily attributable to an extensive poisoning program by government agencies, that threatens the ferret. This poisoning is unnecessary, and if the black-footed ferret survives it will be because this national monument is a wildlife refuge where no poisons are permitted.

The Badlands is a harsh and inhospitable environment for all plants because moisture is scarce and rainfall sometimes runs off without soaking into the ground. High temperatures in summer and relatively cold temperatures in winter also limit plant life.

Nonetheless, some three hundred kinds of plants grow here. Although cliffsides and peaks are barren

A few members of the pine family find footing among the pinnacles and spires (above), though grasses are the main ground cover.

Distinctive black markings on his huge six-to-seven-inch ears identify the black-tailed jackrabbit (right), whose length may reach 21 inches.

because erosion tears out most plants attempting to root, about half of the monument surfaces are covered with carpets of grass, cactus and other growth.

The light-colored sediments that compose the Badlands were washed in by flooding ancient rivers. This material is now being washed away continually by the White, Cheyenne and Badlands rivers whose waters show thick white sediments, particularly after rains or winter snow melts. This erosion has made the giant mud flat into a jumble of milky waterways constantly reshaped and redirected.

Rocks in the monument are largely mudstones and siltstones so closely compacted they look and feel like stone, although they dissolve in water. Occasional outcrops of resistant sandstone and some thin layers of limestone are found. Nodules and lumps resembling concrete appear in some formations laid down millions of years ago.

The delicately colored saw-edged succession of hundreds of spires and peaks in an unvegetated zone from Cedar Pass to Sage Creek is called the Wall. It divides the upper (northern) grasslands from those on the lower (southern) side. Average elevation difference be-

19

Parching sun glints off the white layers of fragmented material deposited by ancient volcanic activity to the west.

low these spectacular pinnacles is about two hundred feet. In Cedar Pass and Castle Butte areas, the Wall towers up to 150 feet above the upper grasslands and as much as 450 feet over the lower area.

Sometime in the past several hundred years, a wide part of the towering cliff near Cedar Pass broke loose, slumping down and away from the foot of the cliff. The formerly horizontal layers were split, crushed, tilted and dumped atop each other, disrupting the normal drainage pattern. This type of disturbed area is called a slump, and this particular slump is named Cliff Shelf.

Holes, pits and even seasonal ponds formed as a result of rains and melting snows seeking outlets through the tumbled clay and rocks. Deep pits, located only a few yards south of the Cliff Shelf Nature Trail, are a dramatic illustration of the drastic erosion taking place through slumps. Because of the scrambled formations and the resulting interruption of former drainage canals, moisture is now trapped in the area and creates conditions favorable for the lush growth of grass, shrubs and trees.

Faults -- cracks in the earth's crust -- intensify the foreboding Badlands aura. Many of these are visible between Cedar Pass and Norbeck Pass further west. The alternating bands of dark and light sedimentation

are broken and exposed making these faults easily recognizable. Most of this faulting has resulted in vertical movement of only a few feet, but near Dillon Pass the fault is up to forty-nine feet high.

Homesteaders had occupied only half of the Badlands by 1922 and drought caused most of them to leave in the 1930's. The state legislature petitioned the Federal Government to make the area a national park as early as 1909. But it was not until 1939 that President Franklin D. Roosevelt established Badlands National Monument.

Campgrounds, picnic areas and visitor centers are near most points of the monument while private lodgings and camp areas are plentiful in nearby communities. During rainy weather, mud is adhesive and hard to drive on, but many roads are paved. Days are hot in summer but nights are cool and most winter days are warm enough for short hikes.

"Here today, gone tomorrow," has a literal application in this peculiar area of raw and arid landscape called the Badlands, where erosion by wind, water and winter storm holds full sway; some peaks lose height at rates of up to six inches a year. Mudslides, new erosions, slumps and changed drainage patterns continue to tear away the surfaces of this changing region.

Miller

A keen sense of hearing, aggressive hunting habits and
general hyperactivity are characteristic of the long-tailed weasel
(above), which is notably slender and has a thick, soft coat.

Prickly pear is a widespread cactus species in the U. S. Its
flowers are large, with yellow petals and many stamens; the red, sweet
and juicy fruit is edible if the barbed hairs are removed from the exterior.

NPS

Rough coral-rock shores (above) in Biscayne monument stretch among waters submerging a tropical preserve which, seen from aerial perspective (below left), appears as a vast marine meadow. Biscayne is a nursery for reef and pelagic fish as well as for corals, shells, crabs and other varieties (below).

Biscayne

Florida

Wild bird calls and the splash of marine life are the only interruptions to the peaceful silence of the narrow, low-lying islands and barrier reefs of the upper Florida Keys. The higher ground of these keys, nine or ten feet above the tidal marshes, has rare Sargent palms, as well as mahoganies and dense mangrove thickets. This subtropical forest area, in combination with the bay-ocean habitat, supports ecological communities unique in the Western Hemisphere.

Here in the northern limits of living coral reefs along United States coasts -- protected at last by national park conservation practices -- small numbers of the rare and endangered North American crocodiles may still maintain haunts in the quiet waters. Land mammals, although few, include the opossum, raccoon and the red-bellied squirrel, a creature introduced here from central Mexico. The rare manatee (sea cow) and bottle-nosed dolphin share the waters surrounding the keys with the many colorful and varied fish. Although seabirds and shorebirds are common, this locale is also the northernmost breeding area for several species of rare West Indian land birds.

Biscayne National Monument, one of the newest national monuments, contains about 4,200 acres of uplands and more than 92,000 acres of submerged reefs. Located a few miles south of Miami, this combination of barrier islands, coral reefs and coastal waters sets aside a section of the Florida Keys to remain unspoiled for all time.

Elliott Key, Adams Key, Old Rhodes Key and Sands Key form an almost continuous island barrier bisecting the submerged areas of the monument. The submerged lands form two broad, divided habitats. On the Biscayne Bay side, the bottom is a deposit of marl mud and marine grasses. The shallow bank areas and dense grassy meadows here are an extremely important East Coast breeding and hatching grounds for at least 250 kinds of marine game and food fish.

Underwater terrain on the Atlantic Ocean side of the islands is more variable with the bottom gradually deepening to the edge of the rubble reefs. On this sea side, turtle grass grows in the warm shallows. The rocky limestone outcroppings, bottom shoals, coral, coralline algae and marine grasses support an extremely rich and varied tropical marine biota. The ecosystems here are so fragile that any distinct major disturbance by man would damage them irreparably.

The entire area of the monument, including the broad tidal meadows, provides shelter for deep sea fish as well as amphibian and terrestrial creatures. Many types of coral, sea grasses, shellfish, crabs, starfish and sponges can be observed in their natural habitat.

Although this area has been near a well-traveled sector of the Atlantic Coast since the beginning of European occupation, and in earlier times by Indians, it remains relatively undisturbed. Relics of the boisterous era of Spanish galleons, loaded to the gunwales with gold bullion, and English sea rovers searching the seas for the loot lie rotting in these reefs. Several ship hulks, wrecked on these treacherous shoals, are within the monument boundaries.

To the south, John Pennekamp Coral Reef State Park provides a splendid extension to the monument. Homestead Bayfront Park, set aside on the mainland side of the bay in Dade County, complements the monument, and a short distance inland is the entrance to Everglades National Park. Within the monument itself is ninety-acre Elliott Key Park with boat docks and a marina. No other facilities are now available, although general development and land acquisition has begun. The State of Florida has provided an eighty-acre site for the National Park Service visitor center and other monument facilities on the mainland, but completion dates have not been set.

Yet the peace and solitude of these isles can be shared with birds, fish and wildlife visible in sudden flashes of bright color. The brilliant green subtropical forests lend a feeling of tranquillity, making this a remarkable barrier reef preserved as a national treasure.

Weber

Black Canyon of the Gunnison

Colorado

From the rim, this gigantic slash in the mountains of southwestern Colorado appears like the jagged jaws of some natural cataclysm. The Gunnison River has carved forbidding rock walls that rise almost perpendicular for more than two thousand feet above the river's surface as it slices its way from high in the Rocky Mountains to its confluence with the Colorado River.

A mist frequently hangs over the river, and the sun, even in summer, strikes the bottom of the dark, tortuous gorge for only a few minutes each day. Here and there, the towering walls have zig-zag patterns of white where molten rock has pushed its way into the formations. Huge, angular slabs of rock lying in the river attest to the continual collapse of the walls.

A feeling of wildness and uncontrolled power pervades this cleft between the Uncompahgre and West Elk mountains. Fifty miles in total length, the canyon's most spectacular section is within the boundaries of Black Canyon of the Gunnison National Monument,

proclaimed by President Herbert Hoover in 1933.

The monument sector of the river has walls as close as 1,300 feet and as wide as 3,300 feet at the rim. Narrowest point in the gorge bottom is about 40 feet. The erosive force necessary to channel this deep path through solid rock formations can be partially conceived in hearing the roar from the depths. Occasionally sounds of rock slides add a reverberation to the din.

From either the north or the south rim, the geologic story of the river becomes plain. Gentle slopes above the gorge prove a much wider, slower river once flowed here. Sediments show these upper layers are 180 million years old. However, as the level of the area rose during an upthrust, the river -- already in its earlier channel -- had no choice but to cut through the hard core strata beneath its former bed.

The rock in the walls is mostly crystalline-textured granite in which feldspar, quartz and mica form an intricate tracery. The various formations are stained

Above: Among the vegetation on the canyon's rim, Indian paintbrush colors the mountain cover with its scarlet-tipped bracts.

Short

Black Canyon winters slightly modify the wild depths of the Gunnison River's gorge in western Colorado with snowy layers of white scattered on the underlying dark walls and ledges.

black and streaked by the elements, thus the name Black Canyon.

The Painted Wall area in the western end of the monument shows how eroding water, channeling its way through bedrock that is uniform and unbroken, leaves nearly smooth, vertical cliffs. But dramatic differences occur upstream in the fractured areas where "block" islands and pinnacles have been left. In this area, differential weathering has caused the softer sectors of the rock to be eroded away, leaving the harder parts standing clear of the walls.

The Gunnison River eroded through the rock more rapidly than its tributaries, leaving many side valleys literally "hanging" high above the river surface. Since the tributaries lacked the sustained flow and steep incline of the Gunnison, the valley facing at the Gunnison juncture gradually was shorn off. A few of these tributary valleys, however, extend to the valley floor.

Some spear points ten thousand years old were discovered in the Uncompahgre Valley, and ancient pictographs and petroglyphs are seen in other nearby valleys. These findings lead archeologists to believe the area was once the home of ancient Indians. But by the time the first non-Indian explorers came, only small numbers of Ute Indians roamed this region.

The first modern history of the canyon originated with Juan Maris de Rivera, who visited the area under orders from the Spanish governor in 1765. Eleven years later, two Franciscan priests tried a trip down the river but gave up. In 1853, after the area became U. S. territory, Captain John W. Gunnison came looking for a

likely railroad route. He shied away from close exploration of the canyon, but put his name to the river.

Finally, in 1881, a Denver and Rio Grande Western railroad engineer, Byron H. Bryant, led a small party through the canyon. He wrote later, "It was like feeling one's way blindfolded through an interminable Inferno."

His party found that the bare walls above the narrow confines of the river channel amplified sound so harshly that the noise of the water and the sound of the

While the black folds of the canyon walls appear to envelop the Gunnison River below, sunlight on the rim outlines stands of aged pinyon, juniper and flowering shrubs.

falling rocks were nearly unbearable. Midway in the length of the chasm, they discovered that their greatest danger was from falling rocks and landslides. Huge slabs of rock were balanced precariously the length of the canyon, they reported, and any sudden sound would cause them to tumble down to the bottom of the gorge. They found the sound of an avalanche either nearby or far away to be a blood-chilling, fearful experience.

Two decades later, a two-man team traveled down this canyon in the only other recorded tour, even today, of its dangerous, dismal length. A. L. Fellows of the Bureau of Reclamation and W. W. Torrence, his guide, were looking for a likely spot to dig a tunnel to release some of the river's life-giving water into the plains nearby. Although the two men found a spot for their irrigation tunnel, which was completed in 1909 and is outside of the monument, they very nearly did not get out alive to tell about it:

> The river at the bottom is icy, wild and raging, filled with rocks and sucks like no other river I have ever seen [Fellows wrote later]. There are only two hours a day, at best, when vision is unimpaired. During the afternoon the canyon fills with a chilling mist that doesn't dissipate entirely until sunshine time the next day -- and if it be a cloudy day, the mist stays on.

Both plant life and animals in this wilderness are intensely interesting. Deer and smaller kinds of wildlife are often seen and cougar, bear, bobcat, fox and coyote exist here in small numbers. Amphibians, many lizards and birds, including both golden and bald eagles, also inhabit the region.

Trees top the rimrock with a mantle of green despite the more than eight-thousand-foot altitude. Pinyon-juniper forests give way at the upper levels to a remarkable stand of rugged and ancient pinyon pines. In 1940 borings indicated that the ages of these patriarchs ranged from 550 to 750 years. During autumn a landscape of bright color prevails at Black Canyon. Gambel oak and mountain mahogany turn scarlet, and groves of aspen and willow mix in their fluttering yellows. Even the dark pine, spruce and the walls of the canyon seem to be bright under the blue Colorado sky. Sun glistens on the blacks, pinks, reds and whites of the granite cliffs. Even in winter, snow, contrasting with the colors of the cliffs, clings to every protrusion of rock.

Eight miles of scenic drives, plus hiking trails and numerous overlooks on both rims, provide ample opportunity to view this panorama. A ranger station and campground are maintained on each rim. Access to the 13,176-acre monument is sometimes limited by heavy snowfalls in winter.

The folds and veins of Black Canyon's walls vary in thickness, texture, color and direction from vertical to horizontal. Formations are bent and arched like a gigantic web, cut by the roaring fury of the Gunnison River charging through the chasm below.

Maslowski

Common to the canyon and entire Southwest is the small gray fox (above), peculiar for his ability to climb trees and to evade pursuit.

The whites, pinks, reds and blacks of the sheer granite canyon walls (below) are streaked with flakes of mica and veins of pastel feldspar and quartz.

Hyde

27

Buck Island Reef

Virgin Islands

A coral city in a turquoise world of tropical sunlight and quiet shadows populated by colorful, incredibly varied forms of marine life is one description of the horseshoe-shaped barrier reef called Buck Island. The living coral, just beneath the ocean surface only a few yards offshore, forms a lagoon of quiet waters reflecting the humpbacked reaches of Buck Island itself. These underwater reefs and their amazing array of fish life make it a tropical underwater wilderness that is unsurpassed in the Caribbean.

Sea water, washing softly across the reef, freshens the lagoon constantly and maintains its salinity and crystal clearness. The uninhabited island maintains the lushness of tropical isles and has been kept free from the pollution of mankind. This minute piece of land, one and one-half miles northeast of St. Croix, Virgin Islands, is part of the bulwark chain of islands between the Caribbean and Atlantic Ocean. It was declared Buck Island National Monument in 1961.

The lagoon, walled by glistening coral through which are seen twisting alleys paved with shimmering white sand, provides a near perfect backdrop for viewing both plant and animal life near the bottom. The water has such pristine clarity that coral masses, plants and fish may be seen through glass-bottom boxes towed behind rowboats or by skin divers and swimmers equipped with snorkels in water depths ranging from ten to fifteen feet generally and from thirty-five to fifty feet at deeper points in the monument area.

Coral is of three main types: staghorn, elkhorn and brain coral, each formed by a distinctive species of polyp. It takes thousands of years to form a large reef such as this one, and the "building code" is strict because coral is formed only in water where temperatures seldom, if ever, go below seventy-two degrees. Coral forms on solid bottoms, never further than twenty-two degrees latitude from the Equator and at depths of no more than 150 to 200 feet. Water movement needs to be gentle enough to furnish the tiny coral polyp with plankton, its only food source.

The polyps exude a limestone exterior skeleton, produce more polyps attached to themselves and so make a larger base to provide a rigid structure for more coral and other animals and plants. These live polyps contain multitudes of microscopic plants in a mutually beneficial arrangement. The polyp digests plankton and releases carbon dioxide, which, in turn, is used by the plants to provide oxygen for the polyp. This exchange, called symbiosis, is responsible for the fantastic beauty of tropical reefs.

Soon after the coral polyps begin building their carefully made dwellings, near relatives, such as sea fans, sea whips, gorgonians and sea anemones, join the community. Millions of tiny plants and animals, followed by larger fish and marine animals, rapidly come along to complete the ecological balance. The coral itself ranges from the glistening white to golden browns and yellows, aqua-marine and blue viewed through the depths. Branches of the staghorn coral, in deep golden browns, form treelike shapes, while the elkhorn formations are unbranched and look slightly different. The grayish-white brain coral bulges up from the bottom in wrinkled domes sometimes as large as an automobile.

Into this water environment comes the community of fish, in a rainbow variety of colors, each with its individualistic habits and shapes. A close-up look at a clump of sea whips may reveal a trumpet fish, shaped almost exactly like the stems of the plant, head down and swaying gently in identical rhythm with the currents, thus displaying its own peculiar defensive tactic in hiding from larger, predator fish.

Both the blue and the green tang fish -- sometimes called doctor, or surgeon, fish because of a razor-like bone projection at the base of its tail -- dart among the coral projections. On occasion, one may see a sharp-toothed moray eel crouched under a shadowy coral projection awaiting an unwary spiny crab. French angel fish, queen trigger fish and vari-colored parrot fish create a kaleidoscopic shimmer in the water as they nibble at plankton and pieces of coral. Wrasse -- which includes a group of multi-colored small fish -- also are common, along with Atlantic spade fish, striped port fish, damsel fish and four-eyed butterfly fish with their two simulated eyes near the tail, making them appear

A magnificent barrier reef of staghorn coral surrounds Buck Island, which is just off the eastern tip of St. Croix in the Virgin Islands. It hosts a marine garden of colonial animals, other corals, fish and sea turtles among its maze of jagged formations.

Tropical fish (below) are among the most incredibly colored and shaped animals. They inhabit reef communities populated by various fish and plant life that cooperate in symbiotic associations, exchanging food, protection and grooming services.

to be swimming backward. Goatfish, many mollusks, starfish and yellow grunt move carefully among the coral. Outside in deeper waters, amberjacks, sharks and barracuda await choice snacks from among the less watchful quarry.

The endangered green sea turtle is relatively common here in the safe preserves of the monument. Starfish move slowly, meeting an occasional trunk fish that is boxlike and colored white with black polka dots. It secretes a poison that keeps most predators away. Sea urchins move calmly, knowing their spiny backs provide a bristly protection.

In the lagoon and surrounding ocean are underwater worlds of color and movement, while above are thousands of frigate birds (sometimes called man-of-war birds) floating effortlessly for hours high in the air on the easterly trade winds. Pelican rookeries are also on the island.

In upper reaches of the island, rising 344 feet above the surface, several other birds are common -- varieties of bananaquits, as well as emerald-throated hummingbirds and warblers. The land-bound mongoose and land crabs also frequent the island.

Tropical growth on Buck Island is scrubby, jungle-like vegetation of plants and trees. Turpentine trees, grotesquely twisted, appear as if they writhed and entwined about themselves as they grew. Many kinds of cacti are here along with brilliant green acacias and poisonous manchineel trees. Sap from the manchineel tree is milky in color, but burns like lye on the skin.

A diver makes his way around elkhorn coral and reef fish. Built and maintained by the tiny bodies of polyps accumulated into colonies, this elkhorn reef is found on the seaward side of the island and forms a bulwark against the Atlantic Ocean.

The entire monument presents a display of nature in a virtually untouched setting. Access is by boat and native seamen from St. Croix ply the ways between docks there and Buck Island pier in a variety of sailing craft. Motorized launches from there and other nearby areas also make the trip. Picnic tables are provided, but fires are allowed only in the picnic area. No overnight camping is permitted on the island, but boats may anchor on the west beach.

The National Park Service has provided an efficient system for guiding swimmers about the interesting points of the lagoon. Arrowed markers on the bottom point and guide snorkellers to the variety of undersea sights and views. Except for the inexperienced, dangers are minimal, although coral scratches (especially those from the stinging coral) are painful, as are the stings from the Portugese man-of-war jellyfish. Spines on sea urchins are sharp and piercing. But sharks and barracuda seldom invade the shallow lagoon and no mishaps have ever been recorded amid the startlingly clear blue waters. This is, in truth, an underwater wonderland non-pareil!

A covering of vines and epiphytes spreads through the hardwood forest on Buck Island which also supports several species of cacti.

31

Capitol Reef

Utah

On the slope of Chimney Rock (above), the rainbow bands of color for which Capitol Reef is justly famous display rich variation along the many terraces which resemble great underwater limestone reefs.

Towering above a shallow river bed (opposite), a great dome of erosion-sculpted rock rises like a capitol building. The formation's lower shale is ripple marked, while the upper range is topped with white sandstone.

The violent upthrust of multi-colored barrier cliffs stretching one hundred miles across the south-central Utah desert looks like a huge ocean wave suspended between the Fremont River and its two tributaries. These interruptions in the striking shale and sandstone escarpments resemble the clustered buildings of a city -- hence the appellation Capitol Reef given to this area by Captain John C. Frémont, who viewed the area from the side of Thousand Lake Mountain in 1854.

This magnificent escarpment is the western face of a folding of the earth's crust that occurred in some ancient upheaval. Major John Wesley Powell, a geologist who first explored this region in 1869, called this upthrust the Waterpocket Fold because of its unique geologic characteristics. Capitol Reef National Monument preserves a quarter of a million acres of the most picturesque parts of this geological museum. Here the term "paintbrush of nature" takes on special meaning with vermilion-hued shale layers and walls of glowing pink and white mixing with splatters of orange and ocher. The brilliance deepens to "a land of horizontal rainbows" as day wears on.

The surging and folding of the earth's surface caused the eastern segment of the fold to top the western side and erosion has exposed the stratified crust formation. Cliffs range from one thousand to two thousand feet high, making an almost impassable barrier to crossing the desert from west to east. At the base of the cliffs natural cisterns called potholes catch and retain the only fresh water to be found for many miles across the desert. These water catchments caused Powell to call it the Waterpocket Fold. Fremont River Gorge, breeching the walls with Sulphur, Pleasant and Oak creeks, provides the only perennial water supplies in the monument area.

Petroglyphs chipped into the walls of the scarp or in caves hollowed into the sandstone provide a record of the prehistoric eras. Small bands of Indians grew corn on the valley floor, and artifacts, including bone tools, pottery stone implements and rough fabrics, are kept in a museum at the monument's visitor center.

Fain

Hyde

Above: The cool greens of pin-yon-juniper growths, plus the ground cover of sagebrush, saltbush and squawbush, off-set the warmer colors of the rock layers.

The remarkable "slickrock" garden (left) is a part of the Waterpocket Fold where the earth's once-level crust was tilted to form an eastward-sloping plain.

The peculiar geographic isolation of Capitol Reef caused it to be one of the last areas of Utah to be explored and settled. It was, however, scarcities of both water and arable land that kept settlement sparse. The legendary Butch Cassidy and the Sundance Kid maintained an isolated hideaway cabin in Grand Wash. A nearby natural arch recalls this early-day outlaw with the name Cassidy Arch.

For a time in earlier years, Cohab Canyon was the site for seclusion among Mormons whose strong belief in plural marriage caused them to maintain hidden residences in the area.

Thin soils in the valleys and gorges, plus the paucity of rainfall, has maintained Capitol Reef's ecology as a typical sample of the plants and wildlife of the Colorado Plateau. Pinyon-juniper communities, along with sage, saltbush and squawbush are dominant. Deer, foxes, bobcats and porcupines as well as small rodents and numerous lizards comprise the wildlife. Upland species of birds also inhabit the area.

Grand Wash, where early-day travelers crossed the huge monocline, shows the difficulties of traveling through the twisting and labrynthian countryside. Here, the layers of shale and sandstone show some of the grandest detailing in the country of geological periods, which spanned sixty million years.

At Capitol Gorge early settler Cutler Behunin decided to make a wagon trail in 1880. He entered the gorge with tools and wagons, but eight days later he had progressed only three and a half miles. Yet until recent years, his trail was the only traverse of the fold in that area. At the head of this trail on the cliff face is a "Pioneer Register" where travelers who followed Behunin's lead carved their names when they negotiated the difficult road way he started.

The lonely isolation of Capitol Reef is captured by the view across the desert to the Henry Mountains in the distance. This was the last major mountain range to be named in the United States. Big Thompson Mesa, near the south end of the monument, provides a spectacular viewpoint for Grand Gulch, which is a deep valley separating the mesa from the 1,500-foot-high escarpment of the fold.

Spectacularly eroded cliff faces are constantly changing patterns and colors according to time of day and perspective. The Motorman, Twin Rocks and Chimney Rock bear close resemblence to their namesakes. From the side of Sulphur Creek Gorge, The Castle is seen as a result of centuries of the chiseling and shaping action of winds, moisture and freezing conditions forming the spire and buttresses of a medieval fortress. Shapes of temples are in Cathedral Valley nearby.

Perhaps one of the most beautiful sights in the monument is Hickman Natural Bridge, towering seventy-two feet above the watershed of Whiskey Spring. This span of fine-grained sandstone is gracefully balanced for 133 feet between cliffs.

A grayish-white Caprock Formation may be most responsible for the peculiar domelike forms erosion has made in the monument. This hardened sandstone has

"Butch" Cassidy is reported to have kept a regular hideout about the turn of the century in a back country cabin and left his mark (top) in the Capitol Reef area. Earlier inhabitants in the Fremont River region left curious petroglyphs (bottom), some of which retain a hint of primitive paint; diggings have also exposed utensils.

acted as a shield for the softer layers in a way that causes wind and water to shape them into official-looking building towers. One layer of the geologic formation at the base of the cliffs contains a number of reptile and amphibian fossils. Great boulders of volcanic origin are also found in the valleys of the monument. These may have been pushed into the area by the glacial incursions of ancient times.

Isolated and desolate, this part of the mile-high land of southern Utah was first set aside in 1937. In 1969, President Lyndon B. Johnson extended it by more than 200,000 acres to preserve the most spectacular parts of the Waterpocket Fold. A visitor center, public camping and picnic areas, plus two private motel and lodge areas inside the monument, assist travelers in seeing this out-of-the-way sector of North America.

Capitol Reef today remains almost exactly as it was when geologist C. E. Dutton said of it a century ago: "The colors are such as no pigments can portray. They are deep, rich and variegated; and so luminous are they, that light seems to flow or shine out of the rock rather than to be reflected from it."

Lone Capulin Mountain (left) rises as a landmark above the surrounding plateau in northeastern New Mexico.

Below: Looking north and east from the summit of Capulin peak, the edge of the Great Plains is visible in the distance.

Capulin Mountain

New Mexico

A mantle of green trees and grass softens the violence which built this cone-shaped mountain of cinders and ashes. The reds, rusty-browns and blacks of the thousand-foot-high crater come from material thrown from inside the earth in volcanic eruptions many centuries ago. Although vegetation has partially stabilized the slopes, continuing rock slides in some places show this crater to be young in the stream of geologic time. It is one of the largest, most symmetrical cinder cones in the United States.

This is Capulin Mountain National Monument, 775 acres of recent geological history, established in 1916. Rising from a relatively level plain in northeastern New Mexico, it had become a conspicuous landmark as early as the nineteenth century during the days of the Cimarron Cut-off to the Santa Fe Trail. The main cut-off trail was about thirty miles to the east.

The cone's steep sides of ash and cinder, little modified by time, indicate that the volcanic eruptions which formed it occurred relatively recently, perhaps about seven thousand years ago. Successive eruptions at that time spewed out cinders and ash but little lava. Only two lava flows can be observed, one north and one south of the mountain. The heavier parts of the volcanic material fell back alongside the eruption vent, thus forming the cone, while the rest were blown away by the wind. Lava "bombs," tear-shaped or rounded stones, some nearly a foot in diameter, show how pressure hurled drops of molten lava high enough into the air so that it cooled into stone before falling. The mountain is quiet now, and although there is some question about future volcanic activity, many scientists believe it is unlikely.

An abundance of stabilizing vegetation enhances Capulin's quiet beauty with patches of ponderosa and pinyon pine, Rocky Mountain juniper and mountain mahogany. On the higher slopes are chokecherry, Gambel (scrub) oak and squawbush. The mountain ac-tually was named after the Spanish word for chokecherry -- *capulin.* From May through July many wildflowers bloom on the slopes including Indian paintbrush, bluebonnets (lupines), bluebells and daisies.

During late summer, ladybugs are hatched on the mountain by the millions. They are predators of mealybugs, scale insects and aphids and many are raised commercially outside the monument for use in fields and orchards.

Occasionally a great golden eagle can be seen soaring overhead, and many other species of birds and animals may be observed in the area also. In winter months, the relatively large porcupine population is evident by the teeth-slashed trunks of trees and bushes.

Blustery, southwest winds prevail in the area, yet inside the crater trees seem to lean defiantly into that wind and away from the crater bottom, which ranges from 100 to 415 feet in depth. This strange phenomenon is caused by winds entering the crater at its lower edge on the southwest, circling inside the crater and then blowing the trees in the opposite direction as it spills over the rim. Although some of these wind-twisted trees are as much as 375 years old, a major part of the vegetation has grown in the past half century.

Many of the rocks have gray-green and orange lichens growing on them. These communities of fungus and algae aid each other in breaking down the stone into soil with each feeding the other in a cooperative existence.

A visitor center is located alongside a road which leads to the top of Capulin Mountain, where a rim trail circles the crater. The monument has a picnic area but no campground. Privately operated campgrounds and other lodging are available in nearby towns.

Here in the midst of mostly dun-colored northeastern New Mexico, the bright hues of flowers and trees on a dark cinder mountain make the eras of the relatively recent geologic past easy to read.

Cedar Breaks

Utah

A gigantic natural amphitheater, carved from multi-hued stone, slopes steeply westward from two-mile-high Markagunt Plateau in southwestern Utah. This is a spectacular example of the deterioration of limestone formations uptilted by ancient shiftings of the earth's crust. The gently rolling rim of this grotesquely eroded area is covered by a verdant growth of trees interspersed with lush meadows which display mountain wildflowers soon after the retreat of melting snow. Color, both from various metallic mixes in the limestone and from the lush plant growth, is probably the dominant characteristic of this dramatic area only two and a half miles from Brian Head Peak, the highest point in southwestern Utah.

Early Mormon settlers called the area "breaks" or "badlands." That early name became Cedar Breaks because settlers mistakenly identified the mountain juniper of the area as cedar. This scenic display of erosion became part of Dixie National Forest in 1905, and about ten square miles was established as Cedar Breaks National Monument in 1933. From the rim of the plateau at 10,300 to 10,400 feet above sea level, the amphitheater drops almost half a mile to its lowest point.

Bold rock shapes and cliffs carved from stone layers two thousand feet thick are revealed from outlook points along the rim. Sidewalls are furrowed, corroded and broken into massive ridges that seem to radiate from the center like spokes of a wheel. This geologic display of color starts at the top with white or orange limestone ranging downward through rose and coral tints. Yellows, lavenders and even purples and chocolate hues are seen in many sections of the prodigious natural bowl. The Indians called it "circle of painted cliffs." An artist once counted forty-seven different tints in the stones of the monument.

Even the brilliant coloring, however, is surpassed by the grotesque sculpturing of wind and water in the monument. Formations of columns, pinnacles, standing walls, gateways and terraces suggest structures ranging from cathedrals to tombstones. An outline of a woman with a baby at her breast is shaped in one area. In another spot, erosion has carved the rock into the appearance of a group of people kneeling to pray. Solitary spires, knife-thin walls and crumbling towers seem like the desolation of an ancient city of giants. At sunset the colors soften, and twilight shadows lengthen into blues and purples, making ghostly shapes of the giant obelisks.

The layers of rock from which the amphitheater was eroded were formed some fifty-five million years ago as limy ooze at the bottom of shallow lakes in the region, then near sea level. In the past thirteen million years, the lake bottoms were uplifted to a height of more than ten thousand feet, and a westward-facing escarpment of limestone was created.

With the lifting of the plateau, erosion began, and during intermittent volcanic activity, lava boiled through fissures in the earth adding to the variety of scenes in the area. Many of the newer lava beds still do not support vegetation. Here, in a region where summer heat on the desert below is nearly unbearable, temperatures are cool in July, with snow flurries occasionally taking place in midsummer.

From mid-July through August, mountain wildflowers compete with the desolated beauty of the amphitheater as a major attraction of the monument. Marsh marigold, mountain buttercup, green and fringed gentian, columbine, larkspur, monkshood, mountain bluebell, lupine, sunflower and fields of Indian paintbrush grace the hills.

All photos in this chapter by James Fain.

Above: Cedar Breaks in southern Utah is outstanding for its splendid natural amphitheatre.

Overleaf: Patches of snow mix with the golden orange on the limestone walls to give an abstract effect.

Some of the true ancients of the forest world, bristle-cone pines, are found in sizable groves along the rim. Many of these patriarchs of the wilderness, clinging tenaciously to the near barren soil at the upper edge of the amphitheater, are more than 1,600 years old. Alpine fir and Engelmann spruce are in thick stands in the alpine meadow areas near the rim, and heavy forests of pine, fir, spruce and quaking aspen cloak large sections of the rim and spill down into the formations.

Mountain snows, nearby lakes and the lush vegetation support many wild animals. This is one of the few places the cony, a rodent-like creature mentioned in the Bible, can be seen frequently. Native to the area, these hardy little animals, also called pikas and similar in size to small rabbits but without the ears, eke out their living near the rim. Chipmunks and red squirrels gather pine cones for their winter feeding; but the conies cut grass, cure it in the summer sun and then store it for their winter use. Mule deer are the largest mammals in the monument and can be seen often at morning and evening grazing quietly in the meadows. Weasels, badgers and porcupines are common throughout the area.

Birds find this region a good habitat, better than most sectors of the Western mountain-desert country. Perhaps the most conspicuous is Clark's nutcracker, a handsome bird with a light gray body and bright white patches on its black wings and tail. It is a regular guest at picnic tables and pecks away at campground crumbs. Two species of birds, the violet-green swallow and the white-throated swift, seem to flit untiringly near the rim with never a pause.

Camping is allowed in the monument, usually from June through early September, although no utility connections are available for trailers, and a visitor center is located on the rim near Point Supreme. The Utah Parks Company operates a snack bar, lodge, dining room and cabins in the area. Motels and hotels are available at Parowan and Cedar City, each about twenty miles away. Roads and rim trails provide good scenic views.

The amphitheater at Cedar Breaks is always spectacular, with its eroded limestone cliffs cutting into the Markagunt Plateau. This monument offers an unusual array of attractions with its lush meadows, forests, alpine lakes, wildlife and dramatic landscapes.

Channel Islands

California

A brilliant expanse of treelike sunflowers on the springtime meadows and hills of Santa Barbara Island, thirty-eight miles west of San Pedro, California, serves as a golden beacon to ships at sea. This gleam is from the largest known stands of giant coreopsis in the world. Forty miles northwest, three tiny islets comprise Anacapa Island, a chain tipped on the eastern point by Arch Rock, a forty-foot-high wave sculpture, and isolated as a preserve where thousands of seabirds, rare seals and other marine creatures nest and breed. The barking of the sea lions and the occasional earth-shaking bellow of an angered northern elephant seal bull blend with the cry of gulls and crashing waves.

These two islands are part of the Channel Islands chain which stretches from due west of San Diego northward to Point Conception and carries the archeo-logical threads of prehistory for early man, plants and wildlife. Santa Barbara and Anacapa, like the other six Channel Islands, are mountaintops which were sur-rounded by ocean after the western parts of the ancient Santa Monica Mountains were submerged about a half-million years ago. Almost completely girded by star-tling cliffs, some rising vertically more than five hundred feet, these two islands were set aside as the

Channel Islands National Monument in 1938.

Santa Barbara and Anacapa, comprising almost 18,-000 acres, are a pristine outpost in polluted southern California and provide refuge for numerous species of marine life easily visible in quiet coves and sunny pools below the cliffs. The surrounding ocean temperatures range between fifty-five and sixty-five degrees, offering a moderate climate advantageous to the many marine mammals.

Geographical isolation has offered a splendid oppor-tunity for scientists to study life forms in areas rela-tively unchanged by mankind since the intervening land submerged. The islands have been called an "evo-lution factory" because disassociation from the main-land for upwards of half a million years has allowed subtle changes to occur in generations of both plants and animals. Taxonomists have described distinctive characteristics and recognize new species and subspe-cies known only to the islands. One of these subspecies is the Channel Island fox. Several other small land plants, animals and lizards also show subspecies dif-ferentiation.

Huge flocks of a variety of seabirds nest on cliff tops and the interior highlands of both islands. Anacapa

Sheer cliffs dominate the beaches on both Anacapa (above) and Santa Barbara islands and offer nesting areas for seabirds.

Island is one of the few surviving nesting grounds for the brown pelican and double-crested cormorants. Below, on narrow beaches and in sea caves gouged from sheer cliffs by the surging seas, the almost extinct Guadalupe seal finds hauling-out beaches. Sleek, brown California sea lions are common, while clumsy-appearing elephant seals, each of the bulls sporting a foot-long proboscis, populate coves and quiet beaches. Although sea otters are no longer found here because of exploitation during the nineteenth century by those who wanted their valuable pelts, naturalists believe these beautiful sea animals will eventually return and increase within the safety of the monument preserve. The smallest of the marine mammals, sea otters are larger than the more familiar river otters and reach a maximum weight of one hundred pounds. Although they mate in the water, they bear their young on beaches. Among sea mammals, the otter is unique in depending entirely on an insulating blanket of air trapped in its dense coat for its body warmth. Seals and whales are kept warm by a subcutaneous layer of fat.

The six-to-eight-foot giant coreopsis is perhaps the most distinctive plant on Channel Islands, with its thick bark, gray, rigid trunk and stubby branches that appear lifeless during the dry summers. But come the winter rains, the plants show signs of life, and beginning in early April, bright green leaves appear with a gorgeous canopy of intensely golden-yellow blossoms. The spring months also bring a profusion of wildflowers rivaling any mainland landscape; some 175 distinctive plants have been identified on Santa Barbara and Anacapa. Some of these subspecies discovered are types of oak, poppy, cherry, mountain lilac, morning glory and two species of painted-cup (paintbrush).

The monument areas offer outstanding undersea environments for marine biological research in the tidal pools, coves and in the deeper surrounding waters. The islands are a museum of geological structures where one can find examples of faulting, fossils, volcanic action and canyon development as well as erosion of many kinds. Archeologists have speculated the islands may be one of North America's oldest inhabited areas. George F. Carter, geographer of Johns Hopkins University, unearthed evidence and has theorized that "men were broiling dwarf mammoths" more than 29,000 years ago on what is now Santa Rosa Island. This discovery, by using carbon dating techniques, places man in the area more than twenty thousand years sooner than earlier estimations.

The Channel Islands were occupied at various periods by the Canalino Indians prior to the voyage of Juan Rodriquez Cabrillo, who anchored off Anacapa in 1542. The islands continued to be populated; three of them, Santa Rosa, Santa Cruz and Santa Catalina, now are privately owned, while the other three are controlled by the U. S. Navy.

The monument is accessible only by boat, has no piers and, quite rightly, contains few man-made "improvements." Public camping is allowed, but firewood, food, water, and other supplies must be brought in by rough-it campers. Scuba diving off of either island is most rewarding. National Park Service personnel staff the areas only in summer months, though they patrol both islands year around.

These islands should be combined with the two largest Channel Islands, Santa Rosa and Santa Cruz, and be made into a true national park. This is the last national park option in southern California; it will be a sad chapter of conservation history if these islands are not converted into a superb park that will keep these unique island sanctuaries inviolate for future generations.

A golden brown California sea lion rests on a mossy rock in the islands. The species is quite common and best known as the "trained seal" of circuses and other shows.

NPS, Stoughton

Organ-pipe forms in Chiricahua evolved as widening vertical breaches in hardened lava carved these huge pillars.

Chiricahua

Arizona

Grotesquely eroded spires, pinnacles, towers and massive battlements guard the canyons and shaded glens of the Chiricahua Mountains in the southeast corner of Arizona. In this fascinating wonderland of rocks, Cochise and Geronimo, famous Chiricahua Apache warrior leaders, fought against overwhelming odds to hold their Indian ancestral lands against settlement by outsiders. But the battle in the forces of nature forming these magnificent bulwarks against the arid grasslands below began millions of years ago -- and continues changing the many faces of this ancient upheaval.

Rising steeply from the dry sparseness of southwestern New Mexico and northern Mexico into the corner of Arizona, this mountain range presents a verdant, forest island in a sea of grass. In 1924, after a bloody earlier period of American settlement, some seventeen square miles of the most spectacular sector was set aside as Chiricahua National Monument. The fierce beauty of the monument fires the remembrance of the past of these mountains -- a phantasmagoria of terrestrial upheaval and lean Indians hunting still abundant wildlife, their women picking herbs and flowers.

Mighty geological forces created the basic structures of these peculiar pinnacles and delicately balanced rocks during intermittent volcanic eruptions at least twenty-five million years ago. The explosive force of the eruptions shows now where various beds of lava and white-hot ash later cooled and were pressured into stone in Rhyolite Canyon. Remissions and recurring eruptions caused varying thicknesses in the lava layers, and during some longer periods of inactivity, allowed sediment layers to be formed in prehistoric lakebeds. These layers now show in the rocky ramparts which range in height from 5,160 feet to 7,365 feet. One explosive eruption must have caused a volcanic hail-

storm. Marble-size volcanic pellets cemented into a peculiar formation called "peanut brittle" rock have been eroded and are open for modern inspection.

An uplift and tilting of the earth's crust caused the mountainous terrain. Fissures and faults became wider and eventually became valleys and canyons. Changing climate, resulting in heavy summer downpours, eroded the cliff faces, while the winds, rain and storm continued the constant struggle between weathering elements and stone.

In the changeless pace of ages, these breaches in the lava crust eroded, and rain water channels carved the stone masses into a myriad of sizes and shapes. Other eroded shapes resemble a huge Duck on a Rock, the Old Maid, Punch and Judy and a variety of amazing likenesses of giant beasts and men in a ridge and canyon area of volcanic rock. Spires crumble, balanced rocks crash down -- and while a generation sees little change, in geologic time, erosion extends its weird reformation of the rocky terrain. Softer rock parts were cut away and what remained balanced huge monoliths, wrinkled and etched.

As the rock weathered, soil formed and collected. Plants gained a foothold, then spread and began accumulating more soil. This activity caused the development of ecological niches and communities of varying altitudinal requirements that are a fascinating part of the monument today. Furthermore, because of their isolation in an arid grassland, the Chiricahua Mountains afford a haven for many plants and animals which are rare in the entire surrounding area. Climatic conditions vary considerably -- shaded slopes have much vegetation and varieties of both plant and animal life not found on the more arid slopes exposed to direct sunlight. Rainfall averages about eighteen inches annually, mostly in July and August. Temperatures have a mean of forty degrees in January and seventy-four in

NPS, Mang, Jr.

A view toward the northeast horizon of the monument includes the recumbent profile of Cochise Head, named for one of the two great Apaches who roamed the Chiricahua range in the mid 1800's.

July. Each winter there are two or three snowfalls.

The biological consequences of the variety of elevations and exposures to sunlight have caused some botanists to estimate there is a greater range of plant life in Chiricahua National Monument than in any area of like size in the United States. For example, more than five hundred plant species are found here. Biologists learned, too, that the isolation meant that some forms of both plants and animals are distinctly different here than anywhere else.

Sunny slopes are characterized by desert type plants including the creamy-blossomed yucca, Palmer agave (century plant) and catclaw acacia, among others. These sun-exposed slopes meet the shaded declines which have scrub chapparal, a covering of oak, red-stemmed manzanita and bark-shedding madrones mingling with the chalky white limbs of sycamore and the feathery gray foliage of the Arizona cypress. Douglas fir and quaking aspens at higher elevations in the Chiracahua Mountains reflect the relatively moist conditions of the range. Wildflowers are found abundantly according to their natural elevation, moisture need and other environmental conditions.

The wildlife of the monument is almost as complex

as the plant life. Two distinct species are the Apache fox squirrel and the green rock rattlesnake. "Visiting" species from Mexican highlands also come to the Chiricahuas. Among them are the coppery-tailed trogon and, rarely, the Mexican jaguar. The coatimundi -- a long-tailed animal resembling a raccoon -- also comes across the border to this attractive habitat. Larger animals include the javelina (collared peccary), wild turkeys and the Coues white-tailed deer. An occasional black bear is also seen in the monument.

A multitude of birds provide bright flashes of color and sound among the trees and canyons of the monument. In wooded glens are vermilion flycatchers, orioles, red-faced warblers and painted redstarts. A variety of lizards and other denizens of the Southwest United States and mountain country are plentiful.

There are campsites and picnic areas as well as the National Park Service headquarters and a visitor center. Motels and restaurants are thirty-six miles away.

At Massai Point, in Echo Canyon or Heart of Rocks with its fairyland of imaginative likenesses, this land is vibrant and alive in a way that is little different from those earlier times of Indian stewardship when the sounds of night birds and coyotes closed the day.

46

Young

Above: Massai Point, named for another famous Apache--"Big Foot" Massai, who resisted reservation life long after most of his cohorts in the area had been captured--looks out over a canyon populated by lava blocks of all shapes.

Perched together (below) are two raccoonlike carnivores who frequent Chiricahua --the ringtail on the left, the coatimundi on the right. The first is notable for his splendid tail, the other for his ever-twitching, probing snout.

NPS

Colorado

Colorado

Wind, water and frost have exposed millions of years of geologic time in the vividly colored cliffs and towers carved from the Uncompahgre Plateau, which rises 1,-500 feet above the Grand Valley of the Colorado River in southwestern Colorado. Great cross sections of rock displayed in deep canyons portray eons of formative periods. Nearby, in Grand Valley near the city of Grand Junction, agricultural fields stretch a dozen miles like a checkered carpet on the valley floor. This region of semiarid climates and peculiar geologic formations provides an interesting habitat for a surprising array of wildlife and plants.

Geologists read a progression of more than 225 million years here, from the hard, crystalline rocks on the floor of the valley, through layers of greenish, sedimentary limestone, to brick-red siltstone and buff-hued sandstone. Changes of climate, periods of flooding, deep oceans, shallow lakes and marshy bogs are recorded in these formations.

Scientists have found the records of ancient men in pictographs and in the sites of prehistoric villages, while paleontologists have learned about the age of dinosaurs from skeletal fossils discovered in the area.

Sedimentation found in depths of up to three miles show that the original Uncompahgre Highlands were gigantic mountains. About 100 million years later a prodigious upheaval occurred in the terrestrial crust. Mountains crumbled and ocean floors were raised thousands of feet to put a new look on the face of the Western United States. From Artists Point above the valley, visitors can see the red, green, gray and brown silty shales that once were shallows in an ancient sea. Ripple marks in the formation indicate that a shallow lake or inlet may have done part of this lamination.

These colorful cliffs and towers have been set aside as Colorado National Monument. To the north across the valley, Book Cliffs form the skyline; to the east, Grand Mesa looms on the horizon.

Dramatic names label the formations -- Coke Ovens, No Thoroughfare Canyon, Monument Canyon and Red Canyon. Great rock displacements of an earlier era caused a fault during the uplift period of the region's development. Now this fault is an escarpment hundreds of feet high paralleling the monument. It is one of its most striking sights.

Average rainfall is only about eleven inches annually, yet the natural forces are still at work forming fantastic monoliths, open caves, windowed walls and other forms as they erode the cliffs and highlands sand grain by sand grain, weakening the heights and undercutting huge, delicately balanced rocks. Sentinel Rock, Independence Monument and Balanced Rock all are examples of the results of these weathering processes.

Artifacts, burial grounds and habitations of prehistoric basketmakers have been found throughout the monument. Evidence shows that at an even earlier time the Brontosaurus and the eighty-ton Brachiosaurus, the largest dinosaur ever discovered, once lived here.

Ute Indians resided here when a small group of Spaniards arrived in 1776, led by Father Domínguez and Father Escalante. Antoine Robidoux, a St. Louis Frenchman, set up a trading post a short distance to the south in 1830, and fur trappers probed the area during the same period. Modern-day history of the monument began with a pioneer named John Otto, who "discovered" it about the turn of the century and became an enthusiastic road builder and trailblazer.

A view down Monument Canyon opens onto Independence Monument flanked by spectacular escarpments.

Not satisfied with word-of-mouth advertising of the sights and thrilling experiences he found here, he began to write letters. Otto's dream came true in 1911 when President William Howard Taft signed a proclamation establishing Colorado National Monument, and John Otto was named its first custodian.

Park visitors catch fleeting glimpses of wildlife and the brilliant displays of red, purple, pink and white desert and mountain wildflowers suddenly blooming after spring rains.

Plants and animals share a habitat of unusual interest. Three kinds of lizards may share the same locale without friction: One hunts for food in crevices and niches, a second gets his food on the tops of flat rocks, while the third eats food found at the bases of cliffs and in the shade of huge rocks. The yucca, with its creamy white blossoms, depends entirely on a moth for reproduction. The moth burrows into the bloom to lay eggs in the ovary (seed capsules), and while the fruit furnishes food for several larvae, the moth carries pollen to another plant to fertilize it as she burrows to plant more eggs. Tiny birds build nests in the spiny thorns of the few cactus growing here to protect their nests from marauding predators, while the birds themselves protect the cactus from devouring insects.

Forest cover is comprised mostly of Utah juniper and pinyon pine interspersed with some grasses and shrubs, such as sagebrush, serviceberry and mountain mahogany. Deer, foxes and bobcats are plentiful, but cougars and elk (wapiti) are only infrequent visitors. Bison, introduced into the monument in 1926, are limited by forage supply to a herd of not more than ten. There is scarcely a pinyon pine in the monument that remains unscarred by the sharp teeth of the yellow porcupine, which eats the inner bark of the pines.

Only the quick-eyed see most of the desert birds. Rock wrens, magpies, blue-gray gnatcatchers, sage sparrows and green-tailed towhees sometimes are heard without being seen behind special camouflaging markings. The few broad-leafed trees such as cottonwoods, however, attract many birds including red-tailed hawks, ravens, blackbirds and owls. The turkey vulture and the golden eagle nest on the higher crags.

A visitor center, campgrounds and picnic areas with tables, water, fireplaces and firewood are provided in the monument by the National Park Service. The twenty-two-mile Rim Drive, plus interior drives, hiking trails and scenic viewpoints, make the monument's attractions easily accessible.

As ages pass, leveling forces of weathering continue to reshape this area of sheer cliffs and precarious caprocks. But glimpses of an environment made by nature and ignored by man leave a memorable impression of the vastness and changeability of the earth's crust.

America's most common feline, the bobcat (or wildcat, catamount or tiger cat), is an awesome lightweight hunter known for his powerful springs, markedly dappled coloration and noisy caterwauling, yet, contrary to appearance, he lives mostly on rodents and is generally a boon to farmers.

50

NPS

Weber

Monument Canyon (top) was the area settled at the turn of the century by John Otto, the energetic visionary who determined to make this area of wildly colored cliffs, record-bearing stone formations and fascinating wildlife known and preserved for the future.

The mountain cottontail (bottom) is colored a yellowish gray; like all rabbits, he is an indispensable link in the food chain, either as consumer or prey, and eats a great variety of plants.

Craters of the Moon

Idaho

A desolate landscape of unyielding blacks, chocolate-to-golden tans, and sometimes, rusty-reds, has made another world of an eighty-three-square-mile sector of south-central Idaho. Ebony-colored rock rivers, glinting bluish purple in strong sunlight, are guarded by peculiar open cones, startlingly red inside with side slopes of tawny brown shadings.

Characteristics of this strange land on the northern reaches of the Snake River Lava Plain between the Pioneer and the Lost River mountains bears striking resemblence to the craters and darkened valleys of the moon as viewed through telescopes. Therefore, in 1924, when President Coolidge set aside 53,545 acres of this barren wasteland, it was named Craters of the Moon National Monument.

Volcanic eruptions resulting in extensive lava flows during at least three different time periods are responsible for this foreboding wasteland. The molten, gaseous rock killed all growing things in its path, leaving one of the harshest environments known. Time determinations, made from the life span rings of pines found growing in the newest lava flows, indicate the last eruptions ended at least two thousand years ago.

Early westbound settlers avoided the area, but in the 1880's, two venturesome cattlemen, J. W. Powell and Arthur Ferris, explored this wasteland hoping to find a permanent water supply for their livestock. Later studies by the U. S. Geological Survey caused widespread interest resulting in the national monument designation.

The era of volcanism responsible for Craters of the Moon perhaps encompassed a million years. Although the monument resembles a gigantic, cataclysmic convolution, most of these lava flows and cinder cones rose through what they call the Great Rift --a fissure in the earth's crust that can be traced through the monument--in relatively mild fashion. Cinder cones, both large and small, show that the eruptions of the gaseous lava occurred along a definite line pattern.

A marvelous view from atop Big Cinder Butte reveals two distinct forms of basaltic (black) lava involved in these eruptions. The *pahoehoe* (pronounced pah-HO ay -HO ay) and *aa* (ah-ah) are the two. *Pahoehoe* is a billowy, ropy type of lava having many caverns and covers about half of the monument area. Its shiny blue, glassy crusts make some of the flows darkly beautiful in brilliant sunlight. The ropy, wrinkled surfaces are caused by the hardening of a thin crust on the lava flow while the underlying molten rock continues in motion.

In contrast, the *aa* lava is rough, jagged and spiny -- apparently having the same chemical origin, but made up of a different combination of gas and heat. When it is flowing hot this kind of lava is a doughy mass and escaping gas pulls out stringers of lava, causing the spines. The whole flow resembles slush ice on a river in springtime. Flows of *aa* lava in the monument are twenty-five to one hundred feet thick and some of them extend miles into the plains nearby.

A variety of cinder cones, spatter cones and lava domes are seen in the monument. Cones are formed by lava froth or spray from fire fountains at the time of eruptions. Big Cinder Butte is the finest example in the area, with rich browns and tans and undersides composed of smaller cinders which are sometimes a brilliant brick red.

Spatter cones were built by smaller fire fountains when clots of lava were hurled from the eruption hole and moved so slowly in the air for such short distances that they failed to cool, and thus were literally "spattered" when they landed. Lava domes have smooth domelike shapes rising from ten to fifty feet high in the monument. These interesting formations came from continuous, slow-welling lava from the same vent opening along the Great Rift.

One of the strangest landscapes in America is the unearthly wasteland in southern Idaho contained in Craters of the Moon National Monument, where volcanic formations, like these spatter cones, are scattered over an 83-square-mile sea of black lava and cinders, touched with a few grass patches and bounded by distant mountains.

Young

Basalt lava is the only known kind in the Craters area and occurs here in two types called by their Hawaiian names, pahoehoe *and* aa. *The photos above and below show examples of* aa, *distinguishable by its spiny, jagged surface which looks like a mass of lava clinkers -- particularly noticeable in the detail (right) of Devil's Orchard.*

Fain

Spindle, ribbon and bread-crust lava bombs are found in abundance. These were formed from clots of lava hurled into the air, cooled and shaped by either their spinning movement into football shapes called spindles; or, still molten, dropped back onto the ground as ribbonlike rock, remaining plastic enough to wrap itself around whatever object it fell upon. Bread-crust bombs are porous lava blobs, full of gas, that cooled into broken, crust-covered cinders as the gas escaped and the molten rock cooled in the air.

Perhaps the most intriguing parts of the monument are the tunnels and caverns, all occuring in *pahoehoe* lava. The longest, Arco Tunnel, is 1,867 feet long, and was not discovered until about a decade ago. Great Owl Cavern, Indian Tunnel and Needles Cave, along with Boy Scout Cave, are some other caves. Lava stalactites hang from some tunnel ceilings. The tunnels are formed when flowing lava cools on the outside, forming a tube through which still molten lava continues to flow. Near perfect insulation allows the lava flow to continue after the outside of the tube has hardened.

Because of such insulation, on a hot summer day with temperatures in the upper eighties, ice water is seldom more than a few feet away in some caves. They are frost encrusted and have ice-covered pools inside the tunnels year around. Water and snow seeping through cracks into the tunnels and crevices during seven months of winter thaws little in five months of summer. Temperatures in the caves remain at from thirty-four to forty degrees all summer, allowing for year-round ice-skating in some of the larger ones.

Tree molds -- openings where growing trees were surrounded and burned out by the heat of encompassing lava flows -- have retained the complete outlines of trees and branches in sizes from three inches to more than three feet in diameter.

It seems doubtful that living things could exist in this inhospitable environment. Yet, there are more than two hundred species of plants, some animals and a number of birds. The yellow-bellied marmot is a common small mammal. Each spring wildflower displays dot the cinder gardens areas of the monument. Among them are the silvery pads of the leaves of dwarf buckwheat, topped by the yellow or pink pom-pom type flowers. Timber and vegetation are sparse in this semiarid climate which has only ten inches of rainfall annually.

A visitor center and monument headquarters are twenty miles southwest of Arco, Idaho, and a seven-mile automobile drive loop is open year around except during heavy snows. Campgrounds and picnic facilities as well as National Park Service personnel are available from April 15 through October 15.

Some of the most perfect examples of basaltic cinder cones in the world are found at Craters of the Moon National Monument. Here, portrayed in revealing detail, is the dramatic duel between a barren landscape, sterilized in the white heat of volcanic eruptions, and natural reclamation by growing things that rebuild soil from lava rock and blowing dust. This is a fascinating place to study a chapter in the earth's evolution.

NPS

Pahoehoe *lava most often has a ropy, wrinkled surface of blue, vitric crusts. Underneath are many caverns formed when the lava stream hardened on the top and sides, allowing the molten center to flow on.*

For centuries men and women have pitted
their strength against and have tried to live
in Death Valley, from the early Indians through
the pioneers and goldrush prospectors. Now mere
remembrances (above) are left of those brief
communities and attempted exploits.

Death seems a poor name for this valley
(opposite) which may appear with infinite forms of
gracefulness and light where undulating waves
and ripples pattern the sand with shadows.

Death Valley

California, Nevada

Heat waves shimmer in the scorching sun as it beats down upon the flats and crags of this barren valley situated between severe mountain ridges rising from a distant desert. It is a heartless master, this valley, unchanged by the softening touch of time. Man's efforts to tame this wilderness seem puny, dwarfed by heaps of lava, burst stone and many-hued clays cast up from beneath the earth's crust in some ancient cataclysm.

Indians who once dwelled in nearby mountains and attempted to harvest a little food from the sparse vegetation called the valley *tomesha*, meaning "red earth," because it yielded a fire-colored clay that warriors used to produce warpaint for their bodies. Sourdough mountain men claimed the Indian word meant "ground afire." But the name that finally attached itself unshakeably to this harsh valley is Death Valley.

The name is inappropriate, for this is a land of light, color and considerable beauty. Each shift of light, shadow or perspective casts a different spell because of the infinite variations of color, form and texture.

Pioneers in the westward movement of the nineteenth century bypassed this valley, believing -- as its name implies -- that it would sustain no life. Yet, in the vivid contrasts of this landscape, there is abundant desert life -- wild animals, birds, insects and plant life. Although the annual rainfall is scant, only 1.66 inches, if there is enough rain in November, mountain and desert wildflowers provide a burst of color in spring.

In the early spring, one can stand 282 feet below sea level at Badwater in temperatures near one hundred degrees and look westward toward Telescope Peak high in the Panamint Range to see plumes of snow blowing from the peak.

Even in midwinter, temperatures average about ninety degrees in the sunny hours and are sharply cool at night. In summer, average daytime temperatures rise above the 120-degree mark. A temperature of 134 degrees occurred once -- the hottest ever recorded in the Western Hemisphere.

The old sourdough prospectors are gone. But the wry, sometimes grim, humor with which they named the ghost towns that remain in the valley recalls the period when an ore strike would stampede thousands to raw frontier areas in a single day. Panamint City, said to have been started by a band of thieves high in the

Aguereberry Point was named for a prospector, Pete Aguereberry, who became known here after the '49 goldrush.

Roberts

Panamint Mountains, was the roughest of the boom towns in the United States for a few short months. A surging flood from a desert cloudburst washed it away. Greenwater is a litter of rubbish and old bottles today. Ryan was moved en masse to a new location when boom became bust and a new strike was made. Cloudbursts, vandals and dust storms are completing deterioration.

Although the days of the "desert rat" prospector are over, their burros, now wild and abundant, have added to the animal life of the area. These hardy, scruffy-looking creatures roam the mountains and flats, surviving and increasing on the sparse grass and bushes, searching out their own watering places. Sometimes called "rocky mountain canaries," these little beasts, with their ornery antics and braying calls, recall the ribald impudence of those who pioneered Death Valley.

Few of the men who loved and fought the elements in Death Valley became wealthy. But Walter Scott, later known as Death Valley Scotty, was able to combine his love for the valley and a comfortable living in his last thirty years. In 1924, Scott and a wealthy Eastern friend, Albert Johnson, built a huge Moorish castle at about the three-thousand-foot level in Grapevine Canyon. This monstrous spoof, patterned after European castles, had eighteen fireplaces and the added touch of a 185-foot swimming pool. The place Scott called his "shack" remains as a monument to the eccentricities of some who once called Death Valley home.

Seeing Scotty's Castle perched halfway up a stark canyon is no more surprising than the sight of wildflowers blooming in the desert after an early spring rainfall. Golden primroses shine like newly minted coins. Some bright cactus flowers blossom for several days, while others burst into bloom, lose their petals, and drop their seeds in a single day. Because of the unique abilities of desert flowers to adapt, they bloom and seed only when conditions of moisture and temperature are correct. Sometimes, they bloom only at intervals of several years. As late as 1920, many believed Death Valley sustained no life, yet there are actually some six hundred species of plants in the monument. The plants grow from sea level and below near Badwater to the sides of the 11,000-foot Telescope Peak in the Panamints.

Out on the broad mud flats and sand dunes, as well as in the specialized ecological communities of cacti, arrowbush and mesquite brush, the life cycles of birds, plants, animals and insects continue in historic patterns. The plants are capable of withstanding the scorching heat and drought through use of peculiar narrowed leaves, broad, deep root systems and unusual seeding methods. In addition to cactus flowers and

*The polychrome fairyland of Zabriskie Point in the
Black Mountains of the monument lies in an ancient
lake bed into which sand and silt washed from mountains
now disappeared. After the lake dried up, the sediments were exposed for arrangement by wind and rain.*

many mountain wildflowers, botanists have found two
species of orchid in this desolation. In an area called the
Devil's Cornfield, arrowweed has grown into peculiar
shapes because winds have blown the earth from
around its roots.

Mesquite bushes sift dust from blowing storms, forming a layer of fine silt around them. Here packrats,
pocket mice and other small animals burrow. Insects
come to the animals and plants. Then birds become
predators of the insects and the smaller animals. Last
in the chain of life are predator kit foxes, bobcats and
coyotes which feed on the small creatures of this area.

An early morning inspection of sand dunes reveals
tiny prints of many feet which scampered across the
dunes the previous night. Small markings in the sand
trace the path of an antelope ground squirrel, a mouse,
rat or perhaps some insect. But here and there these
tiny paths are interrupted, obliterated in a flurry of
talon and wing scuffs where some nocturnal bird of
prey, possibly an owl, has dropped from the sky on
silent wings to continue the cycle of life and death. The

rare pallid bat is also found here joining the insect
hunters in evening forays.

Peculiarities of wildlife in this desert wilderness are
apparent in the flocks of saltwater marsh birds and
coots that regularly wade and search for food in Salt
Creek and other salt pools. They find "desert sardines,"
the sourdough name for small minnow-sized, silvery
blue pupfish found in the saltwater pools of Death Valley. These rare and endangered fish are believed to be
descended from an ancestral species originally living in
a prehistoric lake of which the valley was bottom. Sa-
line water holes at Salt Creek, about three times as
salty as the ocean, contain some of these fish.

Faulting, helped by volcanoes and rock masses
formed by lava, have arranged and rearranged the area
many times. This faulting, or fracturing of the crust,
caused the slow collapse of a large section of land under
the valley floor and simultaneously, in compensation,
mountain ranges were thrust upward on both east
and west, virtually cutting off the valley from out side.

Myers

*From an oasis of palms (above)
fed by natural springs at Furnace
Creek, to land so dry that it looks
like rubble of broken pottery (below),
Death Valley is a varied terrain
made up of three basins split by ridges.
Actually, it is not a true valley, but
a graben, or block of earth's crust
bounded by faults and dropped down
in relation to the surrounding walls.*

Short

The scrambled convolutions of stone in Death Valley present a complete geological museum containing exhibits of most of the eras of geologic time. If all the rock layers were pieced together in proper sequence, their total thickness would be more than twelve miles, but the strata have been so broken and jumbled in the upheavals of time that this history is difficult to read. But it is at least partially indicated by the bright colors of the many winding canyons, such as the brilliant red inside Ubehebe Crater; and the Artists Palette area and Natural Bridge have a variety of exposed strata. The drab duns and grays of some stone faces, the yellows of Mustard Canyon and the luminescent turquoise and emerald in washes coming from the Black and Funeral mountains also help display the many dramatic periods of geologic change.

Cloudbursts are a dangerous summer phenomenon in the monument despite the mountains that serve as a barrier to Pacific Ocean moisture. High rising thunderheads occasionally dump torrents of rain in the mountains and create flash floods.

These flash floods cause a rushing wall of water to race down the narrow twisting canyons. The pressure of the water carries huge boulders, silt, gravel and chunks of mountainside with the flood. Suddenly, the

Adams

Young

Devils Golf Course (above) lies in the bed of an ancient lake which, when it dried up, left a salt precipitate from 3 to 5 feet thick that is now broken into spiny pinnacles which grow by capillary action, drawing the salt solution from the water tables below to the surface where the salt is free to crystalize.

A cross section of American nationalities contributed to making the famous beehive charcoal kilns (left) in Wildrose Canyon: Swiss engineers designed them, Chinese laborers built them and Paiute Indians stoked them with juniper and pinyon pine trees.

gorge opens into the broad valley and the flood waters discharge their load of rocks and silt in a gentle incline at the mouth of the canyon. A major part of the Death Valley surface is comprised of these fan-shaped alluvial plains at the mouths of canyons where floods have been disgorged.

The erosion caused by these pell-mell floods from the mountains have gradually filled the valley with silt and rock particles. There is nearly as much "fill" below the surface of the valley now as there is height to the mountain ridges above. Bedrock has been estimated to be nine thousand feet below the surface.

Winds, too, are active in the ever-changing appearance of Death Valley. The fourteen square miles of sand dunes near the north end never appear exactly the same, although varying crosswinds always keep the sand dunes in the same location. These dunes are spectacularly tinted purple and gold by the play of early morning sunlight and shadow.

From Aguereberry Point and from Dante's View in the eastern heights, the Devil's Golf Course in the valley below looks like a smooth salt flat. But at floor level one realizes the "flat" consists of crystalline salt which remains when water seeps up to the ground's surface, evaporates and leaves spiked pinnacles as much as two feet high. As the salt pinnacles form, a breaking sound is clearly discernible in the heating and cooling of the valley floor.

Off the 250 miles of paved roadway in the monument, terrain is still raw, wild and threatening. But the rare combinations and complexities of this land beckon to many year round. There are twelve campgrounds in the monument, and other accommodations are available at Furnace Creek and Stove Pipe Wells. A visitor center is located at Furnace Creek.

Although austere and awesome, Death Valley National Monument has a strong attraction for both naturalists and historians. Here, evidence of the ebullience of the frontier period remains alongside the harsh terrain that appears to threaten the fragile beauty of the isolated patches of wildflowers. However, this strange and foreboding landscape with its mysterious beauty makes an impression on the senses and the imagination that is as enduring as the valley itself. Death Valley qualifies in every respect to be a true national park. Someday soon Congress should act to give it this status.

A stark contrast exists between brightness and shadows in the sunrise reflections on Badwater, a pool of bitter water formed by a seepage of spring water that collects Glauber and epsom salts on its way to the surface of the valley. Nearby is the lowest point in the Western Hemisphere -- 282 feet below sea level.

Adams

Devils Postpile

California

The tremendous gray-brown mass of columnar stones, rising vertically from among the lush forests and brilliant wildflower meadows of the high Sierra Nevada, resembles a pipe organ from some legendary age of giants. On a talus slope at the foot of this perpendicular facing are fragmented sections of polygonal columns strewn in a jumbled mass as though the giant, tiring of his prodigious toy, had smashed parts of it in a fit of anger.

Here, 7,600 feet above sea level, this convoluted mass is the remnant of a million-year-old volcanic eruption. Dominating the surrounding forests and meadows, the entire formation is approximately nine hundred feet long, and as much as two hundred feet high. The columns are from forty to sixty feet tall.

This geological oddity, one of the most remarkable of its kind in North America, is formed of dark, basaltic lava flows, and is included in a one-by-three-mile area set aside in 1911 as Devils Postpile National Monument. It lies between Yosemite and Sequoia national parks on the John Muir Trail. Included in the monument are part of the Middle Fork of the San Joaquin River valley and Rainbow Falls on this river. Soda Spring -- carbonated by carbon dioxide gases escaping into the water source from volcanic activity deep in the earth -- also is in the monument, upstream from the Devils Postpile formation.

Volcanic eruptions higher in the Sierra Nevada, to the east of the monument, caused the original flow more than 900,000 years ago. As the mass cooled, the lava cracked (something like drying mud), into forms with three to seven sides. These forms extend from the surface downward into the mass, and seen in cross section, they resemble columns.

Several times in the last million years, glaciers, some as much as a thousand feet thick, flowed down the river valley and quarried away much of the lava deposits, including one side of the postpile. Only the more resistant columns, the ones seen today, remained standing. Most of the columns are vertical, but some are slanted and others curved, probably due to slight differences in composition, thickness and cooling rates. The tops of the remaining columns were exposed at right angles to the glacial movement and were polished to a high sheen, giving the appearance of a mosaic. In most places, however, they have been roughened by weathering during the time since the last glacial period.

Near upper reaches of the monument is a pumice flat which originated in the post-glacial era. This rock will float on water, but as it powders, it creates a fine dust. In some areas of the monument, this pumice is crum-

D. Muench from Roberts

Devils Postpile is a sector of huge basalt pillars, with four to seven sides each, left standing in the Middle Fork of the San Joaquin valley after a glacier removed the greater part of an ancient, column-shaped lava deposit.

bly, making the footing difficult as one walks about. Some evidence of recent volcanic activity such as bubbly, hot springs are found nearby.

Rainbow Falls on the Middle Fork of the San Joaquin River, about two miles downstream from the Devils Postpile, provides a thrilling view of this rushing river as it plunges over a precipice 140 feet into a deep green pool below. At the foot of the falls are clumps of willows, Western white pine, hemlocks, alders, and numerous wildflowers.

A campground, open from mid-June to October, is maintained at the National Park Service ranger station in the monument. Two miles away from the postpile, at Reds Meadow, supplies, cabins, meals and both saddle and pack horses are available.

The awesome natural forces that sculpted this geometrically shaped Devils Postpile and the volcanic rubble from lava flows torn by glaciation make this monument a mecca for scientists and those interested in natural wonders.

NPS

The great stump of fluted, igneous rock called Devils Tower was declared the first national monument in 1906 and has been for ages an object for legends, stunts and mountaineering.

Within the monument, the sociable prairie dog is protected from all but its many natural predators; elsewhere this stout, terrestrial squirrel is treated as an undesirable varmit.

F. G. Irwin, Cyr Agency

Devils Tower

Wyoming

A mighty laccolith resembling a monstrous petrified tree stump thrusts itself eight hundred feet skyward from a rounded hill above the Belle Fourche River Valley in northeast Wyoming. The massive gray and buff stone -- a dramatic natural landmark northwest of Sundance, Wyoming -- has a startling appearance from all sides. It stands alone -- a single sentinel visible for more than a hundred miles above forest-patched hills and valleys of the surrounding countryside.

A geological prodigy, this rock upthrust had a place in Indian legends of the region. The Kiowa Indians called the place *mato teepe,* meaning "bear's lodge." The Cheyenne legend termed it "bad god's tower." Explorers used it as a guide point, and this landmark came under intense scientific interest at the end of the nineteenth century. It was set aside as Devils Tower National Monument in 1906, the first U. S. national monument to be authorized by a president under the Antiquities Act of 1906.

Volcanic activity, deep inside the earth, caused an explosive upsurge of magma here about fifty million years ago. Some of the volcanic forces erupted, venting their pressure in lava flows of the area. Devils Tower was created when the volcanic thrust pushed this particular mass of molten materials only to the surface -- or perhaps somewhat below the surface -- where it cooled. Erosion in the intervening millions of years, possibly during some ancient deluge, gradually eroded away softer formations of surrounding earth and rock, leaving the fluted sides of this gigantic stone standing 865 feet above its base on a hill.

Devils Tower is more than a thousand feet in diameter at its base. Its top, measuring 200 by 400 feet, is 1,280 feet above the Belle Fourche River and 5,117 feet above sea level. It is the tallest rock formation of its kind in the United States, and geologists continue to study its strange origin and peculiarities.

Because it is comprised of crystallized molten rock and some sedimentary forms, the composition of the towering rock has a strikingly multi-colored appearance as seen from various vantage points in its forest-green and grassy setting. Looking from near the base, the giant pillar has a curiously fluted look, appearing as though the middle part of the tower is made of columns bound by well-developed, open joints. These open, smooth joints, however, seem to join in a weld nearer the top as they taper together at the higher points.

Gravity, along with moisture, heating, freezing and thawing, has been responsible for splitting off huge sections of the columns, and a rubble of talus has been formed at the base of the tower. Colors range from dark igneous porphyry to the bright buffs and reds of colorful sedimentary formations at the base.

Both wildlife and plant life in the monument area and on the one and one-half acre top are richly varied. Prairie dogs are among the most frequent native mammals seen, and a prairie dog town near monument headquarters gives a close-up view of these small, burrowing creatures. Mule and white-tailed deer, as well as cottontails, chipmunks and ground squirrels are among other wild animals seen on occasion. Birds frequently seen are canyon wrens, Audubon warblers, hairy woodpeckers, Western flycatchers and black-capped chickadees. Ponderosa pine, juniper and quaking aspen are major species of trees. Sagebrush, currant, squawbush and serviceberry thickets are interspersed with grass and prickly pear, as are the yellow, white and red flowers of cinquefoil, and yarrow.

The legends of the Indians indicate that the rock was a fascination for the first Americans. The Kiowa story detailed how several flower-gathering Indian maidens, being pursued by an angry bear, jumped onto this rock (then normal sized) which was quickly elevated to its present height by their powerful god. The Cheyenne legend, in which young braves were principals, was somewhat similar in that it also involved huge bears. Attempting to scale the heights, the bears were supposed to have left claw marks -- the flutings -- along the tower sides.

On July 4, 1893, at a celebration, two ranchers, William Rogers and Willard Ripley, climbed the tower and unfurled a United States flag. Since then, more than one thousand expert climbers have made the ascent.

Today, with new roads and bridges across streams easing travel hazards, a visitor center, furnished camp and picnic grounds, this geological phenomenon is a fascinating place to visit.

Powers

NPS

*Above: Sunlight glows golden on the rock
canyon eroded by the Green and Yampa rivers
which flow through Dinosaur monument, located
in a corner of Utah and Colorado wilderness.*

*A park paleontologist directs quarrying of a section
of sandstone from an ancient sandbar, a deposit
in the southwest corner of the monument which
makes Dinosaur the richest known fossil bed
in the world, with some bones 140 million years old.*

Dinosaur

Colorado, Utah

Hyde

*Even before the monument area was known
for its fossils, visitors and explorers had
noted the unusual rock formations like
The Indian Family in Hells Canyon
where various rock strata are exposed.*

Straddling the Colorado-Utah border just south of Wyoming is an ancient burial ground containing the world's largest known deposits of petrified skeletons of dinosaurs. Here also are deep canyons cut by swift-flowing rivers, and sculptured land contours carved by centuries of erosion.

Dinosaur National Monument is not all fossil beds, but these remnants of past ages are remarkable in their extent and number. Mostly found in a sandstone ledge in the southwestern corner of the monument, the bones were first discovered in 1909 by Earl Douglass of the Carnegie Museum. From then until 1922 the museum unearthed tons of fossils of ancient animals, from the Nannosaurus, which was about the size of a chicken, to the huge Apatosaurus (Brontosaurus), with a length of seventy feet and a weight of thirty-five tons. These skeletons were shipped to museums in this country and in Europe. Paleontologists thought all discoveries had been made, but others were found, and reliefing work continues even today. Visitors to the unusual Dinosaur Quarry Visitor Center, which is built directly on the quarry face, can see a working archeological project in progress as workmen use jackhammers, chisels and ice picks to cut away the rock and expose more fossils.

This abundance of fossils is found in this one place because an ancient sandbar was once in a stream that ran through this area. Dying or dead animals, from both swampland and dry-land habitats, were washed downstream and stranded on this sandbar, much as bodies of domestic animals are washed downstream onto sandbars during heavy floods today.

The bones accumulated in great numbers and certain conditions existed which caused the organic materials of the bones to be replaced by minerals which would not decay, such as silica. It is much like replacing the red bricks of a house with yellow bricks -- the dimensions and shape of the house are the same, only the material has changed. Eventually about five thousand feet of sandstone and shale were deposited on top of the sandbar and compacted into rock. Then a powerful upthrust, which also lifted the Rocky Mountains, raised this area so erosion could slowly wear away the rock layers -- and the sandbar and its bones, some over 140 million years old, were exposed once again.

Other dinosaur remains unearthed here included the Coelurus, which was about the size of an ostrich; the Ceratosaurus, a large animal with a horn on its nose; and the Camarasaurus, a heavy-bodied dinosaur which probably browsed on the lower branches of the gingko tree. Fossils of two types of crocodiles and three turtle species have also been unearthed in this quarry.

The canyons within the monument are impressive. The Green River, running in a general northeast to southwest direction, has cut deep gorges through the eastern flank of the Uinta Mountains. The Gates of Lodore on the north has long been known for its magnificent, narrow canyon with colorful, deep red walls more than two thousand feet high. Dangerous for the inexperienced river runner, it ends, appropriately enough, near Disaster Falls. Further downriver is Hell's Half Mile.

Whirlpool Canyon, named for the hundreds of eddies in its waters, has walls which tower above the Green, keeping the canyon in dark shadows throughout the day. Further south, the slow waters of Island Park, a large, flat, horseshoe-shaped area of the river, end suddenly as the river enters Split Mountain Canyon.

The Yampa River, running east to west to its junction with the Green River at Echo Park in the center of the monument, has also been active in cutting canyons. It became the center of controversy during the 1950's when engineers proposed construction of a dam there. Congress, however, voted to protect park values and did not permit the dam to be built.

The river first cut into relatively soft rock, and after a long period of erosion, its course was established in many bends or meanders. The soft rocks in the river bed were worn away completely, and with an upthrust of the area, the waters concentrated on cutting into the harder strata beneath. The resulting gorge, while not as deep as those of the Green River, is contorted and twisted with numerous gooseneck turns. Near the junction of these two rivers is famous Steamboat Rock, a massive, thin, elongated piece of rock over a thousand feet high, its sheer faces rising straight above the river, which winds around it in a sharp bend.

Erosion has also played a role in the fantastic contortions of rock that can be seen throughout the monument. All geologic foundations exposed here are sedimentary, having been deposited by winds and water.

Vegetation has adapted admirably to the semiarid environment. At lower elevations sagebrush, shadscale, rabbit brush and greasewood predominate; mountain mahogany, serviceberry and other shrubs grow at the higher elevations. Junipers and pinyon pines survive on the mountain slopes, and ponderosa pines, Douglas fir and quaking aspens flourish in the more moist regions and in shaded, protected canyons. Along the river banks are cottonwoods, willows and box elders.

Several hundred species of wildflowers have been found here. Although the slopes appear barren from a distance, closer examination reveals a covering of pink trailing phlox in early spring, followed by sulphur flowers. Patches of bright red Indian paintbrush, yellow and purple beeplants, balsamroots, lupines, penste-

The Grand Overhang looms above tiny kayaks on the Yampa River, here in one of its quieter sectors.

Hyde

Sunlight glows on the moss-covered antlers of a mule deer (above), an animal about the size and shading of its relation, the white-tailed deer. Both deer walk on their toes with a graceful unguligrade step characteristic of most very fast-running animals.

The brown and white female sage grouse (below) displays protective coloring that blends remarkably well with the environment.

The Whispering Cave is located in Echo Park near the junction of the Green and Yampa rivers.

mons, sego lilies and evening primroses mix with this color blanket.

Larger mammals, such as deer, coyote and bobcat, range in the low country, and rodents -- beaver, musk-rat, porcupine, marmot, chipmunk and prairie dog -- are found throughout the region. Cottontails, jackrab-bits and golden-mantled ground squirrels are often seen. Other animals living in this habitat are badgers, foxes, weasels, minks, skunks and pack rats.

The great range in elevation accounts for the more than eighty species of birds. During the day a turkey vulture or Say's phoebe may be noticed, but it is at dusk when many of the birds come out of their nests, includ-ing the gray-brown rock wren, robin, Western fly-

The view north of Round Top takes in a serpentine section of the Yampa River Canyon.

catcher, Audubon's warbler, red-shafted flicker, cliff swallow and white-throated swift. Permanent residents of this rough, dry land are golden and bald eagles, red-tailed hawks and great horned owls.

Two campgrounds with facilities are near the visitor center and Dinosaur Quarry; two picnic areas are located near Echo Park. Other accommodations may be found just outside the southwestern entrance at Vernal and Jensen, Utah. Numerous primitive river camps on both rivers provide night stopping points for the river runner, and scheduled float trips are made by guides. The rapids in the monument are many and fast, and only the experienced should try a river trip without local authorized guides.

Indians lived in this region long before America was discovered by Europeans. Pieces of charred wood from ancient campfires, as well as pottery fragments, have been found in the sands that cover the floors of caves. Mantle's Cave, a large cliff shelter on the Yampa River, was occupied by agricultural Indians between A. D. 400 and 800, for pieces of corncob have been found there.

Petroglyphs (carved pictures on rock walls) and some pictographs (painted pictures) can be seen along the rivers and in shallow caves. No one knows if these relics of ancient Indians were religious symbols, clan mark-

ings, story narratives, or merely doodles.

A small Spanish expedition led by Father Escalante camped in the area on the bank of the Green River in 1776. They were looking for a land route from Santa Fe, New Mexico, to the missions at Monterey, California. Father Escalante kept the records of the trip and reported that they came to "two high bluffs, which, after forming a sort of corral, come so close together that one can scarcely see the opening through which the river comes." Historians believe that both references are to Split Mountain and its canyon.

In 1823 William Ashley and six trappers came down the Green River from Lodore to Split Mountain Canyon, and explored the region. Major John Wesley Powell, leading expeditions down the Green and Colorado rivers in 1869 and 1871, mapped the area and called attention to it in his writings. In 1915 the dinosaur quarry and eighty acres of surrounding land were made a national monument by President Woodrow Wilson. The monument was enlarged in 1938 to include the spectacular canyon country.

This greatest of the world's fossil finds may have named the monument, but the rivers, scenic canyons and eroded mountains are equally worthy of preservation for the present generations and those to come.

Florissant Fossil Beds
and Agate Fossil Beds

Colorado, Nebraska

The broadly rolling inclines of western Nebraska near Agate Springs and the quiet mountain valley near the town of Florissant, Colorado, give scant evidence of the vast store of paleontologic treasures just beneath their surfaces. Yet these two areas have yielded a wealth of fossilized records from prehistoric eras.

Beside the deep slash of the Niobrara River in Nebraska, paleontologists have discovered thousands of fossils of strange beasts that roamed the earth centuries ago. When the first of the Rocky Mountains surged upward ages ago, they created a semitropical savanna which was crossed by meandering rivers where dinosaurs and other animals thrived and would congregate. In the normal course of events, many died along one of the streams, and seasonal floods carried their remains downriver where they were dropped and entombed in the mud. This process probably continued for centuries until a layer of concentrated fossil bones, nearly three feet thick, had accumulated. Later the Niobrara River cut its channel to unearth the fossils.

These two seemingly common hills thus contain evidence of mammalian ascendency in the animal world of twenty-one million years ago. Among the specimens were remains of Diceratherium, a small, two-horned rhinoceros, and a strange, clawed animal called Moropus, which had the head of a horse, the body of a camel, the front legs of a rhinoceros and the hind legs of a bear. Historically the fossils attracted scientific interest in the late 1880's when white settlers moved into the area, formerly controlled by the Sioux Indians. But it was not designated a national monument until 1965.

Development plans call for Agate Fossil Beds National Monument to be opened to the scrutiny of both scientists and the public. Visitors today can see exposed fossils in their sediment beds at the headquarters area. Because this park is a working outdoor museum, other representative fossils are being exposed so that the exact position of the skeletal remains can be seen as they are reliefed in their beds.

In a gentle valley of the Colorado Rockies, fifteen miles west of Pike's Peak, wildflowers provide a brilliantly colored mantle for sedimentary layers preserving one of the largest deposits of insect and plant fossils in North America. These rich fossil beds have yielded specimens representing more than one thousand species of the plant and animal life of a bygone era.

Scientists studying the formations believe that for many prehistoric centuries the Florissant area experienced periodic volcanic eruptions. These eruptions dropped layer upon layer of volcanic ash which carried birds, leaves and twigs with it to the bottom of the ancient lake in the valley below. Further ash-falls and mud flows covered and preserved the debris.

In recent years, scientists have gained much information by excavating portions of that prehistoric valley. The various "digs" have yielded whole petrified tree trunks, often ancient sequoias up to ten feet in diameter, and trunks of trees similar to modern-day elm, along with bark and leaves of oak, walnut, pine, beech, willow and maple. Almost all the fossil butterflies of the New World have come from this site in the Rocky Mountains.

Agate Fossil Beds National Monument is near Scotts Bluff National Historical Monument and comprises 3,-150 acres. Florissant Fossil Beds National Monument covers about six thousand acres and was added to the National Park System in 1969. Visitor facilities and trails are available at Agate the year around, but only on weekends during winter. Facilities have not yet been developed at Florissant.

Plans for both monuments include development of tourist centers, museums, interpretative trails and wayside exhibits detailing the area's ancient history. Meanwhile, relatively open terrain and easy access at both sites provide an opportunity to view the prairie hills of western Nebraska and the Rocky Mountain valleys, as well as space to ponder the eras of earlier history when huge mammals and tiny insects alike fell victim to geological change.

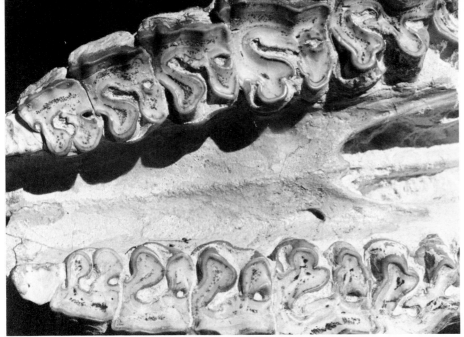

Specimens from Agate Fossil Beds, some over 21 million years old, are in prize collections the world over--like the above set of teeth from Diceratherium, or the two-horned rhinoceros.

The skull and upper jaw of the grass-eating Diceratherium (right) measure 14 inches long.

Volcanic eruptions 40 million years ago in the Florissant area west of Pike's Peak, Colorado, entombed sequoia stumps (lower right), some ten feet in diameter.

A branch of a species of dwarf-cypress (below) left fine details in the volcanic ash.

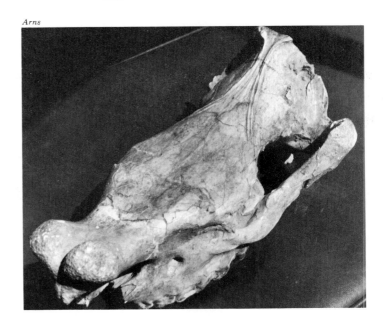

Glacier Bay

Alaska

Usually nature moves so slowly that its effects are not noticeable during the lifetime of a man. But not at Glacier Bay National Monument, located along Alaska's southeast coast in the midst of towering mountains, perpetually clad in snow. Here over twenty tremendous glaciers, hundreds and even thousands of feet thick, move down the mountainsides, carving new valleys in the slopes, pushed by the great weight of the snow and ice constantly accumulating on their tops. Ocean-born storms feed these rivers of ice so consistently that many of them flow all the way to the waters of the bay, where they end in magnificent ice cliffs. Great chunks of ice continually break away from the glacier cliff faces as their support of ice melts or crumbles. When these blocks, some over two hundred feet high, crash into the bay, they cause huge waves. The larger ones fill the tidal inlets with thousands of floating icebergs, many of which could swamp a boat. Muir and Johns Hopkins glaciers are so active in icefalls that it is seldom possible to approach them closer than a couple of miles.

All stages of glacial action can be seen here, from active, moving ice masses to the slowly dying, stagnant ones. Muir Glacier, one of the most active on the entire Alaskan coast and named for famous naturalist-writer John Muir who visited the bay in 1879, has a sheer face rising over two hundred feet from the water and is nearly two miles wide. Most of the fingerlike inlets of the monument terminate at similar cliffs, such as Johns Hopkins Glacier, Grand Pacific Glacier and Plateau Glacier in the bay, monstrous Brady Glacier in Taylor Bay, and Lituya and North Crillon glaciers in Lituya Bay on the Pacific Coast.

A glacier's normal travel rate is one or two inches a day, while a foot or two a day is considered fast and unusual. A rate of twenty or thirty feet a day, however, such as Muir Glacier occasionally achieves, is rare.

In a slower-moving river of ice, if the air in the lower elevations is comparatively warm and there is little accumulation of snow, its lower end (snout) will melt before reaching the waters. Climate and topography thus have much to do with the advance and retreat of glaciers, and in return, the glaciers are sensitive indicators of long-range climatic changes. Glaciers that do not reach the bay deposit their debris at their terminuses in ridges called moraines, and many of the glaciers within the monument are of this type.

The periodic fluctuations of these glaciers have attracted worldwide attention since the 1890's. Ancient, weathered tree stumps, uncovered by retreating glaciers, such as on the shores of Muir Inlet, show that climatic changes take place in a pendulumlike rhythm counted in centuries.

With each recession, the rock-strewn ground left uncovered by the ice was first invaded by fungi, lichens and mosses. Later horsetails began to grow, followed by fireweed, Alpine wildflowers, dwarf willows, and cottonwoods and alders. When the soil had been fertilized by many seasons of growth and decay, giant forests of spruce and hemlock gradually cloaked the land.

Then the pendulum swung, the climate became colder, and the reservoirs of ice among the mountain peaks were filled to the brim; floods washed down tons of sand and gravel, killing the vegetation and leaving only stumps. The glaciers began to grow once again and wind their way down the slopes, covering the stumps with a sheet of ice over their protective gravel layer until the glacier retreated again. The stumps were then washed clean by streams from the glacier or exposed by the clearing processes of the bay's tides.

The glaciers seen in the monument today are remnants of a general ice advance which began about four thousand years ago. This period did not approach the extent of glaciation during the Pleistocene Age, however, and is sometimes referred to as the "little ice age." The ice reached its maximum limits about 1750 and Glacier Bay was completely unknown, covered with an ice cap some three thousand feet thick, even in 1794 when George Vancouver sailed through Cross Sound into Icy Strait, from which Glacier Bay begins. A slow melting trend began, although in 1892 ice still covered Muir and Reid inlets, and Tarr Inlet had not yet been discovered.

An earthquake in 1899 accelerated the downhill advance of the ice flows and upset the balance established by the climate. The bay became choked with floating ice and put an end to the excursions of early tourists who had gone close to the ice faces. The post-quake recession, however, continued until, finally by 1907,

Sunset on Glacier Bay (above), the second largest unit in the park system, silhouettes several of the ice-covered mountains whose snowstorms feed over twenty glaciers in the St. Elias and Fairweather ranges.

Towards the southern end of the monument, a primeval forest of spruce and hemlock is carpeted with thick moss (right). This type of forest is the last and highest development of vegetation which began when the last glacier retreated, leaving the warming land first to mosses and lichens, then to willow and alder thickets, and finally to these forests which are still untouched in many parts of Alaska.

Czolowski

The glaciers flowing into the bay today are remainders of the "little ice age" that began 4,000 years ago and reached its maximum extent into the bay in 1750.

the quake effects had largely been overcome and an equilibrium was established once more.

Another earthquake in 1958 weakened an estimated ninety million tons of rock on the cliffs above the terminus of Lituya Glacier. Avalanching down the mountain, the slide ripped off a thousand feet of the glacier's snout and crashed into the water. On the ridge opposite the slide, a wave surged 1,720 feet high, and as it moved seaward down the bay, it completely stripped four square miles of forest from the shore.

Today some glaciers are retreating, some are advancing, and the remainder fluctuate. Muir Glacier has receded over twenty miles since 1879, leaving John Muir's cabin, originally built close to the snout, far down the inlet. Grand Pacific and Johns Hopkins glaciers, however, have moved forward over the years. If the present trend toward general recession continues, great changes in the configuration of the upper bay area will take place in the next fifty years. Changes equally profound will occur if the ice advances down the bay, which is entirely possible.

Glacier Bay, about seventy miles long and between three to ten miles wide, lies between paralleling mountain ranges higher than any in the continental United States. To the east and north is the largely unmapped, unexplored St. Elias Range which includes Mount St. Elias, one of the world's most spectacular glaciated mountains, reaching a height of eighteen thousand feet 140 miles northwest of the monument. The highest peak on the east shore of the bay in this range is Mount Barnard; it is only 8,214 feet high but rises abruptly from the water.

To the west lies the snowy Fairweather Range, its highest peak, Mount Fairweather, being 15,320 feet on the northwest boundary of the monument. Several other mountains exceed twelve thousand feet on this peninsula between the Pacific and the bay.

Glacier Bay is dotted with islands large and small; some, like the Beardslee Islands at the southern entrance of the bay, are low and densely wooded, and others, such as the Marble Islands just to the north, are steep and mostly treeless, serving as rookeries for thousands of seabirds. The majority of the islands in the mid and upper bay are solid rock, worn and scarred by the ice sheets.

From Cross Sound, Dundas Bay winds its fjordlike waters many miles inland along heavily wooded shores. Further up the Pacific Coast is Lituya Bay, its narrow entrance and violent tidal currents making access extremely difficult.

The southeast portion of the monument, near the National Park Service headquarters at Bartlett Cove, is a veritable paradise -- a luxuriant primeval forest of moss-draped spruce and hemlock.

Alaskan brown bears, black bears and rare glacier bears -- bluish-colored animals which scientists classify as a color phase of the black bear -- may sometimes be observed quite close to the glacier fronts. Also living in

Johns Hopkins Glacier on the northwest of Glacier Bay is highly active: It has steadily retreated since 1892 and often releases 200-foot-high chunks of ice into the bay, making it unsafe to approach by boat closer than two miles.

A small craft passes below Reid Glacier, avoiding icebergs which, if disturbed, could roll over and swamp the boat.

these mountains are minks, martens, otters, coyotes, wolves, lynx, wolverines, foxes, Sitka deer, moose and mountain goats. Hair seals, sea lions, killer and humpback whales, and porpoises may frequently be seen in the waters of the bay. Icebergs sometimes provide resting places for seals.

Various waterfowl inhabit the inlets and islands of the bay -- loons, cormorants, geese, common eiders, guillemots, murrelets, puffins and many gulls, terns and ducks. Bald eagles, ptarmigans, grouse, northwest crows, ravens and hummingbirds dwell along the shorelands.

During the late summer and early autumn spawning season, salmon invade the streams of the monument, attracting many bears, especially in Beartrack Cove, where the bruins have worn broad, winding trails along the stream banks. Dolly Varden and cutthroat trout

live in many of the crystal-clear lakes and streams.

Glacier Bay National Monument, established in 1925 by President Coolidge, is still a primitive wilderness where a hiking party can travel for days without seeing any signs of civilization. Part of the northern boundary is the border between Alaska and Canada, and Tongass National Forest lies adjacent to the monument on the eastern and southern boundaries.

The only way to reach the monument is by boat or plane from the capital city of Juneau, about sixty miles southeast. There are no campgrounds, but the monument's several hundred miles of shoreline provide unlimited camping opportunities, and a small lodge is located at Bartlett Cove, where summer temperatures seldom exceed seventy-two degrees.

John Muir was the first to write about this ice-covered land. Since he did not know the exact location of

the "ice-mountain," he hired a guide who had been there as a boy:

> At length the clouds lifted a little, and beneath their gray fringes I saw the berg-filled expanse of the bay, and the feet of the mountains that stand about it, and the imposing fronts of five huge glaciers, the nearest being immediately beneath me. This was my first general view of Glacier Bay, a solitude of ice and snow and newborn rocks, dim, dreary, mysterious . . . breasting the snow again, crossing the shifting avalanche slopes and torrents, I reached camp about dark, wet and weary . . . and glad.

Muir would be glad today also, for Glacier Bay National Monument has been proposed as a national park. If conservationists prevail and this spectacular land becomes a national park, it will be the largest one in America, exceeding Yellowstone by thousands of acres.

From Mount Abdallah, Reid Glacier (above) is seen across the waters of its inlet which began to form as the glacier retreated after 1892.

The jagged peaks above the cold majesty of Black Rapids Glacier (right) are shrouded by a layer of snow and misty clouds.

Roberts

A tributary of the Colorado River is Havasu Creek located in the Grand Canyon area adjacent to the monument. The creek and its canyon are noted for waterfalls, colorful cliffs and the beautiful blue green tints of the water.

Ornamenting both rims of the Grand Canyon are sego lilies, otherwise called Mariposa tulips.

Grand Canyon

Arizona

The Grand Canyon was once described by the late naturalist, Joseph Wood Krutch, as "the most revealing single page of earth's history anywhere open on the face of the earth." It is all that -- and more. Millions of visitors flock to the Grand Canyon each year. Its north and south rims are flooded with sedentary tourists content to stay on the rims and experience this awesome chasm by peering into its vastness.

In complete contrast to the national park is the Grand Canyon National Monument which adjoins it downriver on its western boundary. A narrow, hot, dusty but graded road -- sometimes impassable after storms and during winter -- leads from both Fredonia and Colorado City on Arizona's Kaibab Plateau (north rim) sixty-five miles to the Tuweep Ranger Station. Six miles further down the road is the canyon rim. This trip is not hazardous, but should not be attempted without ample gasoline, plenty of food and water, camping equipment and tools, for there are no facilities, only a primitive campground at the ranger station.

For the visitor who wishes to enjoy a primitive environment however, the trip is well worth it. The 1,500 people a year who traverse this route stand in fascination at Toroweap Point, overlooking the intersection of the Colorado River and Toroweap Valley. Here the Grand Canyon averages less than a mile wide and nearly three thousand feet in depth. On quiet days the roar of Lava Falls can be heard in the Colorado River.

This section of the Grand Canyon was formed basically the same way as the rest of the canyon -- by the unending force of the waters of the Colorado. But the monument had an extra geologic chapter of volcanic activity. After the canyon had been formed, great masses of molten lava spewed from the sixty or more volcanic craters in the area. Some of the lava flows reached the canyon brink and plunged in fiery torrents down the walls, damming the river at the bottom. Several lakes were thus formed in the canyon (lake deposits of silt have been found in the rock niches far above the river), but the river water spilled over these dams and finally eroded them away, continuing later to cut the bedrock fifty feet deeper.

A Colorado River "dam" built by lava which flowed down Toroweap Canyon (now Toroweap Valley) reached a height of nearly five hundred feet. Remnants of this dam may be seen on both sides of the river and in the rapids of Lava Falls. Another natural dam of lava -- built across Toroweap Canyon and thus it did not reach the river -- is still intact, for the water that once flowed in this canyon was not sufficient to erode the hardened lava. Rock falls and silt have since filled the area behind the dam, forming flat deposits, which caused the canyon to become a valley.

Three thousand feet below the Toroweap overlook, the Colorado River snakes through the Grand Canyon, which is unique here in the monument because the volcanic deposits on the walls are found nowhere else along the river's canyon.

Hardened lava may still be seen clinging to the Grand Canyon's walls, making it one of the most conspicuous features of the monument, and a volcanic cone, Vulcan's Throne, was formed less than a mile from the rim itself.

Plant life in the monument is sparse, but similar to that of the national park with yuccas giving out a shower of white blossoms each spring, and bear grass lifting its yellow-flowered stalk high into the air in June. Sagebrush and greasewood (in Paiute, *toro* refers to greasewood and *weap* means "valley") dominate the northern flats of the region near Mount Trumbull.

Pronghorns, canyon wrens and coyotes are some of the creatures that have made their home in this desolate area. Lizards and a variety of snakes, such as the pink Grand Canyon rattlesnake, also find the desert-like region a good habitat.

Major John Wesley Powell was the monument's first explorer as he traveled down the entire length of the Colorado in 1869. He wrote of his trip through the monument area: "What a conflict of water and fire there must have been here! Just imagine a river of molten lava running down into a river of melted snow. What a seething and a boiling of the waters; what clouds of steam rolled into the heavens!"

Recently the monument was threatened with a proposal that a dam should be built downstream which would have created an artificial lake throughout the western portion of the Grand Canyon, extending even into the national park. Conservationists won this fight in 1968, and the big dam was defeated.

The present monument was established by Presidential proclamation in 1932 and is located primarily on the north rim. The south rim portion is adjacent to Havasu Falls and Creek, the site of a unique tribe of Indians, the Havasupai, who still live in a Shangri-la setting halfway down the canyon.

The monument is a place for those who love rugged, remote regions. This portion of the Grand Canyon is, in effect, reserved for those who want a wilderness-type experience.

85

Great Sand Dunes

Colorado

In sharp contrast with the snow-capped peaks of the mountains nearly surrounding them, the dunes of Great Sand Dunes National Monument stand at the edge of a grasslands valley in southern Colorado, a thousand miles from the nearest ocean or sea. The highest island dunes in the country, they rise over six hundred feet from the San Luis Valley floor and are shifted, sorted, piled and repiled by winds.

Three conditions are generally necessary for the formation of sand dunes -- sand, wind and a natural trap. Here streams fed by melted snow carried sand, silt and gravel into this basin for thousands of years. Most of these streams dropped their loads of material and sunk into the valley floor.

The floor itself had little vegetation, and there was not much to hold the sand in place. Once in the valley the sand and silt were exposed to prevailing southwesterly winds which blew and bounced the sand grains toward the Sangre de Cristo Mountains on the east and northeast of the valley. On reaching the abrupt mountain barrier, the wind swept over and upward through the mountain passes with a subsequent loss in velocity. The sand was then too heavy to be swept through the passes and was dropped at the foot, caught in the curvature of the range. The sand gradually piled up and these dunes were born, stretching ten miles along the base of the mountains.

Today, the ceaseless southwesterly winds sometimes change direction and reshape the dunes, especially when storms blow in from the northeast. The ridges at the tops of the dunes are shifted until they seem to lean backwards, and after the storm is over, the southwest winds restore the ridge contours to their previous shape. Sometimes the winds are strong enough to cause plumes of sand to rise from the ridge tops and curl over the downslopes. Although superficial day-by-day changes are visible in the ripple patterns and in the ridges and slopes, the dunes have remained basically unchanged over the decades.

The San Luis Valley, which ranges from 7,500 to 8,000 feet above sea level and is three times the size of Delaware, owes its horseshoe-shaped configuration to dramatic disturbances in the earth's crust many millions of years ago. At that time an inland sea extended the length of North America from the Gulf of Mexico to the Arctic Ocean, roughly following the line of the later-formed Rocky Mountains. This long, narrow inland sea was marked by zones of weakness in the earth's crust. Interior pressures slowly began to exert themselves, and over a period of a million years the floor of this sea was pushed upward, and what had been sedimentary layers at the bottom of the sea became the peaks of high mountains. Colorado was in the center of this activity, and the San Luis Valley is a product of these upheavals.

Besides the snow-capped Sangre de Cristo peaks on the east and northeast, the valley's horseshoe shape is formed by the San Juan Mountains on the west and the San Luis Hills on the south. The open end of the valley thus faces southwest in the direction of the winds.

Few streams enter the valley, the principal flows occuring in spring when the mountain snow melts. Medano Creek follows the eastern boundary of the dunes for several miles until it suddenly disappears into the sand to appear again five miles away as an immense spring. An area of smaller dunes, formed from sand which blows across the stream bed during dry seasons, is east of the creek. Here are skeletons of a pine forest, called the Ghost Forest, which was covered by these smaller dunes and then uncovered when they moved elsewhere.

Rising over 600 feet from the grassy San Luis Valley floor in southern Colorado, the Great Sand Dunes appear as foothills to the snowy peaks of the Sangre de Cristo Range. The highest inland dunes in the country, they stretch ten miles along the range's base.

Near the campground and Medano Creek is the Ghost Forest, all that remains of a large stand of trees covered over with sand and then uncovered by wind. Here grasses grow sparsely on the sands where once these ancient trees stood tall and provided cool shade.

The sand dunes and Medano Creek provide a variety of living conditions. In addition to the flora and fauna of the valley, foothill slopes and forested mountains, there is the distinctive but sparse vegetation of the dunes themselves. A lack of water and the moving grains of sand prevent plants from gaining a foothold, except in depressions where small patches of grass, a species of low pea plant, and sunflowers find conditions suitable to their growth and stabilize the sands. In certain locations where more sand may blow into these pockets occasionally, the plants have developed extremely long stems, thus adjusting to their barren, changing environment.

Much wildlife characteristic of the rabbit brush and grasslands in the valley can be found along the southwest edge of the dunes area -- rabbits, ground squirrels, coyotes, magpies and other small animals and birds. In the pinyon-juniper-ponderosa pine belt of the foothills in the eastern and northern portions of the monument, chipmunks, mule deer, several types of jays and other creatures typical of this habitat may be observed. Over 150 species of birds have been recorded in the monument region.

Ten thousand years ago this area was occupied by nomadic hunters, and two of their campsites have been excavated, yielding spear points and bones of an extinct species of bison.

Ute Indians largely controlled the valley during relatively recent times, but certain Pueblos and Apaches from the south, and Commanches, Cheyennes and Arapahoes from the north periodically visited here.

Spanish explorers are known to have been in the San Luis Valley, including Juan Bautista de Anza in 1779, who traversed the west side of the valley and the Sangre de Cristo Pass south of the dunes. In 1806-1807 Lieutenant Zebulon Pike, on assignment to explore the lands acquired through the Louisiana Purchase, entered the valley by way of the Medano Pass and wrote a description of the dunes in his journal. Other men later visited the dunes, including Captain John W. Gunnison in 1853, about the time permanent settlement of the valley began. The dunes were made a national monument in 1932.

A campground, picnic area and visitor center are located on the southeastern edge of the dune mass. Visitors may walk anywhere on the dunes; a walk to the top and return takes about three hours. In summer the sand is usually hot during mid-afternoon, but mornings and evenings are pleasant.

These delicately sculptured but massive sand dunes look out of place in the midst of forested, snow-capped mountains. Sunlight plays bizarre games with them, changing their color, texture and shadows every hour, and these misplaced dunes take on a strange beauty not shared with their seaside cousins.

An ideal combination of beautifully curved lines and soft shadows make the dunes a pleasing composition for both the professional and amateur photographer. Although minute changes can be seen in the dunes daily, they have remained basically unchanged over the years.

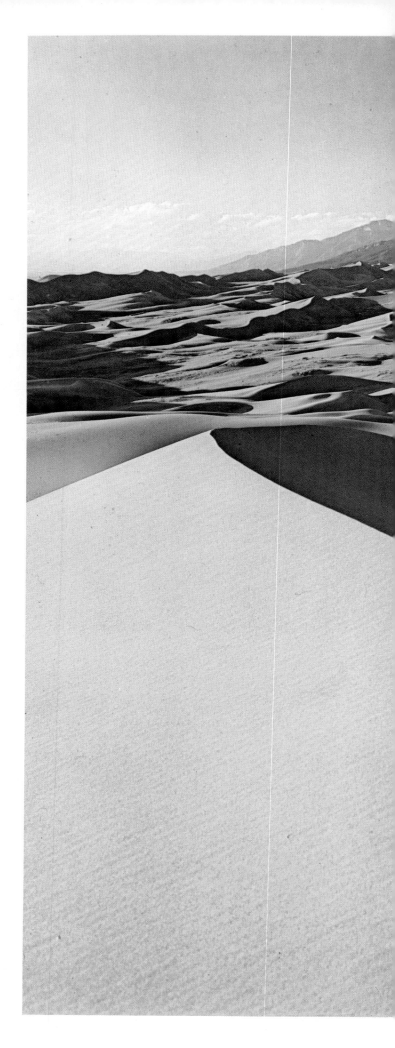

Jewel Cave

South Dakota

Chocolate-colored flowstone drapes a section of a wall in Jewel Cave. The cave is primitive looking with no lights or established trails and few ladders down the steep slopes of the tunnels.

Jewel Cave is for the real spelunker -- one who dislikes electric lights and wide, established trails which look to him like four-lane highways. He leaves these things to nearby almost people-trodden Wind Cave National Park. Located in southwestern South Dakota, Jewel Cave is still not fully explored. There are only a few ladders down steep slopes, and gasoline lanterns, available at the National Park Service headquarters, are necessary to see the fantastic formations.

The entrance of the cave is on the side of a ravine called Hell Canyon. The main passages lead to side galleries and various-sized chambers, the first of which is fine-grained limestone, looking somewhat like Gothic-style architecture. The walls and ceilings of many of the galleries are lined with a thick layer of calcite crystals. Many of them, called dogtooth crystals, are very sharp and sparkle like jewels under a light, thus giving the cave its name. These crystals range in color from light green tints to darker greens and bronze.

Boxlike cavities along the walls and ceilings are covered with minute crystals of many shades of brown, from light bronze to deep chocolate. Globulites, also called cave coral or popcorn, can be seen in clusters of seven or eight inches in depth. Small helictites, resembling deformed pretzels, protrude from the cave walls in every possible direction.

"Soda straws," or very thin, hollow stalactites, of up to thirty-eight inches long but only one-quarter inch in diameter, have been found in Jewel Cave, although many of these near the natural entrance were destroyed by early visitors. Flowstone draperies can be found here in rainbow colors -- yellows, reds, browns, blues and blacks. One curious formation closely resembles a plate of bacon and eggs, the bright yellow "yolks" standing out from the egg "whites" and the red and brown stripes of the "bacon."

Gypsum has several spectacular and rare forms in this cave. Gypsum "flowers" look like toothpaste squeezed through ragged cracks in the walls, and gypsum needles grow upward and outward. These arrow-straight needles are as thin as human hairs and often

*An "egg yolk" stalagmite rises from
a terraced floor. The cave is still not
completely explored, and formations
such as this are being discovered with
each new trip into its dark depths.*

grow in large clusters, looking like a beard. Moonmilk, made of magnesium carbonate compound, is a phosphorescent white material with the consistency of cottage cheese and is not uncommon in caves, but a form of it resembling silver bubblegum exists only here. There are many other unusual formations and more are being discovered with each trip into unexplored sections.

Jewel Cave was formed when the Black Hills were uplifted, thus fracturing the limestone and providing underground channels for water, which dissolved much of the limestone and formed the passages and chambers. After the cave had partially dried, seeping groundwater saturated with calcium carbonate entered the cave, each drip depositing a minute amount of mineral, and over the centuries the deposits took unusual shapes.

The cave was discovered in 1900 by some prospectors, Albert and F. W. Michaud. Although they never found any precious minerals in the cave, they thought they could turn it into a tourist attraction. The venture was not too successful, but the government was interested in making it a national monument, and President Theodore Roosevelt made it part of the National Park System in 1908. It was closed for many decades, however, and much early knowledge of it was lost. Until 1958 the cave was thought to be quite small, but park rangers rediscovered some of the "lost" passages, and other explorers have since gone far beyond those areas. About thirty-five miles of Jewel Cave has thus far been explored, already making it one of the most extensive caves known to man. One of the more spectacular sections of the cave is being developed for use and will be opened to the public for the first time during the National Park Service's centennial celebration in 1972. Elevator service from the new visitor center will provide easy access to the heretofore remote section. No other facilities are present or planned.

The cave lies beneath a rough terrain of gulches, canyons and ravines. The monument includes a virgin stand of ponderosa pine, one of the last remaining such stands in the Black Hills region. Scattered clumps of box elder, snowberry, mountain mahogany and other shrubs thrive on the dry hillsides. Wildflowers bloom profusely during spring and early summer, giving little indication of the underground fairyland below them.

Short

Mormon settlers called this species of yucca the Joshua tree because the branches seemed to point to the promised land.

Joshua Tree

California

Thrue-Yann, Cyr Agency

The Gilia flower's reddish violet and the poppy's yellow are splattered across the arid California country in late spring whenever the winter rains have been good.

These trees that grow up, down and out in every possible direction are called Joshua trees, said to have been named by the Mormons who saw the crooked, a-symmetrical branches as a symbol pointing to the promised land they were seeking, just as the Biblical Joshua pointed the way into the promised land of the Israelites.

In spite of its prickly appearance, the Joshua tree is not a cactus, but a kind of yucca (*Yucca brevifolia*), a member of the greatly varied lily family, and is one of the most spectacular plants of the Southwestern deserts. They grow mostly in southern California, but are also found in a few areas of Nevada, Utah and Arizona. The Joshua tree may attain a height of forty feet and during March and April bears creamy white blossoms in clusters eight to fourteen inches long at the ends of the branches. However, every tree does not bloom every year.

The Joshua tree is often confused with the Mojave yucca (or Spanish dagger) whose leaves are much longer than the Joshua's and also grow at lower elevations. Joshua trees are normally found between three thousand and five thousand feet.

Its sharp, ten-inch-long leaves grow in clusters and when they die, they droop downward and dry into thornlike needles. The branches' strange contortions are caused by the death of the terminal buds after they blossom. Thus each elbow of the crooked arms was at one time the end of the branch where the blossoms died. The twisted arms are also caused by the yucca boring beetle: The tree builds a material over the hole made by the insect, forcing the branch to grow in a different direction.

The Indians found the Joshua tree very useful. They used the buds and flowers for food, the needles on the ends of the branches for sewing, the roots for dye and soap; other parts of the plant were made into rope, sandals, mats and baskets.

One of the best stands of Joshua trees in the world is the focus of Joshua Tree National Monument, one hundred miles east of Los Angeles. Located on the border of the California Mojave (mo-HA-vee) and Colorado deserts, the monument is rich in species of cacti and other desert plant life.

It is phenomenal how these plants survive in the desert with its extreme heat and lack of rain. They give themselves plenty of room to develop extensive root systems, some of which may reach fifty feet from the trunk. The little moisture they do receive -- eight or ten inches a year -- is strictly rationed by the use of thin, hard bark with few pores to let the moisture escape, or soft, spongy bark which holds water inside. Most trees lose much of their water through their leaves, so the desert varieties have developed small leaves which they shed early each year. Cacti do not grow leaves, depending only on their stems for food production.

The creosote bush spreads its roots very close to the ground surface to catch the rainwater before it evaporates, and it has also developed leaves with a heavy, waxy coating. The ocotillo loses its leaves during each period of drought and grows them again after a rain. The mesquite has roots that may reach a depth of fifty or sixty feet to tap underground sources of water.

During spring, if the winter rains have been good, the monument produces a blanket of colorful blossoms -- the bright yellows of the creosote bush and desert senna, the deep purples and pinks of the calico (hedgehog) cactus, the red-tinged greenish yellows of the thorny-fruited cholla cactus, the blues of the sagebrush and the red-purples of the white ratany.

Jumping cholla (CHOH-ya), also called teddybear cholla, is quite conspicuous along the Cholla Cactus Garden Trail in the center of the monument. It is considered the most handsome of the cactus family, but it has many sharp, barbed spines which can easily penetrate the skin. Its name is based on the impression that the spines jump out at anyone who gets too close. The cholla are more friendly to animals, and cactus wrens build their nests in their branches, even adding extra spines for safety against predators. Lizards, crickets, mice and snakes also find haven in jumping cholla.

The Indians used the fruit of the squawbush (or skunkbush) for making a drink which resembled pink lemonade. When the fruit is held in the mouth without being chewed, it tends to quench thirst.

The short, flat cactus with the magenta blossoms visible in the monument is called the beaver tail cactus. Although this plant looks quite smooth from a distance, it has many sharp, tiny spines which readily penetrate the skin.

Joshua Tree National Monument has many oases that contrast sharply with the surrounding desert. The largest, Lost Palms near the southern boundary, contains more than one hundred native California fan palms. To desert travelers, an oasis means water and shade, and an oasis just outside the northern boundary of the monument became popular with early travelers, who founded the town of Twentynine Palms. Another such town is famous Palm Springs, a resort city to the southwest of the monument.

Rocks of several geologic eras are found in the region, but two types dominate -- Pinto gneiss (pronounced "nice") and quartz monzonite. Dark-colored Pinto gneiss makes up the bulk of the mountains, while boulders of light gray or pinkish quartz monzonite are found scattered in heaps, especially in the monument's northern portion.

Indians lived in the area until it was settled about 1900. The first pioneers were prospectors, and old mine shafts and mill sites attest to their activities. Cattle-men built small dams, called tanks, to catch rainwater for their herds, and these dams lent themselves to a number of place-names in the monument, such as Squaw Tank and White Tank.

Most of the monument's animals are nocturnal, but antelope ground squirrels scurry over the sands in the hottest of temperatures. Coyotes are often seen prowling at the outskirts of the campgrounds, but the largest mammal, the desert bighorn sheep, is only occasionally observed.

The brownish kangaroo rats have become so adapted to the dry environment that they can go through their entire lives without ever taking a drink of water. They manufacture water out of their staple diet of dry seeds, grain, and some foliage. Easily recognized by their long, tufted tail, they are neat appearing, unlike some of their cousins living in other areas. Their average size is eight to fifteen inches, but five to nine inches of this is tail. These burrowing rodents make very good pets if they can be caught (not permitted within the monument), for they bound around rapidly and can jump six feet if startled. However, they also have fleas which can carry diseases. These rodents can often be seen at dusk and during the night, but if you look for them, be cautious, for their primary predator, the rattlesnake, is also a nocturnal prowler.

The most commonly seen reptile is the side-blotched lizard (little brown uta), one of many species of lizards in the area. One of the largest, the chuckwalla, can be observed basking on warm rocks in the cooler mornings and late evenings. Most of the 250 species of birds that

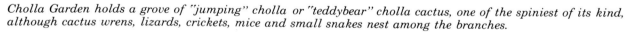

Cholla Garden holds a grove of "jumping" cholla or "teddybear" cholla cactus, one of the spiniest of its kind, although cactus wrens, lizards, crickets, mice and small snakes nest among the branches.

Young

have been sighted in the monument are migrants, and those that remain the year round are usually found near oases.

Many of the trails in the monument, established in 1936, are self-guiding. Eight campgrounds without water are available for use. A visitor center is located at Twentynine Palms on the north and there is a visitor contact station at Cottonwood Spring on the south. Temperatures are variable with hot days and cool nights.

The outstanding scenic point is Salton View at 5,185 feet. Here in one sweep is an impressive panorama of deserts, valleys and mountains, from the hot, barren Salton Sea, 241 feet below sea level, to the snow-capped summits of San Jacinto and San Gorgonio Peaks, both above ten thousand feet. Thus, Joshua Tree country is also a land of contrasts.

Spring clusters of greenish white flowers tip the Joshua tree's quill-like leaves. Indians used these parts for food and fermented beverages and other parts for rope, sandals and mats.

Overleaf: The San Gabriel Mountains in the background lie to the northwest of Joshua Tree monument, which is noted for its sturdy, various and rich desert vegetation.

95

Muench

Katmai

Alaska

Welcome to The Last Wilderness. Although other states may have patches of wilderness, only Alaska's is so primeval and untamed that you could wander for weeks without seeing another human being. It is the kind of wilderness that even people who know they will never see it are deeply satisfied that it still exists. Katmai National Monument, one of the largest units of the National Park System, protects over 4,200 square miles of this wilderness.

Located on the east coast of the peninsula leading to the Aleutian chain, this is one of the least visited of U.S. parks. The annual visitor rate can be counted in the hundreds; in Yosemite National Park that many people may visit every hour. And it is this very lack of human intrusion that keeps Katmai wild and beautiful. With no road or rail access, the monument is out of reach for the casual tourist. Private or chartered planes are needed to see the most scenic spots, for scheduled flights from the King Salmon airport on the Bering Sea side of the peninsula go only to Brooks River lodge and campground. Such isolation guarantees protection of prime wilderness values.

Katmai contains three distinct geographic sections. To the east is the seacoast on Shelikof Strait, a coastline of unsurpassed beauty. The central part is a series of deep fjords nearly surrounded by cliffs rising abruptly one thousand or more feet above the blue waters. One of the fjords, Hidden Harbor, is half a mile across and hundreds of feet deep and is reached through a break in the cliffs less than one hundred feet wide. The northern and southern coasts are comprised of wide, shallow bays with many extensive sandy beaches bordering large marshes and, in Katmai Valley to the south, treacherous quicksand. Offshore are many small islets where Pacific hair seals and northern sea lions rest from the often turbulent waters of the strait. The great gray whale sometimes hunts in the bays and the northern sea otter plays in the shallows.

McCutcheon

Martin Volcano (above) is one in a chain of active volcanoes--Trident,
Mageik and Martin--that lie in the south-central part of the monument
just west of Mount Katmai and south of the Valley of Ten Thousand Smokes.

Katmai Monument is an ideal area for the world's largest bear, the Alaskan brown bear
(left), who finds sanctuary here year around, feeds on salmon and may grow up to 1,500 pounds.

Inland from the coast is the Aleutian Mountain Range, forming the backbone of Katmai. These snow-capped peaks, as high as 7,600 feet, are continually being carved by glaciers and some of them are active volcanos. Two crater lakes exist in the range, Kaguyak on the north and Katmai on the south. There is little vegetation here because of the cold, the high winds and the short growing season; what does exist is of the subarctic tundra variety.

In the western portion of the monument is a huge mixture of grasslands, green forests and large, deep blue lakes. Two life zones meet here as on the seacoast: the Arctic Zone above two thousand feet, comprised of short grasses and other low-lying vegetation; and the Hudsonian Zone of forests of white spruce, balsam poplar, paper birch and dense stands of reed grass. Gradually the woodlands are replacing the grasslands in this part of the monument; the increased rainfall and

Far left: These twisted, bleached trees are located at Dakavak Lake, an area caught in the unexpected 1912 eruption of Novarupta.

Left: Hallo Glacier sweeps down from Mount Dennison toward Hallo Bay, though its front is stagnant in a moraine that keeps it from moving closer than 300 feet above sea level.

Serene waters glistening with touches of sunlight mark the rocky area known as Devils Cove (below), nestling among glaciated peaks.

Lower left: Within Katmai's crater are the brilliantly colored Emerald Lake and a new glacier which is forming slowly, fed by the snows.

NPS, Kauffmann

NPS

milder climate of recent years has induced a rapid growth of trees. Many hills and knolls are covered with blueberry, crowberry and dwarf birch, and numerous rushing, turbulent streams supply the clear lakes with water from the melted snows of the mountains.

Large mammals are numerous. The largest of them, the Alaskan brown bear, can be seen during summer in and along the streams as it fishes for salmon coming up the waters to spawn. In other seasons the bears eat grass on the open slopes, dig for roots or gorge themselves on the wild berries that are abundant in autumn. Moose are common and will always be found near the waters of the lakes or larger streams. Occasionally one may swim across the lakes, its snout, head and antlers the only visible part of the animal. Wolverines, the most far-ranging small mammals -- found from sea level to three thousand feet -- snarl at visitors if their prey is frightened away by man's approach. River otters are numerous on the lakes and along the shores of the bays.

The most abundant meat-eater at Katmai is the red fox, normally found in the lower elevations of the western portions of the monument. The lynx is the only member of the cat family living in this region and sometimes can be seen in the monument headquarters

Two life zones meet in Katmai, and the tundra, or Arctic, zone supports simple plants like mosses, the sporophytes of which are detailed below.

NPS, Keller

area at Brooks River. Beavers "log" the woods near the lakes and build large dams. Caribou and reindeer were once plentiful but have decreased to the point where none have been seen for many years.

Perhaps the most interesting mammal at Katmai is the wolf. This animal's howl is the trademark of the true wilderness. No other species has been so misunderstood by man. We now know that the vicious, man-eating wolf is a myth. Although in rare instances wolves have attacked man, they are wary of him and normally shun all areas where man intrudes. Thus Alaska and Canada are the only places in the Western Hemisphere where large numbers of wolves still exist.

Wolves basically look like large German shepherd dogs. Most of them in North America are dark gray, but they range in color from pure white in the Arctic to black in more southerly reaches. Their sizes vary with region and sex: Wolves of the north are larger than those to the south, and males are larger than females. Their average weight may be seventy-five to one hundred pounds, and from a distance they appear lean and rangy, much like a coyote but larger. These superb beasts are efficient hunters, and generally peaceful.

When running they have more endurance than speed and often have trouble overtaking hoofed animals. A typical family would consist of the parents, mated for life, one or two cubs, and another solitary adult that has been accepted as a part-time cub-sitter and hunting partner. Sometimes during severe weather a few of these families will travel and hunt together, forming a wolf "pack." They seldom quarrel among themselves and are quite friendly toward strangers of their kind, greeting them with play and dog-style tail wagging.

The wolf, like the cougar (mountain lion), usually attacks only the sickly animals for his food, thus weeding out those individuals whose continued existence is a burden on the rest of the herd. A change in man's attitude toward the wolf has been long in coming, but it has started. As protection is expanded, other generations will have a chance to hear his howl in the wilderness areas of North America.

An abundance of nesting sites, plant food, aquatic life and insects make Katmai ideal for birds. Waterfowl -- ducks, loons and gulls -- are plentiful on the lakes, and sea and shorebirds, including colonies of Arctic terns, populate the coasts. Sparrows, warblers and robins are among the some forty species of songbirds recorded here. Bald eagles can be seen along the streams and lakes, and whistling swans inhabit the remote ponds during summer. Species that remain here through the cold winter include the chickadees and ptarmigans.

The monument's lakes and streams are dense with Dolly Varden, grayling, northern pike, whitefish, and rainbow and lake trout, giving both seasoned veterans and beginning fishermen a chance at prize catches. In late summer thousands of bright red salmon navigate up the streams from the Bering Sea to spawn.

In early 1912 no one would have thought that this magnificent, but still far away and unexplored, region would become a national monument six years later.

A female sharp-tailed grouse hides among the foliage where in springtime it feeds on seeds, insects and leaves.

But on June 6, 1912, one of the most violent seizures of volcanic action that modern man has recorded called attention to the area. The few natives were warned by pre-eruption earth tremors and they quickly fled, so there was no known loss of human life. Losses to wildlife, however, must have been enormous.

The activity began when Novarupta Volcano, halfway between the now abandoned villages of Katmai on the coast and Savonoski in the lakes region, blew up, spewing forth great masses of pumice and rock. Soon white ash began blowing out of the fissure, and within a few minutes two and a half *cubic* miles of ash had been tossed into the air. Over forty square miles of a nearby valley was buried in ash seven hundred feet deep, and even Kodiak Island across Shelikof Strait was covered with pumice. Trees on the mountain slopes above the valley were snapped off and carbonized by terrific blasts of scorching wind.

Steam and hot gasses rose through innumerable small holes and cracks in this valley, pushing their way through the ash cover. Expeditions, sponsored by the National Geographic Society, were made into the valley later, and it was called the Valley of the Ten Thousand Smokes. The heat from some of these fumaroles reached nearly eight hundred degrees, high enough to melt zinc! The smokes have dwindled over the decades and very few are active today. The society's published reports on the volcanic occurrence as well as the stark wilderness of the region resulted in Katmai's being established as a national monument in 1918. It qualifies in every respect as a national park, and conservationists have urged Congress to give it this status.

After Novarupta had spent its own volcanic material, the base of Mount Katmai, six miles away, was sucked in by the volcano through an underground conduit. With its support gone, Mount Katmai collapsed with a roar that could be heard hundreds of miles away, creating a chasm three miles long, two miles wide and 3,200 feet deep. The hole has since partially filled with water, making a crater lake warmed by volcanic heat. Inside the crater above the water level a glacier has formed, perhaps the only glacier in the world whose precise age is known. The snows only partially melt each summer, but the lake fluctuates fifteen feet annually.

The last person to leave the doomed valley, the chief of the Savonoski villagers who called himself American Pete, said in 1918 of his experience, "The Katmai mountain blow up with lots of fire, and fire come down trail from Katmai with lots of smoke. . . .Dark. No could see. Hot ash fall. . . .Never can go back to Savonoski to live. Everything ash."

Katmai is one of our finest remaining wilderness parks. Its remoteness insures that it will always remain as a pristine outpost of nature.

Lava Beds

California

From a distance the land looks fairly level, dotted in places with symmetrical cinder cones and craters. But closer examination reveals that the "level" blackness is extremely rough, jagged and rocky, for this is where the earth vented its anger thousands of years ago. Lava Beds National Monument, located near the California-Oregon border midway between Lassen Volcanic and Crater Lake national parks, is unique among volcanic areas because no large volcano existed here; all the formations were caused by many small holes in the earth's crust.

The eruptions that took place here were of two types -- the more common gaseous type which created the cinder cones and the fissure type, where great masses of thick, *pahoehoe* lava flowed like molasses from deep cracks in the ground. Rivers of molten lava streamed across the region, the outer material cooling and hardening more quickly than the interior, forming a crusty shell or tube through which the hotter matter continued to flow. When the eruptions ceased, the lava shells were emptied, leaving large tunnels or caves.

About three hundred of these lava tubes have been found in the monument, and many more are believed to exist. Many of the cave roofs have collapsed in places to form serpentlike natural trenches 20 to 100 feet deep and 50 to 250 feet wide, with narrow bridges occasionally arching over them.

As the lava flow in the crusty tubes diminished, the cooling lava splashed against the ceilings, creating lava stalactites ("lava-cicles") and some of them were also formed when hot gases remelted pieces of the shell. Rivulets of lava on the walls of the tubes hardened into ribs.

Many of the caves are quite large and contain unusual formations. Catacombs Cave on the paved Cave Loop Road in the southern part of the monument is so named because of the niches in the walls, which resemble the Christian burial caves of ancient Rome. Nearby Sentinel Cave was named for the stone figures which guard its passageway.

Many of the caves are so deep that the cold winter air does not have a chance to warm during summer, and groundwater seeping into the caves freezes. Two of the

Catacombs Cave, so named because the niches in the walls resemble Christian burial caves of ancient Rome, is an excellent example of a lava tube, formed when the outside of a lava flow cooled faster than the interior.

White clouds complement the curve of a black cinder cone, one of many in the monument which rise from 100 to 500 feet above the lava beds. Juniper, ponderosa pine and shrubs sparsely dot the smooth slopes.

Hyde

most spectacular ice caves are Merrill Ice Cave, which contains a frozen waterfall, and Frozen River Cave (not open to the public) named for a sheet of ice five to six feet thick and several hundred feet long.

The smooth, black cinder cones, about seventeen in number, rise from one hundred to over five hundred feet above the lava beds. Many small spatter cones can be seen on the beds, and some of them form deep holes resembling chimneys from the earth's hot core. One such hole, Fleener Chimneys, near the main road, is only three feet in diameter but 130 feet deep.

Plant life among these black lava beds is unexpectedly colorful. During spring and summer about 250 species of wildflowers, including purple sage, scarlet Indian paintbrush and blue wild flax, grow wherever there is sufficient soil. Scattered large spots of green in the beds are juniper, ponderosa pine, wild current, antelope bitterbrush and mountain mahogany. Colorful lichens adorn the rocks in all seasons.

Rocky Mountain mule deer, coyotes, foxes, skunks, weasels and badgers live in the monument area, as do cougars, bobcats and pronghorn antelope, although they are rarely seen.

The National Park Service has developed a campground in the headquarters area and a picnic ground at Fleener Chimneys for the use of visitors at Lava Beds National Monument.

This grim and jagged landscape was unfortunately the scene of one of the most unnecessary, bloody conflicts between Indians and settlers in California.

The Modoc Indians, a fiercely independent people, only numbered between four and eight hundred but they had lived in the Lava Beds region for many centuries, though not in the beds themselves. When settlers began moving into the area, clashes inevitably occurred. Defeated, the Modocs were "given" a reservation of less desirable lands, but their bitter enemies, the

Klamaths, also lived there. Indian agents ignored the bloody friction between the two tribes, and in 1870 about three hundred Modocs, led by an Indian named Captain Jack, returned to their homeland where for two years they roamed without being bothered.

After an attempt was made to return them to the reservation in 1872, Captain Jack and fifty-three other warriors and their families decided to make their stand. Using the lava beds as their hideout because of the difficult but familiar terrain, they were able to hold off over a thousand soldiers for many months. Newly assigned commander General E. R. S. Canby, sympathetic to the Modocs, proposed a peace parley and Captain Jack accepted, but he was later persuaded by the more warlike Indians to murder the peace delegation which included the general. Canby thus became the only general ever killed in an Indian campaign. (Contrary to popular belief, George Custer, who was killed at the Battle of Little Big Horn in 1876, was not a general but a lieutenant colonel.)

After many more skirmishes, Captain Jack and his band surrendered in 1873, and he and three of his warriors were hanged shortly afterward. The remaining Indians were taken to a remote reservation in unfamiliar Oklahoma.

In his plea for peace while in the lava trenches in 1872, Captain Jack said, "It is true we have killed many white men. The Modoc heart is strong. The Modoc guns are sure. But hear me, oh *muck-a-lux* ('my people')! The white men are many. They will come again. No matter how many the Modocs kill, more will come. We will all be killed in the end." Looking out over this landscape today, a visitor can only wonder why the Modocs were not allowed to remain in their homeland and deplore the insatiable appetites which caused white invaders to covet these lands.

105

Lehman Caves

Nevada

Lehman Caves National Monument is in the foothills on the eastern slope of towering Wheeler Peak (13,063 feet), the highest point of the Snake Range of eastern Nevada. It is surrounded by a forest of pinyon pine and Utah juniper that overlooks the sage-covered Snake Valley. This square-mile monument, established in 1922, has an average elevation of seven thousand feet.

Absalom S. Lehman moved into the area in the late 1860's and established a large ranch about a mile and a half from the cave. He guided parties through its underground galleries from about 1885 until his death in 1891, showing them a variety of colorful and curious formations -- including columns twenty feet high.

On opposite sides of the monument are Baker and Lehman creeks flowing out of the glaciated canyons. Wheeler Peak has been carved into its present shape by mountain glaciers (the southernmost in the United States) at the heads of these creeks and by the rushing waters of the streams themselves.

This quartzite peak was originally sandstone and its eastern slopes are covered with layers of limestone. The heat from a granite intrusion changed some of the limestone to its metamorphic state, marble. Lehman Caves was formed from this marble.

Hundreds of thousands of years ago, when the climate was more humid, the formation of the caves began. Water charged with carbon dioxide filled the cracks and joint planes in the marble and gradually widened and enlarged them. The more soluble rock dissolved, leaving large, vaulted rooms, and the joint planes widened into connecting passages. These eventually formed a labyrinth of corridors and small winding tunnels between the larger chambers.

The second stage of cave formation began as the water table lowered, draining the underground cavities. Seeping down through the overlying rock, the calcium-laden water gathered as drops or spread out in thin films on the ceilings and sides of the chambers. Carbon dioxide escaping from the incoming water allowed the mineral to come out of its solution as calcite crystals, gradually forming stalactites on the ceilings. Water dripping from the stalactites built up stubby stalagmites on the floor. In places, water trickling down sloping ceilings has built graceful "draperies" and translucent, ribbonlike "bacon strips." Particularly curious formations are the thin, round disks of calcite, called shields or pallettes, which occur throughout the caves in angular positions on the walls and floors. They are an uncommon cave phenomenon not yet fully explained by geologists.

Water pools on the floor have built miniature rimstone dams around their edges that are beautifully terraced. The huge, fluted columns, with their many "nodes" or terraces, reach from floor to ceiling. Strange-looking mushroomlike lumps, twisting helctites and frosty incrustations grow on many formations, walls and ceilings in a variety of colors -- creamy white, buff, chocolate, orange and red.

Trips through the caves, lasting about one and a half hours, are conducted over a two-thirds-of-a-mile paved trail with several stairways. Temperatures average fifty degrees.

Wherever one goes in these caverns he will see in the myriad of unusual formations shapes resembling animals, toms-toms and figurines, even a "cypress swamp." These outlines of shapes, color-splashed ceilings and enveloping shadows stimulate the imagination as only treasure caves such as Lehman can do.

The Cypress Swamp is one of the beautifully sculptured rooms in Lehman Caves. Thousands of small calcite crystal stalactites hang from the ceiling like Spanish moss. Larger stalactites have sometimes joined with stalagmites on the floor to make a solid column which grows with each calcium-laden drop of water running down its side.

Marble Canyon

Arizona

If this canyon was in any other part of the country, it would have been made into a national park many years ago. But Marble Canyon has the dubious honor of being located adjacent to even more spectacular Grand Canyon. Linking Grand Canyon National Park and National Monument with Glen Canyon National Recreation Area, it was the last major Colorado River canyon to be Federally protected. Under the shadow of a dam proposal for many years, the fifty-two-mile stretch was proclaimed a national monument by President Lyndon B. Johnson the day he left office, January 20, 1969. Two hundred consecutive miles of Colorado River canyons from Utah through Arizona are now preserved from man-made developments.

This chasm has remained so wild that Major John Wesley Powell would immediately recognize it as the place that he named Marble Canyon in 1896. The only way to see the canyon is to ride the rafts through its dangerous rapids. It is an unforgettable experience. Some of the rapids are no more than seventy-five feet wide with a consequent violent churning of water. Leaving Glen Canyon at historic Lee's Ferry (until recent years the only place along the entire river length from Utah to Nevada where a traveler could cross the great river) the adventurous modern visitor must traverse Badger Creek Rapids, Soap Creek Rapids, Cave Springs Rapids, President Harding Rapids and Nankoweap Rapids before he reaches the junction of the Colorado and Little Colorado rivers, where the Grand Canyon begins. Whirlpools in the wide channels are very strong and large, but large rafts are able to navigate through them safely.

In the early part of this century two brothers, Emery and Ellsworth Kolb, followed Major Powell's route from Wyoming to Mexico. They described Marble Canyon:

> [It]was now beginning to narrow up, with a steep, boulder-covered slope on either side, three or four hundred feet high; with a sheer wall of dark red limestone of equal height directly above that. There was also a plateau of red sandstone and distant walls topped with light-coloured rock, the same formations with which we were familiar in the Grand Canyon. The inner gorge had narrowed from a thousand feet or more down to four hundred feet, the slope at the river was growing steeper and gradually disappearing, and each mile of travel had added a hundred feet or more to the height of the walls. Soon after resuming our journey that afternoon, the slope disappeared altogether, and the sheer walls came down close to the water. There were few places where one could climb out, had we desired to do so. This hard limestone wall, which Major Powell had named the marble wall, had a disconcerting way of weathering very smooth and sheer, with a few ledges and fewer breaks. . . .

> The wonderful marble walls now rose from the water's edge to a height of eight or nine hundred feet, the surface of its light blue-gray rock being stained to a dark red, or a light red as the case might be, by the iron from the sandstone walls above. There were a thousand feet of these sandstone layers, red in all its varying hues, capped by the four-hundred-foot cross-bedded sandstone wall, breaking sheer, ranging in tone from a soft buff to a golden yellow, with a bloom, or glow, as though illuminated from within.

A morning sun brightens the various colors of the rocky Marble Canyon walls (above) as a yellow raft floats down one of the calm sections of the Colorado.

The rock walls support little vegetation, only few varieties of yucca and cactus, and it comes as a shock to the river runner to come across Vasey's Paradise. Named by Major Powell for his friend, botanist Dr. George Vasey, it is an oasis in a canyon of emptiness. Beautiful streams gush from holes in the rock walls, which are in turn covered with maidenhair fern, vines and watercress. In front of this green background are willow trees, their leaves flapping in the breeze.

Stanton's Cave, a half mile upriver from Vasey's Paradise, has become an important archeological site in the past thirty years. Robert Stanton, for whom the cave was named, was an engineer who surveyed a water-level railroad route through the Colorado River canyons in 1889, a venture which luckily did not succeed. After three of his party had drowned, he stashed his equipment in this cave and hiked out, returning months later to complete his trip. In 1939 over sixty split-willow twig figurines were discovered just under the dirt cover of Stanton's Cave. Many of them were ritually pierced by tiny wooden spears, leading scientists to believe they were part of some kind of imitative magic. Immediately beneath the figurine level were numerous bones of birds, including the extinct giant vulture and condor, and evidences of an extinct sheep or goat that sought shelter in the cave thousands of years earlier.

The Kolb brothers wrote in their journal many years ago as they camped in Marble Canyon:

The air turned decidedly cold this day, a hard wind swept up the river, the sky was overcast, and we had little doubt that snow was falling on the Kaibab Plateau, which we could not see, but which we knew rose to the height of 5,500 feet above us. . . .The sheer walls directly above the river dropped down considerably at this point, and a break or two permitted us to climb up as high as we cared to go on the red sandstone wall, which had lost its level character, and now rose in a steep slope over a thousand feet above us.

This deep canyon is secure from human intrusions, and it is hoped that it will soon be added to the Grand Canyon National Park.

109

NPS, Grant

Sunlight filters through tall, stately coastal redwoods which protect lush growths of ferns on the forest floor.

Many Pacific giant salamanders live among the numerous mushrooms, moss and redwood needles.

Muir Woods

California

*John Muir (1838-1914) was
a famous author, naturalist
and conservationist.*

From the hillsides of San Francisco you can see it, touching the sky twenty miles to the north. This is Mount Tamalpais, the Fujiyama of the Golden Gate, and in a valley at its foot is Muir Woods, a virgin stand of California coast redwoods.

To walk through a virgin forest is an experience in itself. Great varieties of plants do not clutter up the ground here; this is a forest that knows where it is going and has weeded out those plants which do not fit in with its natural scheme. Tall, stately redwoods stretch over two hundred feet above the soft, spongy forest floor, covered with redwood needles and cones, green ferns and rainbow-colored mushrooms of all shapes and sizes. The growth is so thick that only single shafts of sunlight can reach through and brighten the forest floor. Fog often covers the treetops during fall and winter, and a soft, misty rain permeates every inch of this evergreen park.

Many years ago, this relatively small forest was threatened by commercial timber cutting and to save it, Congressman William Kent of Marin County and his wife, Elizabeth Thatcher Kent, purchased the woods outright and donated it to the Federal Government on condition that it be designated a national monument in honor of John Muir (1838-1914). Muir was the famed writer, naturalist and conservationist who roamed the Western wilderness for many years and whom Kent greatly admired. Theodore Roosevelt proclaimed the woods a national monument in 1908.

Muir wrote Kent in gratitude: "This is the best tree-lover's monument that could be found in all the forests of the world. . . . Saving these redwoods from the axe and saw . . . is in many ways the most notable service to God and man I have heard. . . ."

The coast redwood's scientific name is *Sequoia sempervirens.* Sequoia comes from the Cherokee Indian, Sequoyah, who invented an Indian alphabet and taught his people to read and write; *sempervirens* means evergreen. This tree differs from its close relative, the Sierra redwood, *Sequoia gigantea*, primarily in that the *gigantea* is larger in girth and much older, while the *sempervirens* is taller. The tallest living thing on earth is a *sempervirens* in Redwoods National Park in northern California. The trees at Muir Woods are not as tall as those further north along the coast, but they are no less impressive, the tallest tree reaching a height of 236 feet near the Bohemian Grove. The foliage of the *gigantea* somewhat resembles that of juniper, while the *sempervirens* foliage is more like hemlock. The bark of the Sierra tree is a bright sienna, while the coast version's bark is a dull chocolate; finally, *sempervirens'* cones are only one-third the size of its cousin's to the east.

The redwood's reproduction is unique in that it is one of the few coniferous trees that reproduces by sprouting from its own root system. Although seeds germinate readily, they cannot establish a strong root system fast enough to carry it through the summer drought season. The stump sprout already has a developed root system, however, and will quickly mature when the parent dies. This is a primary reason why the forest survives today, for there is evidence that, over many centuries, a large fire would sweep the woods at least once every hundred years or so, killing many great trees but not the roots which supplied the new sprouts with life. The redwoods also resist fire by having a large amount of water in their wood, a very thick, asbestoslike bark and almost no flammable pitch. The charred stumps and deep scars easily visible in the woods resulted from the last major fire which occurred about 1845. Now with man's care these present redwoods will continue to grow even taller.

Muir Woods is noted for its redwood peculiarities of burls and albino shoots. Burls are large, lumpy growths on the sides of the trees. They are not caused by disease but rather by some kind of genetic disorder. Rare albino shoots are caused by the lack of chlorophyll, the chemical responsible for a plant's green color.

Other trees mixing with the redwoods include Douglas fir, California laurel, tanbark oak (tan oak), red alder and California buckeye. Ferns cover the forest floors, the most common being Western sword fern, ladyfern, Western bracken and giant chain fern.

The only large mammal here is the black-tailed deer, a cousin of the mule deer. Birds are numerous and active during the morning hours. Redwood Creek is also a spawning bed of silver salmon and steelhead trout, which can be seen in winter fighting their way upstream from the Pacific Ocean.

Muir Woods has no picnic areas or campgrounds (campgrounds are in surrounding Mount Tamalpais State Park), and is only open during daylight hours. However, a peaceful walk along these six miles of trails is all that is needed to induce feelings of serenity and remind visitors that these great trees are one of the natural masterpieces of this planet.

Natural Bridges

Utah

NPS, Grant

A fine example of wind erosion is the Goblet (above), a sandstone formation near Cottonwood Canyon. No one knows how much longer the stem will hold its heavy mass.

Owachomo Bridge (opposite) is the oldest of the three natural bridges in the monument, thus its life expectancy is less. Only nine feet thick, it is flat on the top.

Southern Utah is reknowned throughout the world for its fantastic landscape of brilliantly colored cliffs, tortuous box canyons, sandstone arches, pinnacles, towers and natural bridges. Three of the most impressive bridges are the principal features of Natural Bridges National Monument. Although smaller than Rainbow Bridge sixty miles southwest, these bridges are among the largest known natural bridges in the world.

Located in rugged country, the mammoth stone wonders were formed like most natural bridges: A meandering river gouged out a canyon and gradually wore away the canyon wall of the inside part of a sharp bend. The waters then flowed through the hole and created a natural bridge. Although similar in looks, arches differ from natural bridges in that they were not formed by river erosion, but by wind, rain and frost erosion.

Cass Hite, exploring this inaccessible area for minerals, viewed the three bridges in 1883. Hite named the bridges, in decreasing size, the President, the Senator and the Congressman. Cowboy James Scorup saw the stone bridges in 1895 but didn't name them under the assumption they had already been discovered. In 1903 Horace Long, a mining engineer, stopped at Hite's cabin and met Scorup, who volunteered to guide him to the bridges provided one was named for his mother, Caroline. A few days later the two men reached the bridges, naming the first one Caroline. The President was renamed the Augusta after Long's wife. The smallest bridge was renamed Edwin two years later, in honor of Colonel Edwin Holmes, a prominent Salt Lake City resident.

Dr. Byron Cummings of the University of Utah organized an expedition in 1907 to explore the bridges area and turned in a report to the Federal authorities. That report formed the basis for President Theodore Roosevelt's 1908 proclamation establishing Natural Bridges National Monument.

Not content with the data on hand, a Government surveyor, W. B. Douglass, obtained an assignment to further explore the monument region and try to find out the original Indian names for the bridges. The latter proved difficult because there were no Indian names. Paiutes, who still live in the region, called all bridges, natural and man-made, *ma-vah-talk-tump*, or "under the horse's belly." At the time it was thought that the cliff ruins of southern Utah were once the dwellings of the ancestors of the Hopis, so it was natural, since Paiute names were not forthcoming, that the bridge's names should be Hopi. Thus in 1909 President William Howard Taft enlarged the monument and officially assigned Hopi names to the stone wonders.

In White Canyon, the Sipapu Bridge (formerly the Augusta) stretches 268 feet across at a height of 220 feet and is the largest and most graceful. Its abutments are far enough from the stream bed that the waters have little or no erosive effect on the bridge. The symmetrical arch suggested to those who named it the *sipapu*, a hole through which the Hopis believe their ancestors emerged from a lower, dark world into the present one.

Kachina Bridge, at the junction of White and Armstrong canyons, reaches 210 feet above the stream bed and 206 feet between the cliffs; it is the bulkiest bridge, though still in its youth geologically as flood waters continue to enlarge the opening. On one of the abutments are numerous pictographs, some of which resemble Hopi masked dancers or *kachinas*, thus the change in name from Caroline.

The last and smallest bridge, Owachomo, is located in Armstrong Canyon and was known as the Edwin Bridge. It is the thinnest (nine feet thick) and the oldest bridge of the three, no longer being eroded by stream waters. Named for the large rounded rock mesa near one end (*owachomo* means "rock mound"), its life expectancy is less; perhaps the fatal crack may already have started. The fate of all natural bridges is illustrated a short distance from Sipapu Bridge, where damaged abutments and faint scars indicate the spot where a fourth mammoth bridge once stood.

A cliff dwelling of about twenty rooms, whose occupants were early Anasazi Indians, can be seen along the trail between the Sipapu and Kachina bridges.

Deer are numerous in the pinyon-juniper forests surrounding the monument, and bighorn sheep summer in the canyons. Coyotes, bobcats and smaller mammals are plentiful also.

Although the monument roads are paved, the approach roads are dirt and sometimes impassible during heavy snows and rainstorms. An eight-mile loop road links the bridges with the visitor center and the campground at the east entrance.

It is fitting that these bridges were given Indian names, for this is an unspoiled, solitary landscape, and its natural wonders in a wilderness setting has much appeal to those who are attracted to this region and its Indian history.

Oregon Caves

Oregon

Oregon Caves National Monument is on the slopes of Mount Elijah, a peak of almost 6,400 feet in the Siskiyou Mountains of southwestern Oregon. Although long called Oregon Caves, it is in fact a single marble cavern consisting of an intricate complex of corridors. The main entrance is the northernmost and lowest point in the cave at an elevation of four thousand feet. The chambers in the southern regions of the cave are at considerably higher levels.

Located between the Rogue and Klamath rivers, the area is a transitional one between the California mountains and the Northwest evergreen forest. The region usually receives several feet of snow each winter.

Elijah J. Davidson discovered Oregon Cave in 1874 while in pursuit of a bear, and explorers were soon attracted to the cavern. Frank M. Nickerson found four different levels and opened several galleries blocked by stalactites. He served as a part owner of the cave and guide for several years. Joaquin Miller, the "poet of the Sierras," visited the cave in 1907 with a party that included Chandler B. Watson, a geologist. Miller made the cave so well known through his writings that it was established as a national monument in 1909. Joaquin Miller's Chapel and Watson's Grotto are chambers in the cave named for these two men.

The formation of the cave covers a vast period of geologic time. A shallow arm of the ancient ocean that covered the area 180 million years ago deposited a thick bed of calcium carbonate which later hardened into limestone. The intense heat and pressure created during the periods of mountain building transformed the limestone into marble, and it was raised above the sea as part of a mountain range. The uplifting process that formed the mountains fractured the marble in many places, and even though the openings along these fractures may have been relatively small, they allowed the passage of water. Groundwater, charged with acids from decaying vegetation, moved along the fractures and dissolved the marble. Thus the fractures were eventually enlarged to the present cave.

The later stage of cave development began as streams in the region cut their valleys deeper and the water table gradually fell below the level of the caverns. They were drained, allowing the entrance of air. The resulting process of natural deposition created the decorative beauty that fascinates today's visitor. Drops of water reached the caverns and evaporated into the air, leaving minute deposits of calcium carbonate. Deep inside the cave, where humidity reaches ninety-eight percent, evaporation was minimal but much the same deposition process took place due to the loss of carbon dioxide. Eventually millions of drops left thick deposits covering the walls, ceiling and floors of Oregon Cave. Where the drops dripped slowly from the ceiling, stalactites were formed; where water fell to the floor, stalagmites were built up. In some places stalactites and stalagmites joined and formed columns and many odd and fantastic shapes. Imperceptibly, this deposition process continues today for Oregon Cave is literally a "live" cave.

The myriad of shapes found in the cavern have caused many of the galleries to bear highly descriptive names. Passageway of the Whale is a fine example of an enlarged crevice. The Wigwam Room has a formation called Chief Rain-in-the-Face. In the Banana Grove and Potato Patch is flowstone drapery that resembles bunches of bananas. Niagara Falls provides an example of cascading flowstone. One chamber, reminiscent of an undersea cave and thus known as Neptune's Grotto, has a vertical shaft, called a domepit or chimney, formed by water flowing from a sinkhole above, down to the water table. The Ghost Chamber, measuring forty feet high, fifty feet wide and over three hundred feet in length, is the largest known room in the cave. Paradise Lost, with its five great cones in a line and three formations of flowstone drapery extending from floor to ceiling, is frequently called the most beautiful room in the cave.

Life in the cave is not abundant but rabbits are frequently seen, and a ringtail or foot-long Pacific giant

salamander wanders in occasionally. But of course the only mammals truly at home here are the eight species of bats. One of them is the Western lump-nosed bat, also called the long-eared bat. During hibernation it curls its large ears in spirals and folds them down against its neck, perhaps to reduce water loss from the thin membrane of the ears. Simple forms of plant life -- algae, mosses and ferns -- grow near the electric lights that have been placed in parts of the cave.

Guide service in the cave is furnished by a concessioner. Children under six are not permitted in the cave but a nursery is available. There are no facilities for camping or picnicking.

Joaquin Miller's "marble halls of Oregon," in their setting high on the slopes of the Siskiyous, easily live up to their reputation as being one of the most unusual caves in the entire West.

Milky white deposits of calcium carbonate have coalesced to form this structure known as The White House, found in a chamber of the marble cavern called Oregon Caves, located high on the slopes of Mount Elijah in southwest Oregon.

Organ Pipe Cactus

Arizona

In 1853 under the terms of the Gadsden Purchase, the United States bought from Mexico a large tract of land at the southern extremity of Arizona Territory and so acquired a portion of desert unlike that of any in the country. The Sonoran Desert ranges from northern Baja California through the Mexican State of Sonora into the borders area of southern Arizona. Although most of this desert is in Mexico, Organ Pipe Cactus National Monument preserves a representative portion of 516 square miles of stark mountains, sweeping bajadas (outwash plains), rocky canyons, flats, dry washes and distinctive plants and animals.

The area is the merging point of three different kinds of desert vegetation -- the drought-ridden California Microphyll (small-leaved) Desert, the upland Arizona Succulent Desert and the tall-cactus Gulf Coast Desert of the Gulf of California.

The most common plant is cactus. There are over thirty species here, and outstanding among these is the organ-pipe cactus (*Lemaireocereus thurberi*), found nowhere else in the United States. The second largest cactus in the country, it may produce over thirty unbranched stems up to twenty feet tall from one plant, bearing close resemblance to a church organ. This curious plant dominates the landscape on the lower slopes of mountains and along the ridges of the bajadas. In May and June each of the small greenish-white-to-pink blossoms bloom on the tips of the stems for only one night, opening after dark and dying shortly after sunrise. In midsummer fruits with a reddish, juicy sweet pulp mature and provide a plentiful source of nutrition for birds and small animals. Papago Indians call the fruit *pitahaya dulce* and they use it in many ways. Some is eaten fresh, some made into a native wine, and some is cooked, thus separating the pulp and seeds from the juice, which is then boiled down to a thick syrup. The pulp is dried and used to make jam, and the seeds are ground up for paste.

The rarest large cactus in the monument, the senita, meaning "old one," closely resembles the organ pipe except that it has very deep ridges between the vertical ribs. Clusters of long gray spines cover the tips of older stems, giving it the local name of whisker cactus. Found only along the southern boundary of the monument near the Mexican border, it sometimes spreads over many square yards along the bottoms and edges of washes and flats.

Other cacti found here are the large saguaro, several species of cholla and the barrel, hedgehog and prickly-pear cactus, all of which produce spectacular blooms of crimson, orange, pink, yellow, lavender, purple and pale green.

Above: Mount Ajo forms a scenic backdrop for the organ-pipe cactus to spread its tall stems above other desert plants. Each organ pipe may produce over thirty of these stems, reaching heights of twenty feet. One of the most unusual desert plants, it is at its northern limits in the monument. Left: A black-throated sparrow ignores bristling cactus needles. Some birds even make their nests in cactus, for the spines provide protection from predators.

Cactus is not the only type of vegetation in the monument. If winter rains have been sufficient, spring may bring with it an array of desert colors -- the bright red, showy flowers of the ocotillo; the greenish-yellow, nearly inconspicuous blossoms of the holacantha or crucifixion-thorn; and the pale yellow of the creosote bush. The brilliant red flowers of the desert honeysuckle attract many hummingbirds, and insects swarm over the drooping, pale yellow flower clusters of the mesquite. The leafless smokethorn or smoke tree from the California Microphyll Desert is covered in late spring with small, violet-to-indigo flowers, and in early summer the large white, fragrant flowers of the night-blooming cereus open at dusk. The paloverde, with its dense mantle of yellow blossoms, forms a ribbon of gold over the land for many spring months.

The large variety of vegetation supports an equal variety of wildlife, and one of the most unusual is the javelina (collared peccary), which is a wild hairy pig that thrives in the monument. Other mammals roaming the monument include coyotes, ring-tailed cats, bobcats, cottontails, jackrabbits, foxes, mule deer and an occasional mountain lion. The raccoonlike ringtail is often confused with the coatimundi, though the former is much smaller and is distinguished by its fluffy, ringed tail. Swift pronghorn antelope may sometimes be seen in valleys, and several bands of bighorn sheep live near the mountaintops. Adjoining the monument on the western edge is the huge Cabeza Prieta Game Range, which is managed by the U. S. Fish and Wildlife Service and protects the habitat of a herd of bighorns.

The rare, inch-long, shiny desert pupfish can be seen swimming in Quitobaquito Springs in the southern portion of the monument. As living proof that this area was once connected to the Gulf of California by the Sonoyta River, they also exist in some waters of Death Valley National Monument. A great variety of lizards and insects inhabit the area, and birds are surprisingly plentiful for a desert. Thrashers are one of the most common, and others include white-winged doves, black-throated sparrows, gilded flickers and warblers, as well as predators like the red-tailed hawk and the golden eagle. The gila woodpecker drills nesting holes in saguaros and then abandons them, leaving them for elf owls who sleep in them during the day. Both turkey and black vultures are a common sight as they soar over the land or congregate at a dead animal's carcass. A great number of waterfowl use the springs at Quitobaquito, and larger birds include Gambel's quail and the roadrunner.

Looking like a skinny, long-tailed chicken, the roadrunner, a member of the cuckoo family, is best known for its comical appearance and striking behavior. Some Indians so admired its prowess as a rattlesnake killer that warriors would carry its feathers into battle. The bird dances, dodges and stabs at the snake's head until it finally grabs the head in its long beak, thrashes it on a rock and then gulps it down. Roadrunners use almost anything that moves in the desert for food--lizards, grasshoppers, mice, sparrows. It is estimated that these birds can sprint up to fifteen miles an hour for a brief stretch.

The first European to visit the upper Sonoran Desert area was Melchior Dias, a Spanish officer sent by Coronado in 1540 to make contact with Alarcon who was exploring the waters of the Gulf of California. In 1699 Father Eusebio Kino established a cattle ranch in the area, and later a small Jesuit mission at Sonoyta, Mexico, just outside the monument. He pioneered the route paralleling the U. S. -Mexican border from the interior of Mexico to lower California; it was later called *El Camino del Diablo* ("The Devil's Highway") because of the brutal desert country that it traversed. During the California gold rush as many as five hundred men may have died of thirst along this roadway. The area is so sparsely settled that even today, aside from Government personnel at the monument and the game range, there are only a few human beings inhabiting some three thousand square miles of land along the border west of the Papago Indian Reservation.

Established in 1937, Organ Pipe Cactus National Monument has a visitor center and campground beside

the main road through the monument. The National Park Service has constructed two loop roads of twenty and fifty miles to take visitors along the base of Mount Ajo, at 4,800 feet the highest point in the monument, and through the washes and plains to Quitobaquito Springs. No visa is needed to cross the border to Sonoyta or to drive the now-paved *El Camino del Diablo,* however a visa is necessary to go farther south into the interior.

This monument and the Cabeza Prieta Game Range to the west have been proposed to be merged into a Sonoran Desert National Park. Conservationists should hope this plan comes to fulfillment soon.

Grossman

Young

The sun backlights a stand of jumping cholla cactus (above) accentuating the sharp needles of the many branches and at the same time throwing a bluish shadow on the craggy peaks of the monument.

A rising full moon in the late minutes of dusk (right) brings out the delicate, cool tones which are in sharp contrast with the blistering, dry colors of daylight.

PINNACLES

California

The shaded path called the Moses Spring Trail that skirts the Bear Gulch is invitingly cool on a hot May afternoon. A soft breeze rustles the tree leaves slightly and twitterings of warblers and wrens are heard overhead. Suddenly, as the trail goes under a broad, overhanging rock face, a loud screech echoes from across the small gulch. Near the treetops is a large hawk, repeatedly swooping down on a boulder, as if protecting her nest from some unknown predator. The bushes near the boulder move and you are soon gazing at the prince of the wilderness, the rare cougar. For a half hour he roams along the rim, paying no attention to his observer across the gulch.

In Pinnacles National Monument, as in many of the wilderness areas in the West, the cougar is present but rarely seen. People lucky enough to view this splendid cat in the wilds never forget their thrilling experience.

The monument is a prime example of the type of habitat the cougar loves. Arid, rocky and rough, the Pinnacles region is located in the Gabilan Range a short distance east of the Monterey and Big Sur peninsulas. It was named for the spectacular spires, columns and jagged peaks, many over one thousand feet high, which are found throughout the monument. Formed when water eroded the volcanic-laid rock many centuries ago, they contrast sharply with the smooth contours of the surrounding area.

Mantling these rugged slopes is a dense, brushy plant cover called chaparral. The stiff-branched, leathery-leaved shrubs have many of the characteristics of desert plants and often grow quite large, thus chaparral is sometimes called a pygmy forest. The chaparral at Pinnacles is considered the best of the entire National Park System and is comprised chiefly of greasewood chamise, mixed with smaller amounts of manzanita, buckbrush (*Ceanothus*) and hollyleaf cherry.

The reasons for this widespread chaparral are the hot, dry climate and the periodic fires. For thousands of years fire has swept the region, and only plants able to tolerate these burnings can survive, adapting to the environment by sprouting from a deep root crown after the rest of the plant has been destroyed, or by producing seeds which are stimulated to germinate by the heat of the fire which kills the parent plant. Man's suppression of these natural fires has allowed other vegetation to take root, such as Digger pine which is spreading and may someday replace the chaparral.

In December bright red berries top the toyon plant, and the California live oak, sycamore, blue oak and California buckeye, which drops its leaves in July so as to avoid the loss of water, can also be found mixed with chaparral or in canyons.

In spring the rocky slopes are dotted with a multitude of colorful wildflowers. Some of the over one hundred species blooming in the monument are the yellow California poppy, the state flower, the pink shooting star, the chaparral nightshade, the butterfly mariposa and the Indian warrior, a bright red flower resembling Indian paintbrush.

The chaparral furnishes cover and food for numerous species of wildlife. The mountain lion is the prince of the predatory animals of the Western Hemisphere. It is perhaps the most mysterious and misunderstood of all the world's large carnivores. Although cougars avoid human beings at all costs, they have been hunted as though they were mortal enemies of man. California paid bounties on this magnificent creature, and even today Arizona still has a bounty on dead mountain lions. These laws have led to the decimation of cougars in some areas, but there is now hope that this persecution is coming to an end.

Strong and ultrasecretive, the males may weigh up to two hundred pounds with a length of eight feet. The female gives birth to one to five young every two years. They are so wide ranging that when a female wishes to mate, she must leave a "calling card" near a lion trail intersection, which doubles as a scent post where they frequently rest. After mating they split up, probably never to see each other again.

A truly rare experience is the sighting of a secretive cougar, or mountain lion, in the wilds. The arid, rocky and rough landscape of Pinnacles, composed chiefly of a chaparral cover, is a prime example of the type of habitat this splendid member of the cat family likes. The cougar is very strong and will avoid man to any extent.

Rock pinnacles, California live oaks and Digger pines are reflected abstractly in the shimmering waters of Bear Gulch Reservoir, easily reached by trail. At the far end of the reservoir Bear Gulch Caves begin, formed when large boulders were wedged between narrow canyon walls.

Young

Cougars travel in large circuits of up to one hundred miles in radius. They often make the route regularly, arriving at a given point within a few hours consistently year after year.

The cougar is a solitary animal who subsists on rabbits, squirrels, mice, wood rats, coyotes, deer and elk. They rely on stealth to achieve their kills, and there are very few recorded instances of attack on human beings -- despite much folklore to the contrary. The cougar prefers to stay to himself in the high country, as recent scientific studies of his habits have shown.

Hopefully, the sad chapter in man's history when the cougar was almost eradicated is almost over, and with a little care and adequate wilderness habitat preservation, the huge cat should gradually increase once more.

Black-tailed deer live in the Pinnacles area, as do gray foxes, bobcats, ground squirrels, chipmunks and several species of bats, mice and rabbits. The raccoon is a frequent visitor to the campgrounds in the monument. This cute but strong and quick-tempered burglar will help himself to any food available, eating fried chicken, peaches and chocolate cake with equal gusto.

Birds are extremely numerous. Out of the 130 species recorded within the monument, seven are owls; there are twelve each of hawks and warblers, six hummingbirds, nine flycatchers and phoebes, and five wrens. Soaring vultures glide over steep canyons, ridges and mountaintops, sometimes not flapping their wings for several hours. The vulture need not be quick because his food is already dead or dying, but the peregrine falcon is another matter. This predacious bird, of which there are few in the monument, feeds nearly exclusively on other birds and is surprisingly fast. A pilot of a small plane once reported executing a dive at 175 miles an hour and seeing a falcon flash past him to chase a duck below.

Entrance to Pinnacles National Monument can be easily reached only on the eastern boundary where a road leads to a visitor center, a picnic area and a campground at Chalone Creek. Fifteen miles of trails take the hiker through the chaparral range.

Not far from the picnic area is Bear Gulch Caves, one of two series of talus caves in the monument, the other being at the Old Pinnacles campground at the end of a dirt road in the northern portion. These caves were formed when earthquakes tossed huge boulders into a narrow canyon, where they were wedged between the two cliffs. The streams still flowing through the caves keep the air refrigerated, a welcome relief from the hot temperatures outside, which in summer usually average one hundred degrees. Trails wind through the caves, but flashlights are a necessity.

Pfleiderer

Sheer rock faces of jagged mountain peaks are a common sight in Pinnacles. Many of these rock columns are over a thousand feet high.

If it is solitude that is needed, Pinnacles has plenty. Although easy to reach by paved road, the monument has few visitors on the weekdays. The High Peaks Trail leads directly to the best of the rocky pinnacles and spires where the visitor can be alone with the wilderness and perhaps catch a fleeting glimpse of its prince, the North American mountain lion.

123

Rainbow Bridge

Utah

Navaho Indians called it *nonnezoshi*, meaning "rainbow-turned-to-stone." Today it is known as Rainbow Bridge, but no matter what name is used, it remains the same -- a soaring, massive pink arch between two cliffs near the Arizona-Utah border.

The dimensions of the bridge are staggering. It is the largest, most spectacular natural bridge in the world -- 278 feet long, nearly the length of a football field. At a height of 309 feet, the Capitol Building in Washington, D. C., would fit underneath. It is 42 feet thick, more than the height of a three-story building, and 33 feet wide, enough to accommodate a two-lane highway.

Unlike most natural bridges, which are straightened and flat at the top, Rainbow Bridge is a true symmetrical arch. It was formed by a stream, Bridge Creek, which meandered through canyons in Utah's red "slickrock" country. One of the sharp bends was nearly a complete circle and ages of slow erosion wore away the thin piece of canyon wall separating the two sections of stream until the water broke through and gradually enlarged the opening to its present size.

The bridge is composed of salmon-pink Navaho sandstone, with dark stains caused by iron oxide and hematite. During rainstorms hematite in the sandstone is washed down the sides of the arch and deposited by evaporation, leaving streaks of reds and browns.

While on a field trip in 1908, Dr. Byron Cummings of the University of Utah heard rumors of a great stone arch somewhere in the ten-thousand-square-mile wilderness along the Colorado River. A Paiute Indian, Nascha Begay, said he knew where it was and offered to guide a small party to it. The next year they were joined by John Wetherill, a local trader, and W. B. Douglass, a Government surveyor, and they climbed in and out of numerous "slickrock" canyons until finally they stood beneath Rainbow Bridge. Their enthusiastic reports gained national attention, and only a year later, in 1910, President Taft proclaimed the bridge a national monument.

For fifty years the bridge proved too inaccessible for any but the hardiest hikers and riders willing to traverse the fourteen rough miles from Rainbow Lodge. The Rainbow Trail has been called one of the most rugged in the United States because it breaches deep chasms and zigzags over the rock formations.

In 1962 the Glen Canyon Dam was completed downriver from Rainbow Bridge, and the Colorado backed up (forming Lake Powell) to within a half mile of the bridge. It is now easily accessible by a short trail from the Lake Powell docks in Rainbow Bridge Canyon, but there are no facilities except for a campground.

Although mostly barren, small springs exist in gouges of sandstone around the bridge and support a variety of plant life. Maidenhair fern and wild orchid thrive in the shade, and growing on the drier slopes are Indian paintbrush, lupine, aster, daisy, yucca, sunflower, evening primrose and sego lily.

Utah Highway Department

Early travelers claimed Rainbow Bridge was one of the great wonders of the world, ranking as high in esteem as Grand Canyon and the Yellowstone geyser beds. The present-day visitor, arriving via boat on Lake Powell as the evening sun sets the pink arch afire, finds it easy to see why the Indians called it a "rainbow-turned-to-stone."

Young

The soaring arch of nonnezoshi (above), or "rainbow-turned-to-stone," rises above the creek which carved it. Rainbow Bridge is the largest and most spectacular natural bridge in the world.

The redbud (left) blooms along Bridge Creek in April, adding another shade of reddish-pink to this red-rock country.

Saguaro

Arizona

The saguaro is the epitome of the North American desert. Because it has been silhouetted against a lavender sunset in travel folders and pictured in old cowboy movies, the saguaro has become famous all over the world as a landmark of the American Southwest. Actually, this cactus is the epitome of only one of the four North American deserts -- the Soronan Desert. But the saguaro -- the name (pronounced sa-wah-ro) believed to be a Spanish corruption of an Indian word -- is in trouble. It is slowly disappearing from some areas of the desert scene in the Southwest. A look at its life cycle will show why.

A mature saguaro produces one hundred or more fruits each year, each fruit containing about two thousand tiny black seeds, which, once on the ground, quickly disappear. They are eaten or carried away to be stored by ground squirrels, coyotes, pack rats and insects. The few seeds that survive must overcome the lack of protective ground cover and the absence of topsoil. Saguaro seedlings cannot survive in sunny, uncovered ground; they must have a cover of vegetative litter, such as that found under paloverde or mesquite, in order to grow and mature. If a plant does take hold in the sandy soil, it grows extremely slowly. After ten years it may be only seven or eight inches tall, and after thirty years, five feet. It is so fragile and delicate during these years that the least disturbance will kill it, as will excessive heat, frost, disease or lack of sufficient water.

All of this slow growth and frailty begins to reap its reward after seventy-five years when the plant's height may be fifteen or twenty feet. Already a giant among desert vegetation, it continues to grow, occasionally reaching fifty feet above the ground.

For hundreds of years an ecological balance existed between the saguaros and the factors which contributed to their growth, but the killing off of coyotes and other larger mammals in certain regions has enabled the smaller animals to rapidly increase in numbers. In some areas grazing has also destroyed the protective vegetative cover that nurtured saguaros.

One place where these unusual plants are now protected from extensive grazing and civilization is Saguaro National Monument. Consisting of two sections on either side of Tucson, the Rincon and Tucson Mountain sections, the monument preserves the unique environment of the Arizona Upland or Succulent Desert, a sub-division of the Sonoran Desert.

The largest cactus in the United States, the saguaro's stem is composed of a skeleton of twelve to thirty slender, vertical ribs that support a mass of spongy tissue covered with a thick green skin that is waxy to retard evaporation and pleated to permit expansion for water storage. Although ranging over most of the Sonoran Desert of northwestern Mexico, in this country it may be seen only in Arizona -- with the exception of a few specimens growing west of the Colorado River in California. Known botanically as *Carnegiea gigantea* or *Cereus giganteus,* it may live up to two hundred years and, at maturity, weigh six or seven tons when taking on water through its widespread root system during summer rains. The water is stored inside for use during the dry seasons, when it gradually loses weight.

The familiar branches or arms begin growing when the stem is between sixteen and twenty-two feet high. No one can explain why the arms grow where they do, except that it apparently has nothing to do with balance. Genetic disorders sometimes force the saguaro to assume weird contortions -- arms growing downward, or great numbers of small arms shaped like basketballs growing at the apex of the stem.

In May clusters of creamy white flowers, the Arizona State Flower, appear at the tips of the branches. These large, cup-shaped blossoms contain nectar which attracts the white-winged dove and other birds, the long-nose bat and many insects, all of which provide for pollination. Like most cactus flowers, they stay open for a short time -- from a few hours after sunset to the following afternoon. Each plant produces about four blossoms a day for a month, and five weeks later the scarlet fruit ripens. Tasting somewhat like a mango, the fruit is more sugary than maple sap and, not surprisingly, it is prized as an excellent foodstuff by animals and man alike. The Papago Indians considered the fruit so essential to their economy that they established its harvest season as the start of their new year.

As the apartment building of the desert, the saguaro provides living space for several species of birds. The Gila woodpecker, elf owl, gilded flicker, sparrow hawk,

Yellow blossoms open at the tips of the branches of jumping cholla cactus, which got its name from the impression that the needles jump at anyone too close.

As monarchs of the desert, saguaros (right) bloom with creamy white flowers up to fifty feet above the arid ground. These giants grow extremely slowly and only under certain conditions of climate, ground cover and ecological balance.

purple martin and flycatcher nest inside the stems, while larger birds such as the red-tailed hawk and great horned owl live among the branches.

There are four distinct plant communities in the monument. The Desert Scrub Belt, below 4,000 feet, is typified by creosote bush, saguaro, paloverde, prickly pear and cholla cacti, ocotillo and mesquite. The Grassland Transition Belt, from 3,500 to 4,500 feet, supports beargrass, grama grasses, and sotol, a plant resembling a yucca. From 4,500 to 7,000 feet is the Woodland and Chaparral Belt containing juniper, pinyon pine, scrub oak, mountain mahogany and manzanita. Finally, Gambel oak, ponderosa pine, aspen and Douglas and white fir exist in the Forest Belt above 6,000 feet near the summit of Mica Mountain in the Rincon Mountain (eastern) section.

Mule deer may be seen in the three lower belts, while the white-tailed deer usually stay in the Forest Belt. Javelinas (collared peccaries) are found in the three lower communities, and badgers and coyotes range throughout all elevations. Tarantula hawks, large blue-black, red-winged wasps that prey on tarantula spiders, are one of many species of insects existing in the desert environment. Desert tortoises live in the very low areas.

An uncommon reptile is the famous Gila monster, the largest and only poisonous lizard in the country. Sometimes reaching a length of twenty-two inches, this heavy-bodied but agile descendant of the dinosaur has acquired a reputation far beyond its narrow range of southern Arizona and extreme southwestern New Mexico. It normally eats birds' eggs and small rodents and will bite if provoked.

The Rincon Mountain section was established as Saguaro National Monument in 1933. A road called the Old Spanish Trail leads from Tucson to the picnic area, the visitor center -- with its huge picture windows looking out over the desert -- and the Cactus Forest loop road, all at the west end of the section.

The smaller Tucson Mountain section to the west was added by President John F. Kennedy in 1961. Twenty miles of scenic roads provide easy access to the various features and picnic areas. Just outside the boundary is the privately operated Arizona-Sonoran Desert Museum, which contains a superb presentation of the plants and animals of the Sonoran Desert.

The saguaros in the Rincon section are fully mature but reproduction is not sufficient to replace the dying specimens. Biologists estimate that this forest will be dead by the Year 2000 unless restorative measures can be found which will encourage a new cycle of reproduction. The vigorous saguaro stands in the Tucson Mountain section, however, might be the finest in the whole Sonoran Desert. If their environment is protected they should remain as one of the nation's most unique forests for the long term future.

127

The famous Gila monster (right), relatively uncommon in the monument, is ferocious-looking
when viewed closely. It is the largest and only
poisonous lizard in the country, sometimes reaching
a length of 22 inches. Opposite, top: A full moon
is cradled in the arms of a giant saguaro. A young
saguaro may only be three inches high but four
years old (bottom, right). Protective natural litter,
such as that found around logs, is needed to allow
the seedling to grow to maturity. Sometimes a
mature saguaro may have a genetic disorder
(below), causing two stems to grow from one and
their branches to take odd contortions. The
monstrous size of these plants is easily seen when
compared to a person standing beside them.

Young

129

Sunset Crater

Arizona

In 1065, one year before William the Conquerer and his bands of Normans landed on the British Isles, a few farming Indians called Sinagua lived in the present Little Colorado River basin in north-central Arizona near the San Francisco Peaks. Because of the lack of moisture, these people located their farmlands near the edge of old cinder beds which had the best soils for growing crops.

One day they were startled by a sudden volcanic eruption in their fields. A small earthquake caused a minor break in the earth's crust. Steam and gasses hissed from the hole, and as the vent grew, the increased pressure ripped chunks of rock and dirt from the edge and sides of the vent. Ashes and cinders from deep within the earth were tossed skyward, and the roars and rumbles of the blast could be heard for miles.

The Indians, doubtless fearful of this evidence of some god's anger, must have fled for safety. Turning around, they would probably have seen the pieces of red-hot lava blowing from the eruption vent and a huge black dust cloud blocking the sun from view.

Heavier particles, cinders and lava built up around the hole, forming a small cone which continued to grow as days passed and the eruptions increased with intensity. Boulders, red-hot from within the earth, rolled and bounded down the steep slopes, creating a wider base. Sudden flashes lit up the column of smoke rising from the cone's crater, and heavier ashes and cinders continued to spread a black carpet for hundreds of square miles, covering the Indians' homes and farmlands.

For six months this activity continued as explosive outbreaks were interspersed with outpourings of molten lava from new vents near the base of the cone, creating rivers of lava which hardened in mid-flow. Steaming spatter cones and crusted lava lagoons were formed, and the cinder cone reached a height of a thousand feet before activity slackened.

For years after, hot springs and vapors seeped out from fumaroles around the main vent, and minerals from the vapors stained the cinders at the crater's rim so that the summit seemed to glow with the colors of a sunset.

Gradually vegetation took a tenuous hold in the immediate vicinity of the cone, and some of the hardier Indians moved back to their ash-covered lands, finding that the volcanic materials held the moisture in the soil, and crops grew tall with a much greater yield than before. Word of this productive farmland spread and the Sinagua area became a melting pot of Indian culture -- Pueblo, Hohokam, Mogollon and Cohonimo. Continuous farming and winds, however, soon removed the protective layer of ash, and, archeologists believe, by 1225, only a few Indians remained in the region and villages were left to the elements.

This volcanic cone is now the Sunset Crater National Monument. The sparse vegetation consists mainly of dwarf ponderosa pine and small quaking aspen trees. At the base of the cone is the Bonita Lava Flow, and nearby, visitors may see rare "squeezeups," where putty-like lava was forced through the earth at fantastic pressures. Small caves exist in the west base of the cone, and ice formed in them during winter remains

throughout the summer. The monument, a short distance north of Flagstaff, has a visitor center, and an eighteen-mile road connects Sunset Crater with Wupatki National Historical Monument, where the ruins of the Indian villages have been preserved.

Sunset Crater today is much like it was centuries ago; the fumaroles and spatter cones look like they have barely had time to cool from the violence that formed them nine hundred years ago.

Sparse vegetation, like the gnarled ponderosa pines and aspens above, has taken hold on the foot of Sunset Crater's harsh lava cone. This area in north-central Arizona was not always so barren, for after the volcano erupted in 1065, many Indians worked the nearby land.

Timpanogos Cave

Utah

The picture at left is labeled vertically: *NPS, Keller*

The Great Heart of Timpanogos (above), a huge stalactite, is one of the features of Timpanogos Cave.

Small, delicate aragonite crystals (below) deck the caves' ceilings with frostlike patterns of white.

NPS, Keller

While hunting cougar in the American Fork Canyon of the Wasatch Mountains of Utah in 1887, Martin Hansen came across an entrance to a small cave high up on the slopes of twelve-thousand-foot-high Mount Timpanogos, a Ute Indian word believed to mean "rock river." The cave contained many colorful dripstone formations, but, for the next thirty-four years, it was only locally known. In 1921 two other caves were discovered close by, both larger and more spectacular than the first. They received national attention, and the following year President Warren Harding proclaimed Timpanogos Cave a national monument, preserving these unique limewater formations for future generations.

Much of the interior is covered by pink and white translucent crystals which glow and sparkle in the slightest light. Larger formations are composed of myriads of smaller features -- feathery boas, braided wreaths and needlelike stalactites. Pools of water reflect the sheafs of pink- and brown-striped draperies suspended from dark niches and pendents hanging from the ceiling, while pedestals rise above the cave floor. The walls are encrusted with glistening aragonite crystals and bedecked with tangled masses of root-shaped stone called helictites. Varying amounts of iron, combined with other mineral impurities, tints the odd shapes with hues of lemon yellow, red, brown, green, blue and lavender.

Pressures within the earth pushed the Wasatch Range upwards, separating the Colorado Plateau from the Great Basin of Nevada and western Utah and making an area of broken and pulverized rock through which groundwater could pass. The water eventually carried away the pulverized rock and limestone dissolved from it, forming small tunnels which were finally enlarged to long passageways. Outside, a river flowed at approximately the level of the cave. The river cut a canyon at a faster rate than the cave stream could deepen its bed, so the cave was left high up on the

Water drips slowly from the points of the stalactites hanging from the caves' ceilings and causes ripples in a large pool of cold water, showing that the formation of the caves' intricate features is a constant process. The average temperature here is 43 degrees.

canyon wall. But the stream found other means of reaching the river below, and circulating air gradually dried out the tunnels and caverns. Groundwater continued to seep into the caves, however, carrying an infinitely small amount of dissolved limestone from above. This limewater deposited its minerals drop by drop to form the intricate decorations that can be seen today. The process is continuing, although it may take hundreds of years for the limestone to accumulate.

The names themselves describe the major formations -- The Giant's Comb, Father Time's Jewel Box, Coral Gardens, Hidden Lake, Chocolate Falls, Chimes Chamber, Cavern of Sleep and the Great Heart of Timpanogos, a huge bulbous stalactite.

The three separate caves that make up the monument are connected by man-made tunnels, and tours of these colorfully decorated chambers are regularly conducted by the National Park Service during spring, summer and fall. The temperature in the caves is a chilly forty-three degrees and the humidity is ninety-five percent. A mile-and-a-half trail from the visitor center and picnic grounds zigzags 1,065 feet up Mount Timpanogos by way of the American Fork Canyon to the cave entrance.

The canyon has abundant plant and wildlife typical of the central Rockies. A hike up the top of snow-capped Mount Timpanogos leads to a spectacular view of the Great Basin and Great Salt Lake below, with no visible evidence of the fantasy world that exists deep inside the mountain.

White Sands

New Mexico

White Sands National Monument preserves the most spectacular part of the world's largest gypsum dune field -- great rolling hills of dazzling white sand that provide a severe environment for the animals and plants which have managed to survive in it. The monument is set in the Tularosa Basin of southern New Mexico that extends for over a hundred miles between mountains and highlands, the remnants of a plateau.

These mountains, including the forested Sacramentos to the east and rugged San Andres to the west, contain massive layers of gypsum rock that seasonal rains and melting snows have been eroding for centuries. Dissolved gypsum is eventually carried to Lake Lucero, the lowest part of the basin at the southern end, where the warm sun and dry winds evaporate the lake, leaving it a gypsum-crystal encrusted marsh much of the year. Gypsum also lies beneath the basin floor, evidence that it was once part of the high plateau around it. Capillary action draws the gypsum-laden underground water to the surface which, after evaporation, leaves extensive alkalai flats north of the lake. Persistent, scouring winds from the southwest disintegrate the crystals in the lake bed and the alkalai flats into brilliant white grains of sand, pile them into dunes and push the dunes across the landscape as new ones are constantly formed.

The winds blow the particles of gypsum, sometimes in a visible cloud, up the gentle windward slopes of the dunes as they continue to inch forward sporadically in a northeasterly direction. When the grains reach the dune crest they fall on the steep leeward side. Ripples on the flatter dunes are miniature examples of the same process. The dune area is now about thirty miles long and twelve miles wide. Dune peaks are as high as fifty feet.

Yet life survives, including over a hundred species of hardy plants. Even on the barren alkalai flats some vegetation holds on with amazing tenacity -- such as clumps of pickleweed or iodinebush. Sparse ground cover between the marginal dunes is made up primarily of delicate purple sand verbena, pink centauriums and rice grass. But their existence is temporary, for they are certain to be buried eventually by the advancing dunes.

The groundwater only three or four feet below the surface gives White Sands an advantage over most other dune areas, but it is only a slight one, for few plants can use the gypsum-laden water. Among those that can absorb it are the skunkbush sumac (squawbush), soaptree yucca, shrubby pennyroyal, rubber rabbit brush and cottonwood tree. As the sand begins to accumulate around its base such a plant will put on a burst of growth, thus stretching its "neck" to keep above the sand. As a result of this struggle for survival plants with stems as long as forty feet have been found. As the dunes continue to move, they gradually recede from these plants, leaving them elevated on pedestals of compacted gypsum bound by their tangled roots. The fourwing saltbush grows only among the stable dunes and its salty tasting leaves are palatable to wildlife.

Few animals live in the sands. Coyotes, occasional foxes, and the skunks, porcupines and gophers sometimes seen in the dunes come from the surrounding area. To avoid these predators, two species unique to White Sands have evolved white coloration to help protect them. A small pocket mouse (*Perognathus apache gypsi*) is seldom seen because he is nocturnal. In contrast with this white pocket mouse, the red hills nearby contain a pocket mouse that is a rusty color, and in the black lava beds north of the sands is a black race. The

The marginal areas of White Sands monument support a few vigorous plants like the hybrid varieties of yucca.

NPS

small white lizard (*Holbrookie maculata ruthveni*) can frequently be seen scampering over the sand during the day. It has no external ear openings and has overlapping scales on its upper lip to keep sand out of its mouth.

Prehistoric Indians apparently avoided the White Sands desert, although the remains of their fires, pottery and arrowheads have been found along its rim. Seventeenth-century Spanish explorers left behind a two-wheeled wooden cart, called a *carreta*, now on display in the small interpretive museum at the headquarters visitor center. The site of man's first atomic explosion is outside the monument, about fifty-five miles north of the visitor center.

Established in 1933, the monument has an eight-mile scenic drive into the heart of the dunes. Near the end of the drive is an immense picnic area with fireplaces and shaded tables, but there is no campground. Vehicles are restricted to roads because they can easily bog down if they are driven on the dunes. However, a brief walk to the tops of one of the great dunes can bring you an exhilarating experience in a sea of glistening sand and sky, silent except for the relentless wind.

A huge yucca root has been exposed and isolated by the wind that blows the sand unimpeded and sometimes at gale strengths.

136

Nocturnal animals leave tracks on this desert basin that is covered with gypsum sand which the wind constantly repatterns.

The endless ranks of sand dunes seem still, although these glistening gypsum mounds are always growing and moving.

NPS

Young

Pines frame Devils Lake in south-central Wisconsin. An ancient glacier plowed through the bluffs, making the pass seen in the distance.

The rolling countryside of the North Unit of Kettle Moraine State Forest is composed of glacier-formed moraines, eskers, kames and drumlins.

Ice Age

National Scientific Reserve

Wisconsin

A million years ago an ice cap formed in the region of Hudson Bay and Labrador. The weight of its increasing thickness pressed it outward and the ice began to move. A frozen blanket thousands of feet thick spread southward across North America, going as far as Kansas, Missouri and Ohio. This was the Pleistocene Ice Age. The ice advanced and retreated four different times in one-thousand- and ten-thousand-year stages, each successive stage wiping out most of the effects of the previous ice sheet.

The last stage ended ten thousand years ago and left its mark on America's landscape. It can be seen on Cape Cod and on the hills of Michigan, but nowhere is this ice age stamp more evident and impressive than in Wisconsin. In fact the state lent its name to this last stage of ice, the Wisconsin Stage.

The caliber of glacial features in Wisconsin has prompted a unique concept in conservation--that Federal, state and local governments join to protect cooperatively these glacial marks. Thus the Ice Age National Scientific Reserve was established in 1971. Composed of nine separate units spread across the state, the reserve is administered by the Wisconsin Department of Natural Resources working in close cooperation with the National Park Service and local county governments.

The largest portion is the North Unit of the Kettle Moraine State Forest, a few miles north of Milwaukee. Here the Green Bay and Lake Michigan lobes of the ice sheet crushed together, pushing dirt, rocks and glacial till into large, long heaps called moraines. Similar kinds of moraines, called terminal moraines and marking the farthest southern advance of the ice, can be seen all across the state.

Water channels sometimes developed in the ice sheet, and water-collected debris was dumped, just as silt is dumped on a river bottom, forming long, narrow ridges called eskers. Where melting waters flowed through holes or cracks in the ice or cascaded over the edges, debris was piled into conical masses called kames, which resemble volcanic cinder cones on the landscape. Frequently a large fallen chunk of ice would be covered with a layer of glacial till and dirt, and when the ice finally melted, the layer would collapse, forming a craterlike cavity which soon filled with water. These kettleholes dot the land -- some have dried up, some are in the process of drying up and are marshes and bogs, and others are small lakes. All of these glacial features can easily be seen in the Kettle Moraine area. The most impressive kame is one near the town of Dundee, a symmetrical cone rising from the fields with a kettlehole marsh at its base. Deciduous and evergreen forests cover most of the region and there are numerous recreational facilities at Mauthe Lake.

Nine miles west is the Campbellsport Drumlin Unit. Scientists still puzzle over the origin of drumlins, which are oval hills trending in the direction of the ice movement. The hills are now covered with pasture and farmland which are privately owned. At the northern end of Kettle Moraine near scenic Elkhart Lake is the Sheboygan Marsh Unit, a remnant of glacial Lake Michigan.

Twenty-two miles north of Manitowoc on the shores of Lake Michigan is the Two Creeks Unit, enclosing a buried spruce forest that was once covered by a much larger Lake Michigan before and after two periods of glaciation. Scientists use this forest as the standard for dating geological features by the carbon-14 method.

Six miles northwest of the capital city of Madison in the south-central part of the state is the Cross Plains Unit, which contains terminal moraines deposited at the edge of an unglaciated area.

The most impressive single feature of the Ice Age Reserve is Devils Lake State Park, north of Cross Plains near the famous circus town of Baraboo. Here the ancient Wisconsin River had cut a channel through the mountains of the Baraboo Range, but the ice sheet broke through a gap in the range and dammed up both ends of a section of the river gorge with moraines, forcing the river to run elsewhere and creating a water-filled basin. The gap is clearly visible today, and many rock piles make up the cliffs which were once the gorge walls. An excellent forest of predominately pine and oak covers the area, and many rock pinnacles and balanced rocks can be seen from the trails which skirt the lake on the bluffs and shores. The state park is heavily visited during summer.

Further northwest, near Camp Douglas, is Mill Bluff State Park, once the bed of glacial Lake Wisconsin. The rocky buttes here were islands in this ancient lake.

The Bloomer Unit, about thirty-five miles from Eau Claire in the northwestern part of the state, contains many glacial features left by the Chippewa Ice Lobe, including over fifty large kettlehole lakes.

The Wisconsin portion of the Interstate Park on the St. Croix River, fifty-five miles east of Minneapolis, includes a scenic river gorge, once a principal glacial drainageway. Located adjacent to the St. Croix National Wild and Scenic River, this ninth Ice Age Reserve unit has many recreational facilities.

These are the marks that the ice left on our land, which in geological time was not so long ago. Ice caps on three islands just north of Hudson Bay are still shrinking, proving that the ice sheet has not finished melting even today.

Buffalo find relief from the heat of a warm autumn afternoon on the banks of a stream in the North Dakota badlands.

Theodore Roosevelt

National Memorial Park

North Dakota

Theodore Roosevelt was familiar with the North Dakota badlands, having ranched here in the 1880's. Because of his experience in the badlands, he became a dedicated conservationist. As our 26th President, he established the first sixteen national monuments.

"This country is growing on me more and more," Theodore Roosevelt wrote of the North Dakota badlands. "It has a curious, fantastic beauty of its own." Roosevelt came to love this land of eroded valleys, hills, ridges and gorges in the Little Missouri River basin when he ranched here in the 1880's. It gave him a deep understanding of nature and the importance of conserving it, and Theodore Roosevelt National Memorial Park, the only one of its kind in the country, honors this man, who became our twenty-sixth President, by keeping these badlands he knew so well in their natural state.

At first glance this land seems similar to the more famous badlands of South Dakota, but upon closer observation it is apparent that there are marked differences. Although less spectacular than those in South Dakota, these badlands support more vegetation and are more colorful. The varying shades of tan and gray of the sand and clay layers mix with the greens of trees and the yellows, reds and purples of wildflowers. Erosion played a major role where water has cut away the plains terrain, leaving a rugged land, inhospitable in appearance.

Throughout the area are isolated buttes, the tops of which were once the level of the prairies; because of a protecting layer of rock or the hardness of the clay, they have withstood erosion. In the North Unit of the park are great masses of bluish bentonite, a claylike rock which becomes soft when saturated with moisture during rainstorms and slides down the hillsides.

Another curious feature are the lignite coal beds. Millions of years ago the dense vegetation that grew here was deposited in layers, which in time formed large beds of soft, lignite coal. Occasionally the lignite beds catch fire from lightning or other natural causes, burning for years and baking the nearby clay layers into a bricklike substance locally called scoria (although true scoria is the result of volcanic action). In his book, *Ranch Life and the Hunting Trail*, Roosevelt describes the lignite beds: "A strong smell of sulphur hangs round them, the heated earth crumbles and cracks, and through the long clefts that form in it we can see the lurid glow of the subterranean fires, with here and there tongues of blue or cherry colored flame dancing up to the surface." One such burning vein can be seen today in the South Unit.

Plant life in the badlands is varied. The northern slopes, cooler and more moist than the southern slopes because of less sun, support woodlands in which juniper is common. Only semiarid vegetation, such as grasses, yucca and pricky-pear cacti, grow on the southern slopes. Cottonwoods, green ash and box elders are plentiful along the Little Missouri River.

During early summer bright splashes of the small prairie rose, the North Dakota State Flower, can be seen along with goldenrod, aster, scoria and mariposa lily, pasqueflower and phlox.

Wildlife has been sharply reduced since Roosevelt's day. Due to man's depredations, within the last century elk, grizzly and black bear and wolf have disappeared from the area, while buffalo, pronghorn antelope and bighorn sheep were "replanted" in the region in recent years. Smaller animals are still found in the badlands, such as the beaver, coyote, bobcat, jackrabbit, badger, red fox, weasel, muskrat and porcupine. As in the South Dakota badlands, many black-tailed prairie dogs scatter their towns on the flats. Prairie rattlesnakes are sometimes encountered along the roads.

There are 116 species of birds in the badlands. Hawks, falcons and golden eagles soar high above the gullies and buttes, while magpies, woodpeckers, sparrows, larks, swallows, wrens and owls congregate in the trees and vegetation.

In the South Unit, as well as in the rest of the badlands, are the petrified remains of a large forest. Fossils of snail-like creatures have been discovered here, and occasionally a rock will break open to expose leaf impressions of ancient oaks, maples, magnolias, sassafras and elms.

Spring and fall are pleasant, summers hot and dry, but winters are severe. Roosevelt writes:

Sometimes furious gales blow out of

141

The rugged North Dakota badlands stand out in bold relief at sunset, their varied colors taking on a beauty not seen in midday. Sparse vegetation grows on the slopes, providing some cover for jackrabbits, badgers, weasels, muskrats and prairie rattlesnakes which thrive here. An early explorer called this area "hell with the fires out."

the north, driving before them the clouds of blinding snowdust, wrapping the mantle of death round every unsheltered being that faces their unshackled anger. They roar in a thunderous bass as they sweep across the prairie or whirl through the naked cañons; they shiver the great brittle cottonwoods.... Again, in the coldest midwinter weather, not a breath of wind may stir; and then the still, merciless, terrible cold that broods over the earth like the shadow of silent death seems even more dreadful in its gloomy rigor than is the lawless mad-

ness of the storms. All the land is like granite; the great rivers stand still in their beds, as if turned to frosted steel. In the long nights there is no sound to break the lifeless silence. Under the ceaseless, shifting play of the Northern Lights, or lighted only by the wintry brilliance of the stars, the snow-clad plains stretch out into dead and endless wastes of glimmering white.

Little is known of the Indian occupation of these North Dakota badlands until the traders and trappers entered the area in the early 1800's. Various Indian tribes, including the Crow, Cheyenne and Sioux (Dakotah), lived along the banks of the Missouri River then, and in 1804, Canadian Jean Baptiste LePage became the first non-Indian to view the badlands as he traveled through them to join the Lewis and Clark expedition at Fort Mandan north of Bismarck.

It was not until 1864, however, that the area first caught the attention of the American people. Brigadier General Alfred Sully traveled through the Little Missouri basin while on a campaign against the Sioux, and according to legend, he described the land as "hell with the fires out."

Railroad companies began taking notice of the Dakota Territory because their planned railroad from the Great Lakes to the Northwest lumbering country would have to cross the plains. The Indians did not welcome the "iron horse" or the buffalo hunters that came with it, however, and progress on the railroad construction was slow partly due to the Indian resistance to white incursions.

In 1883 Roosevelt came to the badlands to hunt and then decided to enter into a partnership to set up a ranch there, later known as the Maltese Cross Ranch because of its distinctive brand. The next year he set up his own Elkhorn Ranch some distance away. His two cattle operations prospered until the devastating winter of 1886-1887, when severe cold and deep snow wiped out most of the cattle herds. Roosevelt later sold his cattle interests before leaving for Cuba in 1898 to join the famous Rough Riders.

Of his time in the Dakotas, Roosevelt said, "If it had not been for what I learned during those years I spent here in North Dakota, I never in the world would have been made President of the United States." His years in the badlands gave him insights that later made him a conservationist, and his Dakota years made him a Western President as much as an Eastern one. As President, he signed the Antiquities Act of 1906 which empowered Presidents to sign proclamations creating National Monuments out of public domain lands. This was a bold innovation for conservation, and "T. R." used this power to create sixteen monuments himself -- more than any other President.

Theodore Roosevelt National Memorial Park was established in 1947 and contains about 110 square miles of the North Dakota badlands in three units: the South Unit near Medora, the North Unit near Watford City, and the Elkhorn Ranch site midway between the two. The park is open all year and there are campgrounds and picnic areas in both main units. Interpretive programs are presented by the park rangers in the summer, and a visitor center is located at the Medora entrance to the South Unit, with the original Maltese Cross Ranch cabin nearby. The Elkhorn Ranch site can only be reached over a dirt road, and none of the original buildings remain standing.

The seemingly endless miles of gullies and hills convey to visitors today a sense of spaciousness and forlorn beauty, the same sense that Theodore Roosevelt and Alfred Sully must have felt when they saw these badlands, in Sully's words, "grand, dismal, and majestic."

The bright scarlet glow of a burning lignite coal vein in the South Unit of the park, which is believed to have been ignited in 1951, can be seen through a cleft in the rocks. This subterranean fire may burn for many more years.

A mother bison weans her calf one year after its birth in spring. While only a few weeks old, the young calves are able to eat grass and run after their mothers, but it takes eight years for the bulls to reach maturity. Buffalo, once extremely plentiful in the badlands, were nearly killed off within the last century.

143

Aransas

Texas

It is truly a magnificent creature, this tallest of North American birds. Five feet in height, with a seven-foot wingspan, the whooping crane gives a piping cry that can be heard over a mile away. It is noble and stately in appearance, with its gleaming white plumage, red patch of bare skin on the crown, black wing tips and graceful flight. But it is not just its appearance that makes the whooper so unusual. It mates for life and lives in a fiercely guarded privacy with a decorum rarely found in birds. The male, who can sense potential danger a mile away, is always ready to challenge an enemy with bugle calls and a head-on charge.

Every autumn, the world awaits word of the arrival of the whoopers on the Texas Gulf Coast after a 2,500-mile flight from their summer nesting sites in Canada, for these birds have been on the verge of extinction for many years. It is believed that they have not been really numerous for centuries and there may have been only 1,400 dwelling on the continent at the time the Pilgrims landed. By 1938 only fourteen remained and today there are about fifty.

One reason for the modest increase was the establishment in 1937 of the Aransas National Wildlife Refuge at the whoopers' winter grounds on Blackjack Peninsula on the Texas Gulf Coast. Another reason was the sighting in 1955 of a whooper's nest on a swampy island in Canada's vast Wood Buffalo Park, a little-explored area south of Great Slave Lake. It was the first fresh whooping crane nest seen since 1922. It is now believed that for the past decade or so these birds have nested only in Wood or thereabouts; thus we now have information about a vital link in the whoopers' habitats which is necessary to help preserve them. While at their wintering grounds, each pair of birds, including a rusty-colored chick or two if there are offspring, establishes for themselves a territory of about four hundred acres and defends it against other whooping cranes. Because whoopers are so sensitive to intruders, especially human, the public is not allowed to enter the birds' wintering grounds in Aransas, but the birds can be usually viewed with binoculars from an observation tower which overlooks a portion of this coastal area.

Late in the winter, when mates renew their nuptial bonds, one approaches the other with many stiff bows interspersed with cavorting, trumpeting and flapping as he constantly moves in semicircles. Then he leaps into the air stiff-legged, spreading his great wings; this is repeated as he circles more frantically and jumps increasingly higher until his dance is over as suddenly as it began.

Another endangered species, Attwater's prairie chicken, once nested in goodly numbers on the tall-grass prairies of the Texas coast, but as this fertile country was settled, drained and cultivated, all prairie chicken populations were severely depleted and they were forced to survive in isolated patches or on the fringes of their former habitats. Attwater's exist today only on the open coastal prairies and plains of the Texas Gulf Coast, and Aransas is one of their few refuges, although the largest population is in Colorado County, about ninety miles north of Aransas. From a total population of 8,700 in 1937, they had been reduced to about one thousand by 1965.

The marshes, grasslands, brush thickets and woods of Aransas nurture many other species under the supervision of the Bureau of Sport Fisheries and Wildlife. There are several kinds of ducks, geese, herons, egrets and shorebirds, as well as the beautiful roseate spoonbill and the sandhill crane. Among the mammals are an abundance of white-tailed deer and an increasing number of javelinas (collared peccaries). The latter is the only wild native piglike animal in the United States. He ranges from Mexico into Texas, southeastern Arizona and southern New Mexico but is found nowhere else. The javelina weighs between forty and sixty pounds and has coarse gray-black hair which bristles when it is excited, giving the appearance of being larger. Javelinas dwell in patriarchal bands as large as twenty-five or more, and when threatened they fiercely defend themselves. These sturdy beasts favor a terrain in Aransas -- the dense thickets -- quite different from that of the elegant whoopers, but the important fact is that, like the great rare birds, they have found needed sanctuary on this isolated Gulf Coast peninsula appropriately named for the blackjack oak that grows here.

Aransas refuge on Blackjack Peninsula is the nearly extinct whooping crane's winter home (above), to which nearly fifty of the birds migrate each fall from Canada.

Aransas also hosts the endangered Attwater's prairie chicken (right) which the photographer has caught in the midst of its prenuptial dance performed on the "booming grounds."

145

Desert National Wildlife Range

Nevada

The people trying their luck at the gaming tables in Las Vegas are probably little aware that less than ten miles north is a spectacular, vast desert wilderness used primarily for the preservation of one of nature's most intriguing animals, the desert bighorn sheep.

Found in a number of scattered spots in the arid regions of the Southwest and Mexico, the desert bighorn is similar to its cousin farther north, the Rocky Mountain bighorn. Stocky and heavy-bodied, the desert bighorn averages about three feet in height at the shoulder and weighs between 120 and 200 pounds. They are light buff in color with a large white rump patch around the short tail and are one of the most prized hunting trophies in the world because of the massive, curling horns of the rams. These horns may have a circumference of up to sixteen inches at the base and taper sharply to the tip, sometimes measuring nearly forty inches around the outer curls. The ram's horns grow steadily from birth, while the ewe's horns generally do not exceed twelve inches.

Beautifully adapted to their dry desert environment, the sheep go without water for weeks or months during the cooler season and for as long as three to seven days in the hot summer months, sustaining their bodily moisture from food alone. Ewes give birth to a single lamb between February and April when new plant growth is available for the newborn offspring. Twin lambs occur rarely, and only the hardiest of the lambs can survive the rigors of this desert climate.

Grass seems to be their preferred food, but the succulent parts of shrubs and trees are also eaten. Long migrations are infrequent, but seasonal movements resulting in gradual shifts of elevation are common.

Desert bighorns are extremely sure-footed and fast, bounding between rock ledges at speeds up to twenty-five miles an hour. Their only natural predators, the coyote, bobcat, cougar and golden eagle, do not get much chance at the bighorn because of its speed and its superb eyesight. It is reportedly able to see things five miles away. If cornered, it lowers its head and angrily charges, which is usually more than enough warning for an opponent. Predators are not a limiting factor on bighorns on the range.

The battles between bighorn rams are among nature's fiercest spectacles. Somewhat similar to the battles between elk bulls, two rams challenge each other by rising on their hind legs and letting out a trumpeting, bellowing sound. Then they lower their heads and charge into each other with a force that would kill most other animals. The sound of the head-on collision echoes up and down the canyons, sounding something like a two-ton boulder crashing off a cliff. The charge is repeated again and again for hours on end. But it is never a battle to the death, for after they have become tired, they lie down side by side in the shade of a cliff or rock, contentedly chewing their cud as if nothing had happened.

The Desert National Wildlife Range, established in 1936 and containing over a million and a half acres, is the largest Federal refuge in the forty-eight states and one of four ranges whose objective is to protect these sheep in their natural environment. Once numbering about three hundred, the sheep in the range have now increased to one thousand head through the management programs of the Fish and Wildlife Service. The Cabeza Prieta and Kofa game ranges in Arizona and San Andres National Wildlife Refuge in New Mexico also have vigorous herds of bighorns.

The Nevada refuge has a number of mountain ranges, notably the Sheep Range whose highest crest, Hayford Peak, is 9,912 feet high. Vegetation varies with elevation, with saltbrush, creosote bush and mes-

Near White Sage Flat Reservoir (above) in the range, contrasting layers of rock are exposed in this portion of the Mojave Desert which once held inland lakes.

A desert bighorn ewe and her lamb (right) appear to survey the wilderness. They can go for long periods of time without any water, though refuge management has begun to build more water catchments to alleviate the competition between deer, livestock and bighorns for the small supply.

Coyotes (left) are present in the range where they provide the essential service of predation on small rodents, like the jackrabbit in the photo, that would otherwise overpopulate and upset the ecosystem.

Hawaiian Islands

Hawaii

Almost lost in the immensity of the Pacific, the Hawaiian Islands National Wildlife Refuge stretches for almost eight hundred miles to the north and west of the principal Hawaiian Islands, almost to, but not including, Midway Island. Known as the Leeward or Northwestern Hawaiian Islands, the islands, reefs and atolls comprising the refuge are the tops of underwater volcanic peaks and they are older than the inhabited main islands. Here in one of the least known and inaccessible parts of the United States are found species of rare and endangered wildlife and some of the finest seabird nesting colonies in the world.

The refuge, established in 1909 by executive order of President Theodore Roosevelt, contains over 302,000 acres of lands and waters. However, only about 1,765 acres of this is land. The islands vary from flat and sandy terrain to rocky pinnacles rising nine hundred feet high out of the ocean. French Frigate Shoals and Pearl and Hermes Reef are atolls. Size varies from those like Laysan, the largest with two square miles, to islets only a fraction of an acre in size. Vegetation varies; some small islands are bare, while larger ones contain extensive stands on knee-high vegetation interspersed with sandy ridges or rocky outcrops. The palm trees on Nihoa (*Pritchardia remota*) are found nowhere else in the world. Stone house platforms, garden terraces and primitive temples on Nihoa indicate this island was inhabited by ancient Polynesians perhaps as long as seven hundred years ago, although none of the islands is inhabited today except for a coast guard station at French Frigate Shoals.

Because the refuge has been designated as a national research area within the National Wildlife Refuge System, no activities are permitted which could alter the delicate ecosystem of these islands. Insular ecosystems are much more vulnerable to change than those on larger land masses, thus entry to these islands is open only to scientists on a permit basis. When landings are made they frequently occur under hazardous conditions because of rough surf, hidden reefs and the rocky shores of the islands. Sudden squalls are frequent.

Before the islands became a refuge, guano diggers introduced rabbits on Laysan and Lisianski islands that eventually destroyed all the vegetation on the two islands. The resulting alteration of the fragile ecology caused three species of land birds to become extinct, although much of the vegetation has returned. Even today, the introductions of pest insects, weeds or predators could have devastating effects on the islands.

Two small land birds, the wrenlike Nihoa millerbird and bright yellow Nihoa finch, are found nowhere else except on the 156-acre island for which they are named. The former was unknown to science until discovered by Dr. Alexander Wetmore in 1923 and is of Old World origin. The finch, which is really not a finch but a Hawaiian honeycreeper, belongs to a distinctly Hawaiian bird family of New World origin, the Drepanididae. Closely related to the Nihoa finch is the Laysan finch, which looks much like it and is endemic to Laysan. They are numerous on this island, nesting a few inches above the ground in clumps of bunch grass. A teal-sized Laysan duck, also found only on this island, may be the rarest duck in the world. In 1923 there were only seven birds. Today there are perhaps a hundred.

Nesting colonies of hundreds of thousands of seabirds exist on these tiny islands. Most familiar of these are the Laysan and black-footed albatrosses, both known as "gooney birds" because of their strange courtship dances. From late October to late July they nest on Laysan, the largest such colony in the world. The rest of the year they soar over the waters of the Pacific from Japan to the West Coast of the United States, from the Aleutians to Hawaii. Sleek black-and-white sooty terns nest on Laysan in far greater numbers than the albatrosses. Populations may total from 1.5 to 2 million birds in spring and early summer, and it is difficult to walk in many places without stepping on eggs or young. The small white fairy tern, considered the most beautiful seabird of the Pacific, is found on most of the islands. Other seabirds found in large numbers include the greater frigate bird; the blue-faced, the brown and the red-footed boobies; the common, the Hawaiian and the blue-gray noddy terns; the gray-back tern; the tropicbird; and several species of petrels and shearwaters. Hundreds of thousands of wedge-tailed shearwaters, moaning and wailing through the night, make the islands sound like eerie, haunted graveyards.

The sandy beaches of several of the islands provide sanctuaries for the green sea turtle, and here also is the home of the rare Hawaiian monk seal. The turtles, which can weigh as much as five hundred pounds, but are usually about half this size, are sometimes called

the most valuable reptiles in the world. They have been drastically reduced in numbers in much of the world by man's overexploitation. Their eggs and flesh are used as food in many places, and the gelatinous calipee and calapash on the insides of their shells serve as the stock base for green turtle soup so prized by gourmets.

The monk seal is closely related to a species found in the Mediterranean and to the West Indian (or Caribbean) seal that was the first species of wildlife described from the New World. Columbus found them plentiful on his second voyage in 1494, but because of centuries of unrestricted killing there has been no record of their occurrence since 1952. The monk seal is lethargic and unsuspicious, but does not tolerate much disturbance. Because of this and its restricted habitats, it was easy prey for sealers who had almost exterminated the Hawaiian species by 1900. Today there are a little over a thousand monk seals in these islands. The soft, cuddly pups are jet black at birth and possess luminous black eyes. After about seven weeks they become grayish and later a uniform brown tinged with gray. Females can become as heavy as six hundred pounds.

The wildlife in the refuge exhibits a comparative tameness because human disturbances and harassment have not been a factor there for many years. In an overcrowded country still enamored of a growth-is-good ethic, it is fortunate that these unspoiled islands are a part of the United States dedicated not to man but to the welfare of wild creatures.

"Gooney bird" is the common name for the much mythologized Laysan albatross (left, with chick), whose awkward land movements belie its power and grace when it may soar and skim the air on ocean updrafts for days, its narrow wings spanned outward up to twelve feet.

Rare species of birds inhabit the Hawaiian Islands Wildlife Refuge, such as the yellow Nihoa finch (top), which is more correctly called the Hawaiian honeycreeper and is found only on this island.

The red-footed booby with its chick (above) is, like the others of its species, an impressive diver: Keen eyesight and air-sac cushions allow this booby to fish throughout the night and make plunging dives into the sea for fish.

151

Two Kodiak or Alaskan brown bear cubs (left) test their climbing ability in a tree on Kodiak Island. Most of the island is a national wildlife refuge established to protect these cubs and other animals.

Caribou, or reindeer (below), were introduced on Kodiak after the 1920's and now live in limited but increasing numbers. These deer are unique in that they are the only kind that has antlers on both sexes.

Kodiak

Alaska

A mother Kodiak bear prowls through the dense brush of the refuge. These bears are the largest carnivores on earth, standing 10 to 13 feet high on their hind legs.

Kodiak Island, the largest island in the Gulf of Alaska, contains the 2,780 square mile area of Kodiak National Wildlife Refuge, established in 1941. Unlike many other refuges, Kodiak has remained essentially unchanged over the centuries.

The island is wild and mountainous, with snowy peaks reaching four thousand feet above sea level. It is lush with vegetation in some areas while barren in others. Sitka spruce forests dominate the mountains of the northern part of Kodiak, while grassy slopes and rolling Arctic tundra are characteristic of the southern portion.

Numerous clear streams carry the water from the high Alpine lakes to the long, fjordlike bays of the Pacific Coast. Often misty and dismal with low clouds surrounding the peaks, the island averages 105 inches of precipitation annually, and winters, unlike most of Alaska, are mild with temperatures seldom below zero.

The variety of birdlife is extraordinary, and particularily impressive are the almost two hundred pairs of bald eagles, the national emblem, which nest here on rocky pinnacles, cliffs and in cottonwood trees. The willow and the rock ptarmigan, the State Bird of Alaska, are numerous, and the call of the common loon is heard on nearly every lake. Gamefish are plentiful, various and large; on parts of the refuge there are king salmon weighing twenty to sixty pounds.

Animals native to Kodiak are the red fox, land otter, weasel, tundra vole and little brown bat. Transplanted to the island after 1920 and gaining in numbers are black-tailed Sitka deer, snowshoe hare, beaver, muskrat, reindeer, mountain goat, red squirrel and Dall sheep. Sea lions, some weighing a ton, lie on the rocks of several offshore islands as thickly as bathers at Coney Island on a hot day.

But Kodiak Island is best known as the habitat of the Kodiak brown bear, sometimes called the Alaskan brown bear, the largest carnivore on earth. Weighing up to 1,200 pounds and growing to a height of four or more feet at the shoulders, the bear is formidable even without standing erect on its hind legs. When it does, it towers ten to thirteen feet high.

Originally ranging along the entire coastal strip of Alaska and British Columbia, they have been reduced by extensive hunting over the years. The refuge, however, has over 2,400 of these tremendous animals.

The bears den from December to April, and during spring, early summer and fall they are mostly vegetarians. In July and August they are easily seen as they congregate in streams to catch the spawning salmon. Ordinarily solitary creatures, it is possible to see fifty of them within a square mile at this time.

Cubs, weighing less than a pound at birth -- the size of a small squirrel -- are born in the dens during winter. They remain with their mothers for two years before the family ties are broken. Young bears gain weight quickly in summer -- one young bear trapped in July had gained over two hundred pounds when retrapped in a census survey in October.

In spite of their size and clumsy appearance, the bears are quick-moving and agile when necessary, yet silent and cautious in the brush. Tremendously strong animals, they are able to kill a thousand-pound steer with one blow and break a tree four inches in diameter with a sweep of a forearm. They are, however, wary of man and will seldom charge unless cornered or injured.

When discovered by a Russian in 1763, the island was inhabited by people calling themselves Koniags. Numbering over six thousand, they were stronger and hardier than the Aleuts of the mainland, frequently swimming and boating naked in the cold. But imported diseases and ill treatment by the intruding traders gradually reduced their population; today there are only about eight hundred residents of Koniag ancestry left. The Russian influence on Kodiak is still substantial: Many residents of Kodiak speak fluent Russian, and each town and village has a Russian Orthodox Church.

All of the Kodiak refuge is open to the public, but there are no roads. A scheduled airline makes two flights a day from Anchorage to the town of Kodiak, and several bush pilots and a local airline furnish air transportation to almost any part of the refuge. Commercial fishing boats can be chartered for trips around the island and to the beaches.

Loxahatchee

Florida

The Everglades once covered most of southern Florida. Wildlife was extremely plentiful because of a perfectly balanced ecosystem. The Colusa and Seminole Indians living there took care not to upset this balance, but then the Europeans came with their desire to conquer the wilderness. Ponce de Leon trekked over the Everglades looking for his evasive Fountain of Youth and was killed near here by the Colusas in 1521. Then came other Spanish explorers and finally settlers. Conflicts mounted in the early 1800's, and when the Indians were subdued, the glades were open to human despoilment. Today all too few acres of this once great swamp remain undisturbed.

One of the largest remaining areas of glades is Loxahatchee National Wildlife Refuge, containing 220 square miles and located between Lake Okeechobee and Fort Lauderdale. Established in 1951, the refuge preserves the habitat of a fantastic number of birds and animals.

Loxahatchee is roughly pear-shaped, bounded by levees on all sides. Just inside are the canals which expedite the movement of water in or out of the region as called for by the rainfall, which averages sixty-two inches annually. It was originally the bottom of a great sea, but dying vegetation has built up a large body of organic soil rising up to fifteen feet above sea level.

Although crisscrossed with questionable drainage ditches, much of the unique beauty of this section of the Everglades remains. Dense stands of Tracey's beakrush flourish in shallow water flats, and sawgrass continues to cover large areas. Smartweeds, white water lilies and other wet-soil aquatic plants grow here, while the tree islands support mixed stands of redbay, wax-myrtle and holly.

Both wading birds and waterfowl come here by the thousands all year round. The rarest bird found on the refuge is the Everglade kite, of which there are only about one hundred in existance. Medium-sized birds with a black body, white tail bands and, during the breeding season, a red patch between the eyes and the sharply hooked beak, the kites are very sensitive in their eating habits, feeding only on a particular species of freshwater snail. Thus they can survive only in areas where the snails are fairly plentiful. Perching on snags in the marshes after capturing their prey, they deftly pull it from its shell with their specialized beaks.

Two birds that are uncommon outside of the glades are the limpkin and the Florida sandhill crane. The limpkin, a long-legged, long-beaked bird with a brown body and distinctive white arrowhead-shaped spots, feeds on the same species of snail as does the kite, and also other mollusks and insects. The sandhill crane, largest bird found on the refuge, can be easily recognized by its large size and tufted tail. In flight the long neck is outstretched, and its call, once heard, cannot soon be forgotten. During winter a number of cranes may roost in the flooded fields near the refuge headquarters on the eastern boundary near Delray Beach. They build their nests less than a foot above the water, which may be six to eighteen inches deep.

The bald eagle visits Loxahatchee occasionally, but does not normally nest here, preferring instead to travel sixty miles south to Everglades National Park. The American osprey can be found in the region in small numbers most of the year.

The great white heron's breeding range lies south of Loxahatchee, and the number of these graceful long-legged wading birds visiting at any one time is usually small. But the great blue heron is common here, and can be seen along the trails as it stalks through the waters looking for animals to feed upon. A smaller version, the little blue heron, is also numerous.

The Florida sandhill crane (above) is found in this state and in Cuba, and here in Loxahatchee refuge, a part of the Everglades, its numbers are protected.

The common egret (right), like the similar but smaller snowy egret, barely escaped extinction at the turn of the century when plume hunters were greedy for its beautiful, lacy aigrettes.

Portions of Loxahatchee are jungle glades of ferns, semitropical flowers and trees (above), while others are swamps and shallow water flats (opposite, bottom) where water lillies and smartweeds grow. Opposite, top: A great blue heron nests in the refuge. This largest of our herons is distinguished by the two black plumes on either side of its white head and the black patches on its shoulders. The great blue heron fishes standing motionless and will eat nearly any small animal as well as fish. The naturalist Emerson amusingly described its call as, "--a short, coarse, frog-like purring or eructating sound. You might easily mistake it for a frog.... Anything but musical."

A large white bird with yellow beak and black legs seen in the refuge is the common egret, brought to near extinction by plume hunters around the turn of the century. Its smaller cousin, the snowy egret, can be recognized by its black bill and black legs with yellow feet. Egrets feed primarily on small fish, frogs and other water creatures.

During winter one of the most plentiful birds is the coot, a duck-like bird with a white bill. Also abundant at this time of year, and residing here all year round, is the white ibis with its red face and decurved bill. A close relative, the glossy ibis, is identified by its dark bronze plumage.

The roseate spoonbill, a large white and pinkish wader with a bill which flattens out at the tip, is an occasional visitor. Still other birds found in Loxahatchee are common and purple gallinules, anhingas, Louisiana herons, turkey and black vultures, killdeer, mourning doves, smooth-billed anis (normally a bird of the tropics), screech and great horned owls, grackles and mockingbirds.

Loxahatchee is the southern terminus of the Atlantic Flyway, and twenty or more species of ducks migrate here annually. The Florida duck, mottled duck and wood duck nest here, and ring-necked ducks, pintails, blue-winged and green-winged teals, American widgeons, shovellers and baldpates winter in the marshes.

Alligators, though an endangered species nationally, seem to thrive in this refuge. These reptiles can be seen floating partially submerged or sunning on the edge of a canal. Armadillos were introduced into the area about 1920 and forage for insects early or late during day and at night. This odd mammal, with its suit of armor protecting it from all enemies, was named by Spaniards who found it in Mexico and called it the "little fellow in armor."

Rabbits, bobwhite quail, raccoons, river otters, Florida water rats (small, round-tailed versions of the muskrat), bobcats and white-tailed deer also inhabit the glades. An occasional cougar, locally called the Florida panther, may wander into the refuge at times.

Fishing in Loxahatchee is good with largemouth bass, bream and crappies in the ditches and shallows.

Only part of Loxahatchee is open to the public. A concession at the south end carries supplies, and rental boats and guides are available. Boat launching facilities and picnic shelters are located at the extreme northern boundary, and a boat launching ramp is also located near the headquarters building. Accommodations are numerous along Florida's Gold Coast, twelve miles to the east.

This section of the once vast Everglades may yet survive as a natural area if the Florida development "fever" does not encroach upon it further.

BSFW, Snyder

BSFW, Greany

The snowy owl (above), rare in the East and even there seen only in winter, exists in Moosehorn in comparatively large numbers. This large white bird with yellow eyes normally lives on the Arctic tundra, but its range reaches as far south as the upper portions of the United States.

Broad antlers and a large snout are the recognizable characteristics of the tallest mammal in the Americas, the moose (left). This large deer is rarely found away from water.

158

Moosehorn

Maine

Moosehorn National Wildlife Refuge is the essence of Maine. Rocky shores take the shapes of little inlets, bays and secret coves, with evergreens marching right to the sea's edge. The offshore islands are covered with pine, and the ocean waters are crowded with buoys marking the locations of lobster pots. Inland the air is sweet with the smell of balsam fir, hemlock and pine growing on the rolling landscape, and among stands of trees are meadows, lakes, marshes, bogs and streams called flowages, which may be dammed up by enterprising beavers.

Almost all of the East Coast refuges were established for birdlife, and thus were built around marshes, but Moosehorn is mostly uplands. Besides evergreens, the second-growth forests contain sugar maple, white birch, aspen, beech and poplar. The bogs support wild cranberry and blueberry bushes, and the slow-growth black spruce trees are fifty years old although only five or six feet high.

Located on the extreme eastern tip of Maine, Moosehorn is divided into two units: the Baring Unit on the north near the town of Calais (locally pronounced "callous"), and the Edmunds Unit twenty miles south near Whiting. Part of the boundary of the Baring Unit touches the St. Croix River separating Maine from the Canadian province of New Brunswick. The Edmunds Unit borders on Cobscook Bay. Cobscook is an Indian word meaning "boiling tides," and although the tides at Cobscook are large, the biggest tides in the United States (outside of Cook Inlet, Alaska) are at Calais, with a difference of twenty-eight feet between rise and fall.

Although many of the forests are harvested for timber according to a management program established by the Fish and Wildlife Service, tracts have been set aside in each unit as natural areas. A visitor center at the northern entrance to the Baring Unit, open during summer, provides information on the refuge's flora and fauna, which can most easily be seen along the self-guided auto trail.

In spite of its name, Moosehorn was established primarily for the protection of the woodcock, a small, brown nocturnal bird which blends in beautifully with the dead leaves and sticks on the ground. With a short tail and rounded wings, it flies rapidly and erratically when flushed from cover. Feeding on worms which it finds by probing the damp earth with its long, pointed beak, it is extremely hard to see because of its camouflage and is thus a rather secretive creature. Moosehorn is the center of its northeastern nesting grounds, and it winters mostly in the southern Atlantic states. In early spring the male's unusual mating performance may be observed in clearings. When light is at a specific intensity at dawn or dusk, the male woodcock struts around making a "peenting" noise, after which it soars several hundred feet into the air, sings a beautiful warbling song, then plummets straight to the ground, landing softly to begin its strutting again.

Two hundred other species of birds have been identified on the refuge, many of them nesting here. Ring-necked ducks, which do not nest on many of the wildlife refuges, are abundant, along with a great variety of other ducks, teals, grebes, mergansers, loons, hawks, ospreys, warblers, sparrows and the handsome snowy owl, rare in the East and seen only in winter.

Of course, the refuge does have moose, for Maine is one of the few states where one still sees "moose crossing" signs on main highways. Largest of the deer family and tallest mammal of the Americas, it stands six or seven feet at the withers and weighs up to 1,200 pounds. Moose are extremely strong and of uncertain temper. If surprised by man, they will blindly crash through the forest, though normally they are very stealthy. As the largest antlered animals in the world, their horns are immense, spreading up to sixty inches tip to tip. Excellent swimmers, they are rarely found away from water.

Ranging throughout the upper Northern Hemisphere, moose are called elk in Europe. Natural enemies include grizzly bears, cougars and timber wolves (none of which are in Moosehorn) but it is very rare that predators get a chance to down a moose. They are strict vegetarians, dining on twigs, bark, leaves and roots of plants. Being antisocial, they are nearly always found alone, except when mating in the fall. During that time vicious battles take place between bullmoose attracted to the same cow. As much as half an acre of woods can be torn apart by infuriated bulls.

Another interesting animal in the refuge, one that most people have never seen, is the fisher, a large, dark weasel with a bushy tail and rounded ears. Once found in evergreen forests throughout the northern part of the continent, they have been severely reduced by excessive hunting and trapping. Very agile creatures, they are also fine swimmers and will kill almost anything, including raccoons, foxes and deer. They are about the only animals that make a habit of assaulting porcupines. If a fisher eats a porcupine, the quills pass harmlessly through his digestive system, but many fishers carry quills around in their bodies for many weeks as their reward for tangling with this pugnacious rodent.

But the sighting of an adult moose in the wilds of these Maine forests, with its horns sparkling white after ridding itself of their moss, is a memorable experience for any outdoorsman.

National **Bison** Range

Montana

At the southern end of the beautiful Flathead Valley, in the shadows of the majestic Mission Mountains in western Montana, is the home of one of the premiere herds of American buffalo or bison. This herd in the 18,540-acre National Bison Range varies in size from year to year but is generally between three hundred and five hundred.

This huge beast once ranged from Great Slave Lake in Canada to Mexico and from Nevada and Oregon to Tennessee and Pennsylvania, numbering perhaps sixty million animals. What occurred between 1840 and 1880 was a saga of wildlife slaughter that is one of the most savage in U.S. conservation history.

A few buffalo were killed for meat, but millions of others were stripped for their hides and tongues. By the 1870's a widely advertised "sport" was shooting buffalo from the open windows of trains as the animals raced along beside them. The carcasses were left to rot in the prairie sun. The herds were almost completely wiped out by 1882-1883, but the ruthless buffalo hunters apparently did not realize the extent of the massacre for many insisted the herds had gone to Canada and would return. By 1900, only twenty wild bison were known to exist in the United States, with about 250 more in Canada.

Largely through the efforts of the American Bison Society, under the leadership of naturalist Dr. William T. Hornaday, the National Bison Range was established in 1908. In the fall of the following year the first buffalo were released on the range. The bulk of this first herd of thirty-four had been purchased by the Bison Society from the Conrad herd at Kalispell, Montana, which descended in part from four young calves brought back from a hunting expedition in 1873 by Walking Coyote of the Pen d'Oreille Indians.

A member of the cattle family, American bison are cloven hoofed and chew their cud as do their close relatives, domestic sheep and cattle. Their closest wild relative is the European bison. Both sexes have a set of hollow, curved horns and the bulls may weigh a ton or more. Their huge heads and great humps are covered with dark brown wooly hair in fall and winter but they begin shedding their winter coat in spring. To accelerate the shedding and to relieve itching, buffalo rub against large stones and trees. By late spring only the long hairs on head, forelegs and hump remain, and during this period, they are especially vulnerable to harassment by insects. To escape these pests buffalo wallow in dust or sand.

Buffalo are hardy animals with surprising speed and agility. In deep snow they can outdistance a man on snowshoes and in powdery snow they can outrun a dog team. They are excellent swimmers, and their bones have been found on rugged mountain summits. They can root through deep snow with their muzzles and head to find grass for food. In the national refuges they feed primarily on buffalo grass, gramas, bluegrass, bluestems, wheatgrass and fescues.

Buffalo mature at seven or eight years and may live to be twenty-five to thirty years old. During the breeding season in mid to late summer, bulls bellow loudly and become quarrelsome. Many fights occur but they are brief, and much time is spent pawing the earth pugnaciously.

Calves are usually born in April or May, and at birth there is only a hint of the hump they will develop later. Buffalo travel in small herds which, in the nineteenth century, sometimes merged into the great herds occasionally observed then. Only when panicked did these smaller groups lose their identity. Although playful and easily handled as calves, mature buffalo are unpredictable; men who know them best are always wary of them.

As with the buffalo, the other large animal herds on this range are maintained at a more or less constant number: fifty to seventy-five elk (wapiti), two hundred to three hundred mule deer, the same number of white-tailed deer, forty to eighty bighorn sheep and eighty to two hundred pronghorns. All of these animals, except the bighorns, can be seen at headquarters exhibition pastures. For those with more time, a nineteen-mile self-guided tour over graveled road can be taken which includes Headquarters Ridge, Pauline Creek, Elk Creek, Red Sleep Mountain Viewpoint, Trisky Creek, St. Ignatius, Antelope Ridge and Misson Creek.

The range is made up of grasslands, steep hills and narrow canyons. In winter, snow piles deep in nearby hills, but the bison range is so located that it is scantily covered. The grasslands are composed largely of Palouse Prairie vegetation, including the grasses the buffalo feeds on. The area near Pauline Creek is typical of the grasslands and the range generally. Among the

John Allen, Cyr Agency

The American bison (right), in a herd of 300 to 500, roams the National Bison Range in the Flathead Valley of western Montana, a grass and timberland of 18,540 acres preserved for this great species.

A small herd of Rocky Mountain bighorn sheep (below) was introduced in 1911 to provide part of the natural bison environment.

BSFW, Mazzoni

The white-tailed deer (above) inhabits the brushy bottomlands along creeks, browsing among snowberry, willow and cottonwood.

The yellow-bellied marmot (left) shows the white markings which differentiate it in part from its Eastern cousin, the woodchuck.

In the remote Mission Mountains in the eastern range area, the grizzly (below) finds sanctuary equaled only in the national parks and Alaska.

162

species of birds favoring such open areas are rock wrens, horned larks, short-eared owls and many hawks such as the red-tailed, marsh and the prairie falcon. Pronghorns, introduced into the range in 1951 for research purposes, are often seen here also. Mission Creek, frequented by white-tailed deer, is typical of the bottomlands in the range. Trees such as alders, junipers, aspens, birches, cottonwoods, thorn apples and willows are plentiful along such streams, providing habitat for various warblers, thrushes, swallows, woodpeckers, flycatchers and orioles.

The upper hills are in a montane forest zone containing small parklike stands of Douglas fir and Western yellow pine. Here are found several interesting birds, including Western tanagers, Clark's nutcrackers, Lewis' woodpeckers, blue grouse and the spectacular golden eagle. Mule deer inhabit the higher slopes and ridges where the vegetation includes paintbrush, clarkia, several penstemons and bitterroot, the Montana State Flower.

Rocky Mountain elk and gray, or Hungarian, partridge can sometimes be seen at Headquarters Ridge, but the best place to see elk is on the upper reaches of the Elk Creek drainage. Rocky Mountain bighorn sheep, brought into the range in 1922 from Banff National Park, Alberta, are occasionally viewed in the lower reaches of the Trisky Creek drainage. The mountain bighorn is a subspecies of the American bighorn, and its average weight is 185 pounds. The record span for their impressive, corkscrew horns is forty-nine and a half inches. The northern species tend to be grayish brown, while those in southern deserts are pale buff.

During fall and winter wild ducks gather along Misson Creek and ten thousand mallards have been counted there. Furbearers throughout the range include badgers, mink, beavers, muskrats and weasels.

St. Ignatius is the focus of historical interest. Jesuit Fathers founded a mission there in 1854, and the original log-cabin building constructed by them still stands. Before the mission was founded, the site was known as "The Rendezvous" because it was where the Kalispell and Kootenai tribes gathered for bartering and gaming.

Located forty-eight miles north of Missoula, the range has no facilities for camping, but there is a picnic grove inside the main entrance at Moiese, and public fishing is provided on the part of the Jocko River that flows along the southern edge of the range. But perhaps the choicest spot in the range is High Point Lookout on top of Red Sleep Mountain, at an elevation of 4,885 feet the highest point in the range. The lovely valley stretches out below, justifying its Indian name meaning "Land of the Shining Mountains," and sometimes one can see a few tiny dark dots far below, the descendants of Walking Coyote's calves.

A sturdy calf follows the grazing herd in a bunch-grass-covered valley in the foothills beneath snowy mountains.

BSFW

Okefenokee

Georgia

Those who want to study an unimpaired swampland environment should come to Okefenokee. It covers 412,000 acres in extreme southeastern Georgia. One of the largest, oldest and most primitive protected swamps in the United States, it was formed ages ago when the Atlantic Ocean covered most of Florida and southeast Georgia. A sandbar existed offshore which, when the ocean receded to its present shoreline, became a ridge, now called Trail Ridge. A natural depression behind the ridge held some saltwater back, and rainfall over the centuries replaced it with fresh water. Smaller sandbars became islands in this lake, and the whole area supported aquatic vegetation. Decaying plants became peat, which built up above the water surfaces and allowed the growth of larger land plants. Vegetation today includes many huge cypress trees mixed with blackgum and redbay. The uplands around the swamp and the islands within it are covered principally with pine and occasional hardwood patches, called hammocks. From May to October the evergreen foliage of the gordonia, one of the swamp's most distinctive trees, is spotted with large white flowers.

About sixty thousand acres of Okefenokee is prairie, or open marsh. During spring these areas are carpeted with white and yellow water lilies, yellow-spiked "neverwet," white floating hearts, purple bladderwort and pickerelweed.

Sometimes a large piece of peat will break away from the swamp bottom and float on the surface. Smaller plants take root until trees and large brush grow on these floating islands. Locally called "houses" because of the many animals and birds that live and nest on them, the islets frequently become anchored by the trees extending their roots down through the water to the bed of peat below, which may be as thick as twenty feet. The stamping of feet on one of these peat islands will cause the nearby trees to shake, thus the Choctaw name *owaquaphenogau* ("Land of the Trembling Earth"). Okefenokee is simply an anglicized version of this Indian word.

A major characteristic of Okefenokee is the Spanish moss, which is actually an air-breathing plant. Found throughout the Southern states, it festoons all the swamp vegetation with long, flowing draperies of brown and gray.

A few small inlets at the north end of the swamp furnish the only source of water streaming into Okefenokee. The water, coffee-colored due to tannic acids from partially submerged trees, moves slowly through the swamp to the two outlets at the south -- the Suwannee River (immortalized in song by Stephen Foster) which drains into the Gulf of Mexico, and St. Mary's River which flows past Jacksonville into the Atlantic. Small natural canals between the houses open out in places into beautiful lakes, formed during drought periods when the peat dried out and burned up from fires caused by lightning or man.

The most readily recognizable animal in the swamp is the American alligator, rare in almost every other part of the country, but abundant here. This holdover from prehistoric times is known throughout the United States, even by small school children ("A is for Alligator"), as a vicious villain; while actually, unlike its cousin the crocodile, it will normally avoid man unless provoked. Until recent laws made their illegal trade unprofitable, poachers sold their hides to handbag and shoe manufacturers, and reduced their numbers until they were becoming an endangered species.

Growing to a length of up to fifteen feet, the alligator feeds primarily on fish, turtles and other aquatic life. During winter it is inactive, denning under banks or in water holes it has made, which benefits all the swamp wildlife during seasons of drought. In the April-May breeding season males call for the female with a loud bellow heard for miles in the swamp. The female builds a nest mound of grass and muck about two feet high and inserts forty to sixty eggs.

Three months later when they hatch, the young gators grunt and the female makes an opening in the nest to let them out. Being only six to ten inches long at birth, and growing a foot every year until maturity at six feet, they become easy prey for herons, fish, mammals and even other alligators. With these odds, only about one in seven baby gators grows to maturity. The

NPS. Williams

BSFW

Okefenokee Swamp is characterized by dark, murky waters and long strings of Spanish moss festooning the trees (above). It is one of the largest, most primitive swamps in the nation. Most of it is protected as a national wildlife refuge.

An immature little blue heron, seen here with food in its mouth (left), is one of the scores of birds finding a haven in Okefenokee. The immature heron is distinguished by its all-white plumage.

young alligators will eat almost anything that moves if it is smaller than they are, such as tadpoles, snails or insects.

Adult male alligators like to wrestle at times and it is an impressive sight to see two of them wildly splashing about in the water, each trying to pin the other.

Other animals in the swamp include opossums hanging from cypress branches, otters silently swimming in the shallow waters, and raccoons foraging for food. White-tailed deer, black bears and wild turkeys inhabit the islands. The Eastern spadefoot toad, with smooth instead of warty skin, rings out its call on spring nights, and the cottonmouth water moccasin, shy but with a deadly poisonous bite, slithers through the waters in search of frogs.

Practically all of the Atlantic Flyway's species of ducks are here in season, and many stay all year. The anhinga, or snakebird, a large black bird that feeds solely on fish, rests frequently on branches with outstretched wings drying in the sun. Its name comes from its ability to swim completely submerged except for its long snakelike neck. Sandhill cranes majestically fly up from the water, long necks extended, and egrets and herons stalk through the swamp waters in search of food. During the day a red-shouldered hawk may scream overhead, and at night barred owls hoot in the darkness, sending echoes among the cypresses.

Four-fifths of the swamp is under the protection of the Bureau of Sport Fisheries and Wildlife as the Okefenokee National Wildlife Refuge. The establishment of this refuge in 1937 marked the culmination of a long fight to save the swamp from "developers." Beginning in the sixteenth century, when Hernando de Soto may have explored the swamp, Okefenokee was threatened with drainage and timber cutting. After the

Seminole Indians, who had villages on many of the islands, were driven out of the swamp in 1838, attempts were made to drain the area to facilitate logging operations. The Suwannee Canal, heading into the swamp from Camp Cornelia on the eastern boundary, was dug but fortunately proved inefficient for logging. In 1909 a railroad made its way into the swamp on sunken pilings and much timber was cut and hauled out. The pilings rot today, and the swamp has reclaimed the land.

Trips into the interior of Okefenokee can be accomplished only by boat, and a guide is required in the closed areas. The Suwannee Canal is open for visitors with private boats, and a campground is maintained at Camp Cornelia. Planned for this area are nature trails and boardwalks, an observation tower and service facilities.

Stephen Foster State Park, in the interior of the refuge, can be reached via a paved road through the southwestern portion, and a number of facilities, including cottages and a picnic area, are available here.

Early-day naturalist William Bartram wrote in 1791

Weber

The American alligator (above) was once nearly an endangered species due to poaching but has made a remarkable comeback in Okefenokee and other swamps in the Southeast. It may look vicious but actually it is not, feeding primarily on fish, turtles and other aquatic life.

The wild turkey (left), although not as abundant as during pioneer times, still dwells in large numbers in areas such as Okefenokee. It nests in trees and is the same species as the barnyard type, although differing in coloration.

of a belief held by the Creek Indians that an island existed in the middle of the great swamp which was the most blissful place on earth. It was inhabited by a tribe whose women were "incomparably beautiful" while the men were fierce and cruel. After gliding silently along on dark waters beneath eerily draped cypresses and seeing alligators peer up from the water surface with inquisitive eyes, a visitor may wonder about this old legend. Certainly there are many unexpected and fascinating pleasures to be seen in this incomparable swampland environment.

Dunn

BSFW, Goldman

Maslowski

A common egret rests in a slash-pine tree (top, right). This yellow-billed bird is larger than any other white heron or egret in the South and has up to fifty long plumes, or aigrettes, on its back during breeding season. Unlike the snowy egret, it waits completely motionless for its prey.

Right: Raccoons are seen all over the country, especially at night, and are easily recognized by their banded tails and black face-masks. These two young raccoons are curiously peeking out of their tree-trunk home.

167

Upper Mississippi River

Wildlife and Fish Refuge

Illinois, Iowa, Minnesota, Wisconsin

BSFW, Blott

*The bald eagle, our national emblem
but on the endangered species list, nests
in the Upper Mississippi Refuge during the winter
where it feeds on crippled waterfowl and fish.*

Of the four basic flyways for migratory birds in the United States -- the Atlantic, Mississippi, Central and Pacific -- the Mississippi Flyway is the most important. Millions of geese, ducks, swans and other birds spend the winter somewhere along it or move through it to winter farther south. One of the most important areas along the flyway is the 194,000-acre Upper Mississippi River Wildlife and Fish Refuge, which has the most extensive boundaries of any inland refuge for waterfowl. Established in 1924, it extends from Wabasha, Minnesota, approximately 280 miles along both sides of the Mississippi to Rock Island, Illinois, where it is adjacent to the Mark Twain National Wildlife Refuge.

Because of its length, covering a number of life zones and differing climatic conditions, the refuge contains an extraordinary number of species of birds, mammals and fish. The extensive marshlands, riverbottom forests, damp slough-grass and sedge meadows and elevated sand prairies provide habitats for 270 kinds of birds, 50 mammals and 113 species of fish. Ranging as far south as Clinton, Iowa, steep wooded slopes of hardwoods with occasional red cedars and precipitous limestone cliffs, some as high as six hundred feet above the valley floor, present some of the most attractive scenery to be seen in mid-America.

In addition to lands owned by the Bureau of Sport Fisheries and Wildlife, lands purchased by the Corps of Engineers for navigational improvements are now included. Thirteen dams in the refuge raised water levels, forming a series of pools from ten to thirty miles long and creating a maze of channels, sloughs, marshlands and open lakes over the bottomlands. Fine stands of aquatic plants have developed to provide excellent habitat for waterfowl and other wildlife.

Although waterfowl are protected in twenty-five percent of the refuge area, the remainder is open to hunting subject to the regulations of each state. Mallards, wood ducks, widgeons and blue-winged teal are the ducks most often killed along the Mississippi River. Free access and launching ramps for boats are available throughout the refuge, and accommodations and guide services can be found in towns and at resorts on both sides of the river.

The wood duck was on the brink of extinction in the early part of this century because of the drainage of

The above island in the Mississippi lies just south of Wabasha, Minnesota, where the refuge flyway for millions of birds has its northern boundary. Right: Relatively few beavers inhabit the refuge, but they are highly impressive as the master engineers of elaborate and strong domed structures.

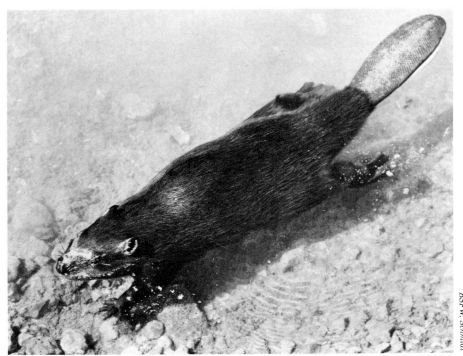

A killdeer stands over its nest of four brown spotted eggs. This species of plover prefers mud flats and open fields near water and is peculiar for its white throat and neck markings, its spectacular nuptial flight and its raucous screaming at intruders.

swamps and the overcutting of forestlands. Commercial hunters also killed thousands for the bird's beautiful feathers. His scientific name, *Aix sponsa*, means "waterfowl in wedding raiment," and without doubt it is America's loveliest water bird. A law was passed in 1918 protecting the wood duck and by the 1940's it had a solid foothold in its native habitat.

The male has a white-striped face, iridescent green, bronze and purple head and back, and a spotted chestnut breast. The flight of wood ducks is swift and direct, and they move with speed and ease through thick timber. The Upper Mississippi refuge is a major nesting area for the "woodie," which favors tree hollows and woodpecker holes as high as fifty feet. The majority of these birds winter on inland ponds in Southern states.

The bald eagle, our national emblem (and, to our shame, also an endangered species of wildlife) nests in numbers in the refuge during the winter when the wood duck is further south. Federal law has protected this magnificent bird since 1940 but results, unlike the case of the wood duck, have been far from satisfying. It is abundant today only in Alaska. In the refuge eagles concentrate below the dams or near the mouths of tributaries where in winter they find crippled waterfowl and fish to feed on.

Although not as fierce as its relative, the golden eagle, the bald eagle has long symbolized strength and, although its courage has been doubted by some, it is the master of its domain. For instance, it will harass the osprey, an excellent fisher occasionally seen in the Upper Mississippi refuge, and force the smaller bird to drop its catch which the bald eagle will occasionally snatch in mid-air.

Eagles remain with the same mate until one or the other dies, and they return annually to the same nest, adding to it each year until some measure ten feet across, twenty feet deep and weigh over one thousand pounds. Adults attain a length of thirty-four to thirty-six inches and a wingspan of seven feet. In the first three months of life eaglets grow from three inches to almost their full mature length of three feet. Their dark brown feathers, bill and eyes become the white head, yellow bill and iris of the adult after four years.

Other birds in the refuge include whistling swans, lesser scaups, ring-necked ducks, redheads, canvasbacks, buffleheads and ruddies, found on open pools above the dams, and mallards, widgeons, gadwalls and teals in the shallow backwaters along river banks. Many herons, egrets, bitterns and rails favor the bottomlands, and in spring and fall, hordes of warblers, vireos, thrushes and sparrows add to the great abundance of birds.

Furbearers, such as the muskrat, mink, beaver, river otter, raccoon, skunk, weasel and fox inhabit the area along the river, and an occasional nutria has been seen in recent years. Of course, the lowlands harbor amphibians and reptiles, including two species of salaman-

Above: A flock of swans spreads out in irregular line over the Mississippi. This bird, of the same order as ducks and geese, has an unmistakably graceful flight and has been subject for both Old and New World legends.

ders, nine frogs, one toad, nine turtles, one lizard and thirteen snakes. Among the snakes is a remnant population of timber rattlers that frequent upper wooded slopes and bluffs. The smaller swamp rattlesnake is found in parts of the river-bottom areas. Fishing for walleye, sauger, bass, perch, sunfish, crappies and catfish is popular below the dams, in sloughs and in channels between the islands.

This area along the mighty river is rich in history, containing the sites of Indian battlegrounds and villages, former trading posts and the routes of early explorers, in addition to some of the earliest towns in the Midwest and many decades of river traffic. Thus it is all the more remarkable that such a relatively large area, so vital to the migratory birds of North America, has been preserved. It provides a place where we can attain some idea of what the Mississippi must have looked like to the first white men with its untrammeled beauty and wealth of wildlife.

Apostle Islands

National Lakeshore

Wisconsin

Lake Superior, the largest of the Great Lakes and the one least polluted by man, has many miles of wilderness shoreline, but nowhere else on Superior is there the scenic variety and wealth of historic association that there is in the Apostle Islands region near the western tip of the lake. Throughout the twenty-three islands and nearby Bayfield Peninsula are heavily forested islands, high lakeside cliffs and wave-sculpted rocky arches, long sandy beaches, marshes, caverns and bays. And yet, despite its primitive, pristine appearance, the Apostle Islands region is rich in history.

The Chippewa Indians entered the region about five hundred years ago, and because of harassment from other tribes, they took refuge on the largest of the Apostle Islands, which they named "The Island of the Golden-Breasted Woodpecker." Today it is called Madeline Island. Here they constructed a great village and remained in comparative peace and safety for 120 years.

Between 1610 and 1622 the French explorers Etienne Brule and Grenoble traversed this area. They called the lake *le lac superieur*, meaning "Upper Lake," and gradually this was corrupted to become "Superior." Medard Chouart, Sieur des Groseilliers, led a fur trading expedition to Lake Superior in 1659. Pierre Radisson wrote of Chequamegon Bay: "...there is a chanell where we take stores of fishes, sturgeons of vast bigness, and Pycks seven feet long."

Des Groseilliers was followed by a stream of travelers, traders, explorers and missionaries. It is believed that it was some French missionaries who named the islands, for an old French map labels them the Twelve Apostles. Perhaps because there are almost twice that number of islands the "Twelve" was eventually dropped.

As the fur trade flourished, the French built a fort on Madeline Island in 1693 called La Pointe. When the Indian allies of the British -- the Sauk, Fox and Kickapoo -- blocked the southern routes, all furs on their way to the East Coast came through Lake Superior, and La Pointe became a bustling trading center. It was from here that the great flotillas of forty-foot canoes manned by the legendary *voyageurs* journeyed to Montreal with furs and returned with trade goods and supplies. After the British came to dominate the area, much of the

Maslowski

The red squirrel (left) is a delightful inhabitant of the Apostle Islands and may be distinguished by his handsome red coat, black side markings and endless chatter.

Pine and birch trees are scattered above the cliff (opposite) which has been eroded by the waves of Lake Superior into arches, caves, pillars and other jagged forms.

172

Eagle Bay on Wisconsin's Bayfield Peninsula is entirely undeveloped and contains a long stretch of sandy beach strewn with boulders, driftwood and gnarled roots of trees that manage a tenuous hold on the rocky soil.

trading shifted further north. Only the aggressive North West Company retained its center of operations at La Pointe. Madeline Island was named for the Indian wife of this company's manager in the 1790's.

With the increasing popularity of the silk hat, La Pointe's decline quickened and trapping ceased by about 1850. Later in the century, logging, commercial fishing -- especially for the prized lake trout -- and quarrying for reddish-brown sandstone became the primary economic activities. Because of uncontrolled timber cutting and forest fires the logging operations were short lived, and in the 1950's the sea lamprey destroyed the lake trout, although, aided by scientific management, they seem to be making a comeback now.

Today Madeline Island is the only island with a permanent settlement, and it has several historic buildings open to the public. The other islands are covered with a luxuriant second-growth forest of mixed hardwoods and conifers, including some beautiful stands of white birch. Wildlife includes black bear, white-tailed deer, raccoon, fox, mink, beaver; bald eagle, osprey, great blue heron, mallard, wood duck, loon, blue-wing teal, gulls and terns. About the only signs of man are a Coast Guard lighthouse on Devil's Island, some tumble-down fishermen's cabins, overgrown quarries and a few summer cottages.

As authorized in 1970, the Apostle Islands National Lakeshore includes twenty of the twenty-three islands, not including the largest, Madeline, and nearly eleven miles along Bayfield Peninsula. Except for Long Island which, until 150 years ago, was part of Chequamegon Point, the islands are the tops of partially submerged sandstone hills of the Bayfield Peninsula's northeasterly extension. They rise above the lake to heights varying from fifty to 480 feet, forming an archipelago about thirty miles long and eighty miles wide, with slightly less than one-fifth of this area in land.

Fortunately, there are few roads either on the mainland or the islands and the water is the lakeshore's main thoroughfare. The only public access today is at Little Sand Bay, at the eastern end of the mainland portion, where there is a campground and fishing dock. The state also operates some facilities on Stockton Island, although it is not part of the lakeshore. An excursion boat makes daily trips through the islands from Bayfield.

The shores on the northeast side of several of the islands, facing the lake and heavy weather, have many cliffs which average about thirty feet in height but occasionally reach sixty feet. On the south and southwest sides beaches are generally sandy, with a few exceptions. In rocky projections from the cliffs, especially on Devil's Island, the northernmost island, erosion by waves has formed arches, caves and pillars of stone along the shore. This island -- called "Evil Spirit Island" by the Indians because they thought the strange

The midland painted turtle, or pond turtle, is constantly alerted to danger by sound vibrations and his keen eyesight.

sounds made by the action of the water in the caves sounded like evil spirits talking -- catches the full force of the ferocious storms that hit Lake Superior.

Stockton Island, containing 10,157 acres, is the largest of the islands within the lakeshore and is one of the most beautiful, with its own lake, an abundance of blueberries and a long beach known as the Singing Sands -- named for the sounds made by the sand as one walks along it. The highest and one of the wildest islands, Oak Island, has deep ravines, clay cliffs over a

hundred feet high, occasional bears and rumors of treasure supposedly left there by pirates who called themselves the Twelve Apostles. Raspberry Bay, about midway along the Bayfield Peninsula unit of the lakeshore, has a superb beach, extensive marsh, pine groves, and sloughs and streams along the Raspberry River, a fine sampling of the many elements that make up this place of diverse beauty and history at the edge of Lake Superior -- one of the largest and least polluted of the world's inland freshwater lakes.

Poet Walt Whitman may have had this scene in mind when he wrote: "The strata of color'd clouds, the long bar of maroon-tint away solitary by itself . . . the horizon's edge, the flying sea-crow, the fragrance of salt marsh and shore mud. . . . ."

Assateague Island

and

Chincoteague National Wildlife Refuge

Maryland, Virginia

A vast expanse of sand and sea makes up Assateague Island National Seashore. Thirty-seven miles long and generally a mile to a mile and a half wide, this barrier island has many moods -- from a quiet summer evening with the soothing wash of waves and the crying of terns the only sounds, to a winter storm raging over the sand, the surf thundering onto the shore.

The island was born of the sea and will die of the sea, as it is rapidly pushed toward the Delmarva Peninsula where three states (Delaware, Maryland and Virginia) share the Atlantic coastline.

The change in topography is phenomenal. Before 1933 Assateague was actually a peninsula, but a storm that year cut an inlet separating it from the barrier island to the north, which has nearly completed its cycle of being pushed into the mainland. At the south end of the island is a small cove called Tom's Cove which did not exist in 1850. The Assateague Beach Coast Guard Station, now abandoned, was built on the very tip of the island in 1922, and since then two more miles of beach have been formed below it, curving around into a "hook." A pier recently exposed on the ocean shore near the north end was actually built on the bay side about thirty years ago.

The sand dunes, built up of grains carried and deposited by ocean currents and surf and then blown above the tide marks by winds, protect the inland portions of the island. The dunes are fragile and unstable, anchored only by grasses that are tolerant of salt spray but vulnerable to feet.

Beyond the dunes, loblolly pines and thickets of wax myrtle, bayberry, sumac, rose and greenbrier have a hold in the packed sand; and deer, foxes, raccoons, and forest birds dwell here. Marshes and many small is-

lands make up the bay shoreline, and in Chincoteague Bay itself, named for a vanished tribe of Indians who lived in this region, are found oysters, clams and crabs which are the source of a substantial fishing industry.

But it is the Assateague beach that draws the most attention. Thirty-seven miles long, it has a gently sloping bottom, fine surf and lack of strong undertow, making it attractive to bathers.

About two-thirds of the national seashore is in Maryland; the Virginia third (the southern third), is comprised of the Chincoteague National Wildlife Refuge. There is a marked difference between the upper and lower portions of Assateague Island -- the lower is greater in vegetation and its marshes are larger, providing excellent cover for more than 225 species of birds. Each season has its own species. In March wintering flocks of ducks, geese, and swans leave the refuge to go north. Other flocks, coming from the south, linger shortly and then continue on. By late April all the waterfowl are gone except for black ducks, blue-winged teals, mallards and gadwalls that nest here.

During April and May enormous numbers of shorebirds, such as sandpipers, plovers, oystercatchers, willets and yellowlegs, gather on mudflats and freshwater ponds. In summer, egrets, herons, ibises, avocets, terns, gulls and black skimmers reside on the ponds and small islands. Shorebirds return in July and August, and autumn is marked by the arrival of hawks and flickers.

On an early, chilly October morning, pintails, widgeons, shovellers, Canada and snow geese and green-winged teals can be seen by the noisy thousands. Scoters in offshore waters parallel the beach for miles, and buffleheads, goldeneyes, mergansers, brants, loons and grebes congregate in Tom's Cove. Many of these

Looking more like a painting than a photograph, this sunset on Assateague's beach is stormy as purple and blue clouds fly over the land on which a wild white pony and others graze among grasses and bayberry in the vicinity of an abandoned farmhouse.

birds terminate their flights at Chincoteague and stay for the winter. Dikes have been constructed around the freshwater pools and marshes at Chincoteague to protect their habitat from storms. These areas provide growths of smartweeds, spikerushes, bulrushes, sago pondweeds and widgeon grass.

One of the most interesting aspects of Assateague Island is its herd of wild ponies. Legend says they are the descendants of ponies that swam ashore from a shipwrecked Spanish galleon, but no one really knows their origin. Most of them are in the refuge, but separate groups are maintained on lands administered by the National Park Service. Their diet consists of marsh grasses and bayberry leaves, and each July a roundup is held by the Chincoteague Volunteer Fire Department, which owns the ponies roaming the refuge portion of the island, to sell some of them and keep the population in balance. Seeing these ponies trotting along the wet sands of the beach is a memorable sight for the visitor.

Sika deer, native to Japan, were introduced onto Assateague in 1923 by some Boy Scouts. Smaller than white-tailed deer, they have flourished under the adverse conditions of the island and can often be seen in marshy meadows.

Assateague Island National Seashore almost failed to become a reality. Although the National Park Service had recommended the island for seashore status in the 1930's, this seemed to be foreclosed when a private developer bought a large section of the island and chopped it into over eight thousand beach homesites and sold them to gullible buyers. But in March 1962, a powerful northeaster storm struck Assateague, destroying most of the man-made structures. This gave conservationists a second chance, and in 1965 President Lyndon B. Johnson signed a bill to make this the largest public seashore on the mid-Atlantic Coast.

Some facilities are located at the south end in Chincoteague refuge, and the "hook" will be developed as a

NPS

In winter the winds pile dry snow into drifts, or "snow dunes," along the beaches. However, the sea knows no season and continues to pound the beach with its powerful breakers, even in the coldest weather. The seashore is deserted at this time, a place of complete solitude.

recreational area. Assateague State Park on the north, within the seashore boundaries but administered by the State of Maryland, contains a campground, picnic areas, a protected beach and other facilities. The extreme northern portion of the island will be left in its natural state.

In her book, *Gift from the Sea*, Anne Morrow Lindbergh might refer to Assateague when she writes:

Rollers on the beach, wind in the pines, the slow flapping of herons across sand dunes, drown out the hectic rhythms of city and suburb, time tables and schedules. One falls under their spell, relaxes, stretches out prone. One becomes, in fact, like the element on which one lies, flattened by the sea; bare, open, empty as the beach, erased by today's tides of all yesterday's scribblings.

Cape Cod and

Monomoy National Wildlife Refuge

Massachusetts

Cape Cod is a slender rampart jutting more than seventy miles from the Massachusetts coast into the wind and waves of the turbulent Atlantic Ocean. A large section of it became part of the National Park System as a result of the interest and leadership of President John F. Kennedy. The storm-lashed seas surge over the shoals and dash against marine scarps and, miles away, these same seas gently lap the slopes of barrier beaches. The Cape, one of the nation's most dramatic headlands, is the northernmost of our national seashores. Its high, shifting dunes, great ponds and historic places make a fascinating outdoor playground in summer or winter.

Cape Cod is shaped much like a man flexing his arm muscles. It was named by explorer Bartholomew Gosnold in 1601 for the "grate stoare" of codfish in the vicinity. The Cape, aided by the lengthening of a sandspit called Monomoy Island which extends south from the "elbow" of the Cape, is responsible for the relatively quieter waters of Cape Cod Bay and Nantucket Sound. Sandbars and shoals surrounding the Cape have been a burying ground for ships from the time of the Pilgrims, who first touched New World soil at what is now Provincetown on the extreme northern tip of the Cape.

The exhilarating aspects of winter storms on Cape Cod moved naturalist Henry David Thoreau to write that these periods were the best time to visit the area. Thoreau is credited with giving the name Great Beach to the seaside sands of the Cape. "A man can stand there and put all America behind him," he wrote. The elemental forces that shape life cycles are evident here in the biting sting of salt water spray borne in the teeth of a northeaster or in the offshore breeze of a quiet July afternoon.

Rooted strongly in sand dunes and silts, the cattails, marsh grass, bearberry, heath and pitch-pine woods stand against the rasping waters, collecting new sand from each windstorm. Glacial movement in the area resulted in an overlapping of northern and southern plant life growing on the Cape. Extensive geological evidence found in the accumulation of glacial drift makes the Cape a lodestone for geo-oceanographers.

Some of the most spectacular sand dune formations are found at Province Lands and Truro at the northern tip. The dunes were formed after glacial action thrust clay and boulders into the coastal plains area while the ocean was still shallow. Erosion of the scarps by wave action caused sandbars, then sandspits and later the dunes. As the dunes were formed, they buried whole forests, and when they moved on, remnants of these forests reappeared. Even today, these forces of nature are clearly visible at Province Lands and Truro.

The wild turkey, once native to this region and traditionally part of the Pilgrims' Thanksgiving, became extirpated in 1850. But the sea gulls on Nauset Light Beach find no shortage of "wild game." They hover fifteen or twenty feet above a rock, drop clams or mussels onto it, and then swoop down to pick the meat from the broken shells. Gone with the wild turkey are the forests the Pilgrims described. However, most of the tree species, possibly in smaller sizes, still are native to the Cape. A remnant of this past, not far from National Park Service headquarters at Wellfleet, is an Atlantic white-cedar swamp considered unusual because it is located so near saltwater. This swamp can be reached by one of the many trails recently established by the park service.

Extensive forests cause an entire change of scene between the highlands and beaches on the west side of the Cape. Here are many deep, freshwater ponds, and

Cape Cod, a long piece of land jutting into the Atlantic from Massachusetts, is a scenic paradise. Sand dunes, beach grasses and the turbulent ocean breakers combine to make this seashore a spectacular meeting place of land and water. The Cape is important historically, for here in 1620 the Pilgrims first landed in the New World.

nearby, the "Cliffs" area arises to a height of 175 feet above Great Beach. In lower altitudes to the south are some of only natural cranberry bogs in the Western Hemisphere.

Ornithologists describe Monomoy Island as an unparalleled area in which to observe shorebirds. Since its establishment as a wildlife refuge in 1944, more than three hundred bird species have been identified here. During seasonal migrations millions of shore, sea and marsh birds stop over at the island regularly. The island is abundant in rich sea life for the birds who visit this 3,300-acre coastal barrier beach.

Such unusual birds as the Hudsonian godwit, the American oystercatcher and the golden plover have been spotted on Monomoy along with thousands of commonly seen Canada geese and black ducks. Monomoy is roadless and entirely undeveloped, and this guarantees any visitor a glimpse of wild nature at its best.

The one who seeks a rare experience of life, whether it be solitude which is indeed becoming rare, or the thrill of seeing a slice of unsullied shoreland, will find both at Cape Cod seashore or Monomoy refuge.

Cape Cod National Seashore, established in 1961, consists of almost 27,000 acres along the outermost one-third of the Cape, primarily facing east and north directly onto the Atlantic. Three large areas have been developed thus far: Province Lands Area on the Cape's tip has a visitor center and provides a splendid panoramic view of the sea from Ocean View Lookout; in the Pilgrim Heights Area a few miles to the east is the spring where the Pilgrims found their first fresh drinking water; and Marconi Station Area contains Thoreau's Great Beach and the site where the first wireless station in the United States was set up in 1903. Smaller areas include Coast Guard Beach Area where, on Nauset Light Beach, there is some of the finest protected saltwater swimming anywhere. A mile and a half inland from this beach is another visitor center and an amphitheater, near the main Cape highway, and just across Salt Pond Bay is Hemenway Landing.

The two visitor centers provide information about exhibits, special programs, guided walks and self-guided nature trails. Six privately operated campgrounds are on the Cape near the national seashore. A number of bicycle trails have also been constructed and one of them, in the Province Lands Area, is nine miles long.

Because Monomoy Refuge is maintained by the Bureau of Sport Fisheries and Wildlife to preserve its wild qualities, there are no facilities. Nearby towns provide accommodations as well as boat rentals.

Fog envelops the Cape, and the ghostly shapes of small boats (top) are reflected in the still waters of Round Cove, an inlet of Pleasant Bay at the southern part of the seashore. Boating is popular on Cape Cod.

Nauset Lighthouse (above) rises above the sand dunes just north of Eastham in the center of the Cape. It is one of four lighthouses along the shores of Cape Cod sending signals out to sea.

Dead pitch-pine trees are being covered with sand (far right) as an active dune moves across the land in the Province Lands Area. Advancing dunes may cover entire forests, only to leave dead trunks when they pass on.

A storm shows its violent nature (right) as wind blows the ocean waters into huge breakers with white spray tails which crash onto the sands of Coast Guard Beach near the Salt Pond Visitor Center.

Cape Hatteras and
Pea Island National Wildlife Refuge
North Carolina

A northeaster storm on Cape Hatteras has to be experienced to be believed. Raging wind blows sand with such force that it can be heard hitting a building, and the brushy plants bend away from the gusts, as if bowing to this master of violent nature. The seas crash their breakers into the shore, spray is hurled into the wind, and skies are ominously dark, the air filled with a cold, misty rain. A walk along the beach at this time is a walk in total loneliness, an experience unique to a place facing the sea such as this.

Hours later, after the storm has passed, the beach takes on a different character. A warm breeze ruffles the drying sea oats and the setting sun plays with the clouds. A ghost crab scurries into the wet sand at your approach; scavenging shorebirds look for culinary delights at the edge of each dying breaker. Small sand dunes now exist where earlier there had been none, and others have disappeared.

The storms of the Cape are so feared that seamen call North Carolina's Outer Banks the Graveyard of the Atlantic. Since 1585, when the British ship *Tiger* was sunk in Ocracoke Inlet to the south of the Cape, and possibly before that, mariners have dreaded passing near Diamond Shoals at the tip of the Cape Hatteras. The clash of warm Gulf Stream and cold Arctic waters, over twelve offshore miles of underwater shifting sandbars, plus enemy submarines in wartime, have combined to send more than seven hundred ships to the bottom from Cape Henry at the entrance of Chesapeake Bay to Cape Fear in southern North Carolina.

Among these relics are the skeletal remains of a World War II LST and U-85, a German submarine sunk in 1942 while preying on Allied shipping. And perhaps someday shifting sands will expose the rusty hulk of the *Monitor,* the first Federal ironclad of the Civil War, which went down with sixteen men somewhere off the Cape in 1862.

The raging storms wreck not only ships but the sands themselves. An especially violent storm on March 7, 1962 (called the Ash Wednesday storm), cut an opening into Hatteras Island at the town of Buxton, creating an inlet which was finally closed a year later with the combined efforts of the Army Corps of Engineers, Federal funds, hundreds of volunteers, two dredges, tens of thousands of sandbags and dozens of junked automobiles. Nature occasionally does this filling-in job herself: Nine miles south of Oregon Inlet at the northern part of the Cape, the road passes over land that just over a decade ago was "New Inlet." The remains of the ill-conceived bridge that once spanned this inlet are visible several hundred yards off the highway.

The history of the Outer Banks, which extend some thirty miles from the mainland at their farthest point at the tip of Cape Hatteras, is nearly a history of the United States. In 1585, and two years later, Sir Walter Raleigh started unsuccessful settlements on Roanoke Island at the northern point of Pamlico Sound which separates the Cape from the mainland. The second English attempt at colonization in the New World was marked by the birth of the first child of English parentage born in America, Virginia Dare, but the settlement mysteriously disappeared. Raleigh had left for England and when he returned in 1590 he found only the word "Croatoan" carved on a stockade post. Fort Raleigh National Historical Site marks the probable spot of the "Lost Colony."

During the eighteenth century, colonials from Virginia and Maryland moved onto the Cape, becoming fishermen, navigators and sailors. They were called "bankers" and they founded the various towns along the Cape.

In 1874 these people started the U. S. Life-Saving Service, and their acts of heroism were commonplace, as in 1899 when a banker on patrol singlehandedly saved ten of the fourteen people on a small cruise ship grounded during a hurricane. The maxim of these volunteer sailors was "The rules say you gotta go, not that you gotta come back," and family cemeteries and scattered lonely graves bear lasting testimony to this conviction.

Bodie Island lighthouse on the northern end of the Hatteras seashore, just above Pea Island refuge, stands sentinel against the treacherous sea of North Carolina's Outer Banks -- Graveyard of the Atlantic.

185

The Life-Saving Service was merged with the Revenue Cutter Service in 1915 to form the U. S. Coast Guard, and the new organization continued the valiant traditions of the old. In 1918 a dramatic sea rescue took place as the men of the Chicamacomico Coast Guard Station saved most of the men of the burning tanker *Mirlo.* During World War II the men had the important job of coastal defense and saving the lives of victims of German submarines.

On December 17, 1903, on a sandy plain called Kitty Hawk near the town of Kill Devil Hill, about ten miles north of the national seashore, Wilbur and Orville Wright flew the world's first successful power-driven airplane.

At the southern tip of the seashore on Ocracoke Island is a spot called Teach's Hole, believed to have been the lair of Edward Teach, better known as the pirate, Blackbeard, feared by merchantmen all along the Atlantic seaboard. By November 1718, after he had terrorized the coasts for six years, Carolinians gave

Lieutenant Robert Maynard of the Royal Navy command of some men and two sloops with orders to find the pirate. A few days later Maynard found Blackbeard's ship *Adventure* anchored near the Ocracoke hideout. One of the sloops ran aground and could not join the battle, so Maynard had most of his men in the other ship stay below deck until the pirates, believing they had killed nearly everyone, swarmed aboard and were subsequently overcome. During the engagement Blackbeard received twenty-five serious wounds, yet he fought powerfully until he suddenly collapsed on the deck. His death marked the end of large-scale piracy in the Atlantic.

Cape Hatteras National Seashore was established in 1953. It covers forty-five square miles stretched along seventy miles of shores of three barrier islands, each separated by an inlet. The eight villages are excluded from the seashore. Visitor centers are located at the Hatteras and Bodie Island lighthouses and at Ocracoke village. Seven campgrounds are within the seashore's

boundaries. The entire beach length is open for swimming. No vehicles of any kind are allowed on the dunes.

At the tip of Cape Hatteras is the tallest lighthouse in the United States, 192 feet above low-tide level. Built in 1870, it is one of three on the Cape and easily recognized by its black and white "barberpole" striping.

Ocracoke, Hatteras and Bodie islands are barrier islands believed to have been formed by ocean currents and wave action on what were originally shoals to the east of the present shoreline. The islands are not more than three miles in width and are covered with sand dunes which have not been stabilized and are still moving. The largest dunes on the Atlantic seaboard are near the town of Nags Head, just north of the seashore. Salt marshes line the western shores of the islands.

Wildflowers grow profusely in this humid climate, even in December when the flats behind the barrier dunes are bright with flowering gaillardia. Growing individually on sand ridges are live oaks and thickets of evergreen yaupon, a species of holly. Sea oats and

The salt marshes of Bodie Island and those in Pea Island's wildlife refuge are one of the winter homes for the greater snow geese, which are protected from hunting and encouraged to browse here among the brushes and weeds, planted to attract a great variety of waterfowl and shorebirds.

187

Dickey

The most common of the "sea gulls" are the herring gulls and the ring-billed gulls, both of which frequent the Hatteras seashore. Neither bird ventures far out to sea, but prefers to scavenge inland and nest on shores or in low trees.

beach grass thrive on the dunes. Near the Hatteras Lighthouse is Buxton Woods, with stands of loblolly pine, American holly and live oak growing on the ridges and slopes. Marshy valleys lie between the ridges and support dense banks of ferns, shrubs and clinging vines.

The head of the Cape, about three miles south of the Hatteras Lighthouse, provides a close-up view of the dangerous Diamond Shoals. The sudden shallow water a couple of hundred feet out from the beach combined with the mixing of the two large ocean currents cause the waves to tumble over each other at angles, making a thunderous roar and much white foam.

Surf fishermen consider the Cape a great spot to catch channel bass, ocean perch, sea mullet (whiting), sea trout, Spanish and king mackerel, flounder and assorted sharks. During the summer, however, fishing is best offshore where marlin, dolphin, bluefish, false albacore and tuna may be caught. Gray trout and flounder swim in Pamlico Sound, and there is some freshwater fishing in ponds which hold largemouth bass and bluegill.

Although animal life is limited to a few deer and some marsh rabbits, birdlife is abundant. Over three hundred species can be found here. Pea Island National Wildlife Refuge -- named after the upper island which existed when New Inlet split Hatteras Island -- is renowned for being the wintering grounds of great numbers of Canada and snow geese. This 6,700 — acre reserve, established in 1938, has the only large concentration of gadwall nesting on the Atlantic seaboard. Other birds found here are royal terns, black skimmers, laughing gulls, black ducks, loons, red-breasted mergansers, glossy ibises, snowy and common egrets, whistling swans, pheasants, grebes, hawks, warblers and many kinds of herons.

From the top of Hatteras Lighthouse, the Cape curves into the horizon on the north and south; to the west lie the fairly calm waters of Pamlico Sound. But your gaze keeps returning to the east -- the wide expanse of the Atlantic and, closer to shore, the herringbone designs of white-capped breakers at Diamond Shoals, spreading scalloped sheets of surf obliquely on the beaches on either side. A dramatic "water confrontation" occurs at Hatteras, and those who know and love this area return again and again because these great sand banks tell important chapters of our history and offer a singular seashore experience.

NPS

The sea along the Outer Banks
has yet to give up all of its
secrets, although centuries of ship-
wrecks have left picturesque re-
minders (above) of scores of ill-
fated schooners and larger ships.

Raging storms can be almost
forgotten when they have passed,
and children play on the beach
between the tumbling waves and
the lines of sturdy beach grass.

Ochsner

Cape Lookout

North Carolina

In the first grays of morning the lighthouse throws its beam many miles into the Atlantic, repeating over and over its set pattern. The eastern sky, rosy pink, reflects onto the foam of the breakers as they hit the beach and spread over the sands. Sandpipers prance on this wet sand, and gradually the light increases until the sun, already above the horizon, finally lifts itself free of the distant clouds.

Dawn on Cape Lookout may be much the same as dawn on other Atlantic barrier beaches with one exception -- here man is no longer an intruder. Unlike Cape Hatteras National Seashore to the north, Cape Lookout National Seashore has no roads, no campgrounds and no thriving towns. Only the lighthouse, the extremely small town of Portsmouth on the north end (with a few summer residents only), and a number of shacks scattered along the shores give evidence of civilization.

It was not always this way. The same colonials from Virginia and Maryland who traveled down Cape Hatteras and established homes and towns came to the lower banks, although there were not as many.

Spanish privateers were a problem for citizens in the 1740's, but after they were gone, the North Carolina Assembly established a "maritime town" named Portsmouth on the island of the same name at Ocracoke Inlet. The town grew to over five hundred residents because Ocracoke Inlet was the only navigable inlet in the central and lower banks, and heavy draught ships had to stop here to transfer their cargos to boats able to navigate Core and Pamlico sounds. In 1846, however, Hatteras and Oregon inlets opened up farther north, and the town's prosperity died until today there are far more homes than people.

The first Cape Lookout Lighthouse was constructed in 1812 and the present one completed in 1859. The lighthouse, 150 feet in height, has a distinctive black and white diamond pattern.

Shackleford Banks, originally heavily forested, was cut over in the nineteenth century for timber to construct ships at Beaufort on the mainland. A town called Diamond City, named after the lighthouse's pattern, prospered until 1899 when a tremendous hurricane washed away the five hundred homes. Three years later everyone had left the area: A few scattered graves are the only remaining traces of what may have been the town.

The U. S. Life-Saving Service, and subsequently the U. S. Coast Guard, maintained patrols along the shores of Core Banks and Portsmouth Island, saving the lives of many victims of the sea whose ships had floundered on the sandbars offshore. With automation and ship safety improvements the patrols no longer proved necessary, and many of the Cape's residents left.

Geographically, Cape Lookout differs from Cape Hatteras in that there are many small islands, mostly tidal marshes, off the west side of the Cape in Core Sound. These marshes support a variety of birdlife, such as sea gulls, terns, boat-tailed grackles, sandpipers and black skimmers. Bottle-nosed dolphins can often be seen playing in the breakwater close offshore, and channel bass, mackerel, bluefish and sea trout are abundant. Shrimp, crabs, oysters and clams are present in large quantities and marsh rabbits and other small mammals inhabit the Cape's islands.

Forests of cedar, holly, live oak, wax myrtle and mulberry are growing on Shackleford Banks, which does not receive the brunt of the Atlantic storms and can support larger vegetation. However, moving sand dunes are slowly engulfing these forests and may in time overrun them.

Most of the lands of Cape Lookout National Seashore were bought and preserved by the State of North Carolina until Congress enacted a law in 1966 making the entire area a national seashore. Under current development plans, Shackleford and Core banks and Portsmouth Island will remain completely roadless, reached only by ferries or private boats. The fifty-eight mile seashore contains about 15,800 acres, although actual acreage fluctuates with each large storm.

On a recent inspection visit to Cape Lookout, National Park Service Director George B. Hartzog reportedly kicked off his shoes and scampered over the dunes, calling the seashore "simply terrific." Terrific for everyone, for the lower banks of North Carolina are now protected against all enemies but nature herself. And if nature decides to change the land a little, that is as it should be. After all, it was hers to begin with!

A setting, hazy sun silhouettes a number of sanderlings as they play touch and go with the foamy white breakers.

Fire Island

New York

Ferns dominate the floor of Sunken Forest at the west end of the seashore. Serviceberry, blackgum and virgin, gnarled American holly provide cover and supply dead leaves for a soft floor mattress. Fire Island seashore is only a short distance from crowded Manhattan.

One-by-one over thousands of years, most of the barrier beaches off the south coast of Long Island have been joined with the mainland. The largest remaining beach, Fire Island, is a narrow divider island between land and the stormy Atlantic. Here are thirty-two miles of white, sandy beaches, wind-twisted pines, grassy wetlands, salt marshes, forests and sand dunes located almost within eyesight of the man-made towers of Manhattan.

Most of this barrier island, from one-half mile to less than two hundred yards wide, has become a national seashore to preserve the last isolated, largely unspoiled shoreline in this densely populated region from the desecrations of "development." It is an island with a delicately balanced ecology, and the few hundred people who live on it know this and are helping preserve its appeal.

Fire Island, like Long Island, is a flat moraine formed by ancient glaciers. The sea and the wind have attacked Fire Island without mercy, constantly but slowly pushing it toward the mainland.

The sand, composed of fine quartz mixed with red garnet and black magnetite, stretches over the horizon on Great South Beach and extends hundreds of feet towards the island's interior. Holding the sand dunes in place are plant communities essential to the island's life -- beach grass, wild rose and beach plum. Bayberry, cedar, ground and pitch pine, sassafras, blueberry and wild cherry also grow in the seashore. Mounds of goldenrod mix with the familiar three-leafed poison ivy. In August rose mallow blooms in the marshes, and pure stands of reed reach heights over six feet.

Toward the west end of the seashore is the unusual Sunken Forest, a virgin woods located a little below sea level. Here may be found unusually large serviceberry, birch, blackgum and gnarled American holly trees, some of which are several hundred years old, with ferns and azalea growing beneath them.

White-tailed deer roam the eastern portion of the island; red foxes hide in the sand dunes, and cottontails scurry through the brush. From October to March the inland waters of Great South Bay, which divides Fire Island from Long Island, come alive with ducks and

Many varied shells from the sea can be collected by beachcombers on Fire Island's 32 miles of white sandy beaches.

geese. Terns nest on the small islands in the bay and black-crowned night herons live in the pine forests.

On the Atlantic side of the seashore, surf fishermen catch mackerel, weakfish and striped bass, and bluefish, winter flounder and fluke can be found on the bay side. Clams and scallops lie in the waters of the bay.

How Fire Island received its name is a mystery. Some romantics argue that huge fires were built here many years ago either to warn ships away or lure them aground to be looted. Others believe whalers built fires to signal the mainland that the blubber was ready. Perhaps the best story, and probably the closest to the truth, tells of a myopic clerk in the tax office who mistakenly copied the original name of Five Islands.

Fire Island National Seashore was authorized by Congress in 1964 after a great storm two years earlier gave conservationists a last chance opportunity to save it from a proposed four-lane highway to be built to stabilize the dunes. A marina, beach and picnic area are located at both Sailor's Haven and Watch Hill. The latter, in the seashore's center, also has a campground. Other campgrounds and bicycle and hiking trails will be constructed at various spots in the seashore. Two roads lead onto the island, one to Robert Moses State Park at the west end, the other to Smith Point County Park on the east end.

About one-tenth of the nation's expanding population lives within a hundred miles of this national seashore. Fire Island is a magnificent beach that was saved in time from the encroachments of "progress."

Gulf Islands

Florida, Mississippi

Wide, gently sloping beaches of unusually fine, white "sugar" sand, clear blue waters reminiscent of Caribbean bays, unique flora and fauna, and several historically important forts are the characteristics of the nation's newest national seashore. Consisting of about 13,600 acres of barrier and offshore islands stretching 150 miles from Florida to Mississippi, Gulf Islands National Seashore is a prime example of what dedicated citizens can do for the preservation of our natural resources.

Citizen interest in these islands was developed in the 1960's when it was learned that sea erosion was undermining Fort Massachusetts on Mississippi's Ship Island, now included within the seashore. They appealed to their Congressmen and Senators for Federal help in preserving the fort, which was further damaged in September 1965 by Hurricane Betsy. National Park Service officials visited the area shortly afterwards and the idea of a national seashore containing islands from Florida to Mississippi was conceived. Erosion would not wait for legislation, however, and local residents formed an organization called Save the Fort, Inc., which gained widespread publicity and enough contributions to erect a protective wall around the old structure. After many discussions, compromises and arguments by Federal, state and local officials and politicians and the residents of Florida and Mississippi's Gulf Coast, a bill authorizing the proposed seashore passed Congress and was signed by President Richard M. Nixon in January 1971.

Saved from further commercial development are some of Mississippi's offshore islands, namely Horn, Petit Bois (meaning "little woods" and locally pronounced "petty boy") and Ship Islands, and in Florida, parts of Santa Rosa Island (formerly the Santa Rosa National Monument which was deactivated by the Secretary of the Interior in 1946), the eastern half of Perdido Key across the channel from Santa Rosa, and sections of Naval Live Oaks Reservation and the Pensacola Naval Air Station, both on the mainland. The two state areas are separated by Alabama's Gulf Coast.

Santa Rosa, a long, thin barrier island, is significant because of its sandy beaches and clear waters. On the western tip of the island lies Fort Pickens, an old brick fort built in 1834 to protect the important deepwater harbor at Pensacola. Before that, the site had been occupied by the Spanish, French and British. The fort's major role was during the Civil War, when it was one of only three forts in the South successfully held by Union forces, the others being Fort Taylor at Key West and Fort Jefferson on Dry Tortugas. In fact its builder, Captain William Chase, a U. S. Army engineer, planned its defenses and strongholds so carefully that, later as a Confederate general, he himself was unable to seize it. For some years after their capture in 1886, Fort Pickens held Geronimo, Nachez and other famous Apache Indian warriors. It was also an active coastal defense fortification during the Spanish-American War, and was even used during the two world wars.

On Perdido Key, across the narrow ship channel from Fort Pickens, are the foundations of Fort McRee, visible only at low tide. Built shortly after Fort Pickens, it was destroyed by tides and pounding surf. The center of the parade grounds, where the flagpole stood in 1852, is now covered by thirty feet of water in the channel.

Across Pensacola Bay on the mainland's Naval Air Station are two other important forts, San Carlos and Barrancas. At one time they were within the boundaries of the planned Pensacola National Monument which was never established. Fort San Carlos was built by the Spanish between 1781 and 1790 on the approximate site of an earlier wooden Spanish fort, completed in 1698. Connected to it by a brick tunnel is Fort Barrancas, built between 1839 and 1844 by the United States and held by the Confederates for a short time during the Civil War. Still a third fort, Redoubt, can be seen a short distance away.

The newest seashore preserves a unique and beautiful piece of shoreline on the Gulf of Mexico (opposite, top).

Beach morning glories (opposite) spread their creamy white-yellow flowers on Horn Island, Mississippi.

The other fort within the seashore is Fort Massachusetts; completed just as the Civil War broke out and seized by the Confederacy, the fort was soon recaptured by Federal troops and was used as an important part of the naval blockade for the duration of the conflict.

Ship Island itself has an intriguing history. The French first settled the island in 1699, and it remained an important stopping point for supplies from France, which were then distributed to all of French Louisiana. After the capital moved from Biloxi to New Orleans, the island's importance declined. In 1815 English General Packenham used the island to launch his ill-fated attack against the forces of General Andrew Jackson and the swashbuckling pirate Jean Lafitte at New Orleans, ending the War of 1812.

Flora in the seashore is extremely varied. For example, Horn Island contains over 204 species of plants. Slim slash-pine trees fight to survive the salt and sand driven by storm winds. Some of the sand dunes have been stabilized by species of magnolia, palmetto and live oak, while the unstabilized dunes are mostly covered with beach grass and sea oats. The 1,300-acre Naval Live Oaks Reservation is a beautiful stand of large live oaks and represents the nation's first attempt at conservation: President John Quincy Adams set aside the area in 1828 to save these rare oaks from being used for shipbuilding.

Marsh plants grow profusely in the ponds, lagoons and marshes of the Mississippi islands. Hurricanes have damaging effects on the seashore; for instance, all of Mississippi's offshore islands were changed considerably by Hurricane Camille in August 1969, and some of the plant life in the new areas has not been scrutinized.

Fur-bearing animals find little on which to survive, and rabbits and opossums are the only two mammals still fairly common on the islands. The monument provides many places for the Gulf's increasingly rare sea turtles to lay their eggs, and it is the only habitat for a species of beach mouse which has developed a very light coloration to blend into the white sand.

A great number of birds nest within the seashore, especially on Horn and Petit Bois islands, two parts of the Gulf Island National Wildlife Refuges. Here the interior ponds, lagoons and marshes serve as wintering grounds for blue and snow geese and several species of ducks. The beaches support laughing gulls and Sandwich and royal terns; redhead ducks are abundant on

the shallow Gulf waters. Other birds include common and snowy egrets; green, great blue and Louisiana herons; willets; snowy and Wilson's plovers; sanderlings; American oystercatchers; killdeer; and occasional ospreys and frigate birds.

The sections of Santa Rosa Island closest to the bridge linking it to the mainland are commercially developed and are not included within the seashore's boundaries, although they contain a number of attractions and facilities for visitors. Other facilities, such as cottages, picnic areas and a campground are located at Fort Pickens State Park at the west end of the island. A boat dock has been built on Ship Island, which, like Horn and Petit Bois, has good smooth beaches to accommodate smaller boats. No facilities are available on these Mississippi islands now, but some, including a visitor center, are planned.

The efforts of citizens of the Florida and Mississippi Gulf Coasts should be deeply appreciated by anyone walking on the "sugar" sands of Santa Rosa, photographing a tern robbing a sea turtle's nest on the beach, or simply imagining how an old fort must have looked in earlier days.

Beach grasses try to stabilize the sand on Horn Island (above, left), but severe storms and hurricanes cause much ecological damage to the offshore islands as well as leaving on the beaches battered relics of their power.

Fort Redoubt (above), on the grounds of the Pensacola Naval Air Station, is one of five old forts included within the seashore. Built by the Spanish and the Americans, the forts were important during the Civil War and after.

197

Top: Lush forest growths of black oak, hickory, chestnut, tamarack, and many vines cover much of the interior of the lakeshore.

A solitary dead leaf (above) lies among the frost-edged leaves of smaller vegetation in the dunes area. The lakeshore contains numerous plant species including cacti.

A moving dune (left) is slowly covering large trees in the east end of the lakeshore. The sand will soon kill the trees and then move further inland, perhaps to cover whole forests which grow on older dunes.

Indiana Dunes

National Lakeshore

Indiana

Through the pines and hardwoods at the tops of the dunes you can see the setting sun silhouetting the impressive skyline of Chicago, thirty-five miles away across Lake Michigan. However, in the same gaze, you can also see the "dark, satanic" steel mills in East Chicago and Gary with smoke billowing from their tall stacks. This is Indiana Dunes -- a natural area squeezed between urbanization and steel mills. In 1919, just after World War I, Stephen T. Mather, the first director of the National Park Service, proposed that forty miles of the Indiana Dunes be preserved as a national park. Mather was ignored and by 1960 those dunes were largely leveled by industry. But a new wave of conservationists took up the cause and the last remnant of these shorelines was saved, less than one third of the original dunes.

These dunes, which reach astonishing heights of up to two hundred feet, were once the sandy shores of a monstrous lake formed by the retreating glaciers. As the lake receded, winds whipped the exposed sand into dunes which "moved" over the area. Through the centuries vegetation gradually covered and immobilized them. New dunes are constantly being formed, however, and sometimes they have gradually covered forests which had established themselves on the older dunes. Occasionally stiff winds blow a niche in a sand ridge, which gradually enlarges to form a "blowout." Five large "blowouts" can be seen in Indiana Dunes State Park, within the lakeshore's boundaries, and the largest one has exposed remnants of a dead forest, killed by the once-advancing sands.

Of equal interest are the bogs and marshes in the area. Large chunks of ice broke off the glaciers as they retreated, and the melting chunks formed kettleholes which were gradually filled with humus, resulting in the marshes. The lakeshore's bogs are significant because of their lush and varied vegetation: over one thousand species of flowering plants and ferns, making Indiana Dunes one of the most interesting botanical areas in the country.

Plants forced to move south because of the glaciers have somehow managed to survive here, mixing with plants from the south which migrated north during the post-glacier warming period. Thus the prickly-pear cactus of the desert mingles with Arctic barberry.

Jack and white pine grow on the dunes and tamarack and birch in the bogs, separated from their normal range to the north by about a hundred miles, while the tulip tree, black gum and sassafras are at their northwestern limits. Dune grass, dwarf willow, sand cherry and cottonwood begin to stabilize the fore dunes near the shoreline. Black oak, pine, hickory, chestnut and some sugar maple and beech grow on the older dunes and in the sand valleys. Wildflowers include the violet, hepatica, buttercup, jack-in-the-pulpit, dune lily and wild rose. Some typical bog and marsh plants are the cattail, blueberry, mayapple, dogwood, raspberry, blackberry and grapevine. White and showy lady's-slippers, rare for the region, are found in Cowles Bog, named for Dr. Henry Cowles who developed the concepts of the science of ecology and who used the dune plant life for much of his studies.

Wildlife was once abundant here, but the overbearing presence of all-conquering man has exterminated the bear, wolf, lynx, bison, elk and the passenger pigeon. The raccoon, opossum, rabbit, fox, mink, squirrel and woodchuck have survived, and deer and beaver have been reintroduced. The six-lined lizard probably migrated here with the cactus and thrives now on the dunes. Many migratory birds stop in the marshes during season, and shorebirds can be seen scavenging on the beach.

Indiana Dunes National Lakeshore contains about 8,200 acres in a number of isolated areas spread along the shore and inland. Eventually, the Ogden Dunes area in the western portion of the lakeshore will be developed for extensive beach recreation, and trails will crisscross the remainder of the lakeshore. The Indiana Dunes State Park has many facilities, including picnic areas, campground, developed beach, bath house and many trails through dunes and marshes. One of them goes to the top of Mount Tom, at 192 feet the highest of the dunes.

USFS

White-water rapids mark the start of the Middle Fork of the Salmon River's journey through the so-called Impassable Canyon in Idaho. The Salmon was one of the original rivers included in the National Wild and Scenic Rivers System and is almost completely primitive.

Eerie morning mists rise from the mirrorlike waters of the Allagash River in Maine's north woods. Pine, spruce, cedar and fir silhouette their pointy tips against the misty sky in the Northeast's last great wilderness.

NPS, Williams

National Wild and Scenic Rivers

ALLAGASH

CLEARWATER

ELEVEN POINT

FEATHER

RIO GRANDE

ROGUE

ST. CROIX

SALMON

WOLF

From the time of the earliest settlers, America's rivers have been an integral part of our history, serving as avenues of commerce, sources of municipal water, and providers of electric power and irrigation for farmlands. They continue to nourish our growth, but these rivers, once also used for recreation, have become increasingly polluted and stripped of their freshness and appeal by all manner of human intrusions.

In an attempt to preserve many tributaries and sections of rivers in an unspoiled condition, a new and different concept of conservation was launched on October 2, 1968, with the passage of the National Wild and Scenic Rivers Act. In this act Congress declared:

> . . . *That certain selected rivers of the Nation which, with their immediate environments, possess outstandingly remarkable scenic, recreational, geologic, fish and wildlife, historic, cultural or other similar values, shall be preserved in free-flowing condition, and that they and their immediate environments shall be protected for the benefit and enjoyment of present and future generations.*

Rivers in the system are classified as wild, scenic or recreational and are administered by various governmental bureaus. It is contemplated that many other rivers will be added to this new system of parklands in the years ahead.

Allagash (Maine)

The most recent river to be included in the system is the Allagash in northern Maine, called the Allagash Wilderness Waterway. The Allagash flows in many changing moods through the Northeast's last great wilderness, a land of forests, mountains, lakes and abundant wildlife. Here the pine, spruce, cedar, balsam fir, birch and beech tower over the smaller plant life, giving protection to moose, deer, black bear, grouse, bobcat, beaver, fox and mink, as well as the rare fisher. It is a region of great beauty, and at the same time a land of excellent recreational opportunities -- superb trout fishing and unmatched canoeing. Administered by the State of Maine, it is wildness in every sense of the word; its waters deep, clear and cold and its air scented with evergreens -- a worthy addition as a wild and scenic river.

Clearwater (Idaho)

The sparkling waters of the Middle Fork of the Clearwater River in northern Idaho and its tributaries, the Selway and Lochsa rivers, are within the Clearwater, Bitterroot and Nezperce national forests and under the management of the U. S. Forest Service. Running westward from the Bitterroot Mountains to the town of Kooskia, the rivers are the most accessible of any in the system. The Lewis and Clark Highway parallels the Middle Fork of the Clearwater and the Lochsa rivers, and another road follows the lower Selway River, but the upper Selway is still quite primitive.

Cutting through heavily forested and partly barren mountains, the rivers alternate from swift rapids to smooth, slow-flowing currents, providing variety for the canoeist or rubber-raft floater. Elk, moose and otters may frequently be observed near the Lewis and Clark Highway, and the Rocky Mountain goat is a common sight in the Black Canyon area. Despite their name, these white, shaggy creatures are not goats, but a relative of the pronghorn antelope. They are more surefooted on the rocky slopes and ledges than any other large North American mammal because of the soft pads in their hooves which give them greater traction. Kids are subject to capture by predators if they wander away from their parents. Adult goats are not likely to be attacked, although eagles have been known to swoop down on them. The goat's curved horns are sharp and can easily kill or injure an unknowing predator. Chinook salmon and steelhead can be found in the clear waters, and a limited number of campgrounds and picnic sites are available along the rivers, with more facilities planned.

Eleven Point (Missouri)

The Eleven Point River meanders without hurry or concern through the picturesque Ozark hills of southern Missouri east of Thomasville, its course cut in the shadows of steep bluffs, through forested sloping valleys and low-lying pasturelands. Springs gushing from the rocky cliffs and rushing up from underground reservoirs provide a continuous source of crystal-clean water. Varying stretches of rapids and clear pools wind beneath shading hardwoods of birch, oak, hickory and sycamore. Intermittently the trees lean far over the river, forming a green canopy, and deep recesses in the surrounding hills contain caves large enough to bring out the spelunker in any visitor, although dangers exist for the visitor untrained in cave exploration. Foxes, raccoons, beavers, muskrats, turtles and water snakes are common near the waters, as are wild turkeys, great blue herons and bobwhite quail. The Eleven Point is within the Mark Twain National Forest and is primarily a float river. Three float camps, or primitive campgrounds accessible only by river or trails, have been built and more are planned. The Eleven Point is a river where man can forget his machines and contemplate the goodness of the earth.

Feather (California)

North of Lake Tahoe in the Sierra Nevada of California is the Middle Fork of the Feather River. From its source at the mouth of Little Last Chance Creek, 108 miles downstream to Lake Oroville, the Middle Fork of the Feather winds its free-flowing waters through Plumas National Forest, with its steep-walled canyons and forested mountains. Different parts of the river are wild, scenic and recreational, the latter sections containing a number of visitor facilities. Although canoeing and raft floating are possible in the calmer upper

Among stately evergreens east of Kooskia, Idaho, the Middle Fork of the Clearwater winds its blue waters, rippled white from underwater rocks.

Roberts

reaches of the river, extended boating is impossible through the lower portions because of churning rapids and many boulders where the water knifes through Bald Rock Canyon. Large numbers of rainbow and brown trout are found in the more inaccessible portions of the river area, and bass, catfish and some trout exist in lesser amounts upstream from Portola. Parts of the river area are key winter ranges for deer which summer at the high elevations of the Sierra Nevada. Evidences of early mining, such as old shacks, can be observed in the wild river sections.

Rio Grande (New Mexico)

From a distance you cannot see the deep, rugged gorge in the barren flats of north-central New Mexico, but it is there, carved by the waters of one of America's famous rivers, the Rio Grande. Deep, tortuous and twisting, the gorge with its carving force, the Rio Grande, and four miles of its tributary, the Red River, are now protected under the administration of the Bureau of Land Management from dams and development. Raft trips down segments of the forty-eight-mile wild river stretch of the Rio Grande are popular. Some reaches are dangerous, with many rapids and boulders, some as large as houses, while other sections are easy and placid. Eagles, owls and countless other birds nest on the cliffsides; muskrats, deer and coyotes roam the banks and rims; and trout swim in the pools.

Most of the river is totally wild, but primitive facilities have been established at Big Arsenic Springs and in some other sections. The lower parts of the river are the roughest and wildest and the only rim bridge along

USFS

Signs along the Lewis and Clark Highway in Idaho
point out sites where mountain goats (opposite, below)
may often be seen. The road parallels the Lochsa River,
part of the Middle Fork of the Clearwater River
and the most accessible of the system's waterways.
Wisconsin's Wolf River (left) beckons canoeists to
explore its rocky waters. In Oregon the Rogue River
cuts through narrow and rough Mule Creek Canyon
(below), one of the scenic wonders of the rivers
system. Two visitors in a kayak (bottom, left) tackle
one of the white-water rapids of the Eleven Point
River in the famous Ozarks of southern Missouri.

USFS, Muir

USFS

USFS

the entire length of the wild river area is the Rio Grande Gorge Bridge connecting Taos with Tres Piedras. This is wild, rocky, high-plains country and there is no other river like the Rio Grande in the wild and scenic river system.

Rogue (Oregon)

Although it starts in the high Cascades near Crater Lake, southwestern Oregon's Rogue River does not complete its course until it cuts through the coastal range to the Pacific Ocean. Here it varies from quiet smoothness to rushing, gurgling rapids, swirling over boulders and racing through narrow rock canyons. Managed by both the Bureau of Land Management and the U. S. Forest Service (the western half is in Siskiyou National Forest), the Rogue River area runs from just west of Grant's Pass to eleven miles short of its ocean mouth. Douglas fir is the dominant tree, and in some places along the river unbroken stands of fir reach several miles to the ridgetops. Side streams are lined with such flowering plants as azalea, rhododendron, Pacific dogwood and Oregon grape. Deer, elk and bears are the most commonly seen large mammals. A large variety of birds make the river area their home, and salmon and steelhead trout use the Rogue as a "fish highway" to travel upstream and spawn. Besides floating down the waters, an excellent way to see this primeval wilderness is to hike the moderately graded Rogue River Trail, which follows the river from Grave Creek to Ilahe, a distance of forty miles. Several primitive campgrounds and private lodges can be found in the river area.

St. Croix (Minnesota-Wisconsin)

Vast stretches of water, boiling up at times into white rapids, cut through the dense northwoods of Wisconsin and Minnesota. This is St. Croix River and its tributary, the Namekagon -- two beautiful, unpolluted waterways which are the essence of the upper Great Lakes country. Administered by the National Park Service, the St. Croix and Namekagon river areas run from the headwaters in Wisconsin downstream to St. Croix Falls. Conifer, birch, sugar maple, oak, aspen and basswood provide cover for numerous deer, waterfowl and game birds, as well as eagles and occasional moose and bear. The trout, muskellunge and smallmouth bass give fishermen many thrills, and the rivers are famous for their excellent canoeing and boating. Interstate Park at the river area's south terminus (the Wisconsin portion of the park is a unit of Ice Age National Scientific Reserve) and many other state parks and preserves lying along the rivers have a number of facilities for visitors, but the sections between them are wild and breathtaking.

Salmon (Idaho)

Snaking its way through central Idaho north of Stanley is the Middle Fork of the Salmon River. This mighty stream flows through one of the deepest gorges in North America, called the "Impassable Canyon" by one early explorer. Born at the confluence of the Marsh and Bear Valley creeks, the Middle Fork runs 106 miles northeast to join the main Salmon. Placid, emerald-colored pools alternate with swift currents and dazzling white water. Managed by the forest service, the river lies within Boise, Challis, Payette and Salmon national forests. Near the headwaters to the south, Douglas fir, lodgepole pine and Engelmann spruce form a forest canopy broken in places by lush meadows. Further north the Ponderosa pine replaces the fir, and the steep slopes of the gorge support mountain mahogany and other shrubs. Elk, bighorn sheep, black bears, mountain goats and deer are some of the wild species living in the river area; salmon and trout are the major fishing attractions. Float trips, though hazardous, are increasing in popularity. All but a small section of the Middle Fork has been classified as wild for reasons obvious to those who have seen this rugged country.

Wolf (Wisconsin)

The Wolf River, running through the famed lakes country of northern Wisconsin northwest of Green Bay, is nationally famous for its white-water boating stretches, its excellent fishing and its spectacular timbered shores of northern hardwoods and conifers. Extending from Keshena north through Menominee County, owned and managed by the Menominee Indians, the Wolf has long been recommended for Federal protection from industrial interests, and with its inclusion in the wild and scenic rivers system this protection is guaranteed. To be managed by the National Park Service with the cooperation of state and local officials,

USFS

A pine tree stands over the splashing white rapids of the Middle Fork of the Feather River (left) in northern California as it flows around the steep slopes and forested mountains of Bald Rock Canyon on its way to Lake Oroville.

Kline

the river remains completely wild and free with only occasional facilities along its banks. On both sides of the river are tall evergreens, the largest concentration of such stands in the state. The Wolf has many interesting scenic spots with names to suit, such as Big Eddy Falls, Spirit Rock, Pine Row, Tea Kettle Rapids, Otter Slide, Shotgun Eddy, and perhaps the most unusual name of all, Gilmores Mistake. One likely story behind this latter name concerns a local logger named Gilmore who at the turn of the century was hired to float some logs down the river to the cutting mills at Oshkosh. The logs jammed up at this point in the Wolf, and using dynamite, Gilmore blasted some rocks out of the water to free the logs. To his chagrin he discovered he had blasted the wrong rocks. His pride was saved, however, when the logs eventually drifted free anyway and continued their trip downstream.

These are only the first nine of America's rapidly disappearing waterways that have been included in this unique system. Among others under consideration for inclusion are portions of the Allegheny in Pennsylvania, the Maumee in Ohio and Indiana, the Upper Iowa in northeast Iowa, the Suwanee in Georgia and Florida and the Skagit in Washington's Cascade Range.

President Richard M. Nixon has said, "We need rivers for commerce and trade; but we also need clean rivers to fish in and sit by." The National Wild and Scenic Rivers System is a step forward to preserve our waterways for just this purpose.

Above: Rubber rafts make their way beneath the Rio Grande Gorge Bridge connecting Taos and Tres Piedras in northern New Mexico. The bridge is the only cliff-to-cliff structure crossing the Rio Grande on the entire length of the wild and scenic river area.

207

A lone canoeist, wrapped warm against the winter cold, glides silently beneath barren branches on the Current River. This area's unpolluted rivers were the first to be specifically preserved for their own merit.

Ozark

National Scenic Riverways

Missouri

This is a place of quiet relaxation and gentle beauty: just two swift-flowing Ozark streams which are undammed, unspoiled and unpolluted.

Ozark National Scenic Riverways protects the Current River, its tributary, Jacks Fork, and their riverbanks as they meander through a portion of the Ozark foothills in southeastern Missouri. These were the first rivers in the country to be specifically preserved as part of the National Park System as scenic rivers. Included within the boundaries are large, natural springs, riverfront caves, limestone bluffs and a great variety of flora and fauna.

The Ozarks are among the oldest mountains in the country. Uplifted and then eroded by wind, water and frost, little remains of their once-spectacular heights. Water, turned into carbonic acid as it seeped into the ground ages ago, dissolved the limestone overlaying the basic granite and formed a honeycombed series of underground caverns. Some of the cave roofs have collapsed, causing sinkholes, a striking example of which is the Sunkland along the upper portions of the Current River, a great hollow several hundred feet across and nearly a mile long produced by the successive fall-in of several interconnected underground chambers.

The caves that have not collapsed are expansive and numerous; domes, stalactites, stalagmites and columns of every conceivable form and color can be found here. Jam-Up Cave, on the banks of the western portion of Jacks Fork and accessible only by river, is the largest of the caverns with six thousand feet of passageways.

In many areas here, groundwater drips into the caverns, collects and circulates through the underground conduits and emerges as springs. At Big Springs, one of the largest single-outlet springs in the country with a maximum flow of 840 million gallons a day, the water rushes with great force from the underwater base of a cliff to the surface, then flows into the Current River several hundred feet downstream.

The streams themselves are strong and transparent, varying in color from sapphire blue to many shades of green, according to depth and the hour of the day. Quiet waters alternate with chutes or rapids as the streams flow through green forests and under rocky bluffs.

A variety of 1,500 plants are found along the riverways. Most of the upland forest is a combination of oak and hickory, but shortleaf pine, maple, sycamore, sassafras, blackgum and birch also grow here. During spring, dogwood, redbud, rose azalea and bush hydran-

Built in 1893, Red Mill on Alley Spring, Jacks Fork, is now used as a demonstration mill and information center.

gea bring forth their blossoms, and gay wildflowers tinge forest floors and limestone bluffs with color.

The wildlife along the riverways nearly disappeared because of early hunting and lumbering, but in the last thirty years deer, beaver, bobcat, opossum, skunk, mink, fox, muskrat and wild turkey have begun to return. One species, however, the rare red wolf, may have left the area permanently. This is unfortunate, for the red wolf is so rare that it does not live in any other unit of the park system.

About two hundred species of birds have been seen in the riverways, even an occasional great blue heron and osprey. The Current and Jacks Fork rivers are among the best smallmouth bass streams in Missouri, and there are ninety-two other species of fish in the rivers, from brilliantly colored darters to largemouth bass.

Indians roamed this area for thousands of years, leaving behind arrowheads and mounds where they buried their dead. French trappers later named one of the rivers in the area *la riviere courante,* "The Running River." During America's westward expansion the

mountains were largely bypassed, but in the 1830's settlers from the hills of Tennessee and Kentucky moved into the Ozarks. Their wants were simple and the Civil War hardly touched their region.

Lumbering in the late 1800's proved the need for a boat suited to the needs of the Ozark rivers, and a long boat with square, upturned ends and a flat bottom was developed. Called the john-boat, it is still used today.

Ozark National Scenic Riverways was authorized by Congress in 1964. It was a pioneering concept for conservation which led to the enactment in 1968 of the Wild and Scenic Rivers Act (see previous chapter). Ozark contains 113 square miles along 140 miles of free-flowing streams. Many public and privately operated campgrounds and picnic grounds are within the riverways' boundaries. A visitor center is located at Powder Mill in the center of the riverways. Canoes and john-boats may be rented at six places within the boundaries and in nearby towns. Love the pure waters of these hills -- and keep them that way for others who follow.

Padre Island

Texas

Along the Texas Gulf Coast is the longest uninterrupted stretch of primitive, warm-weather beach land in the continental United States. For those who are fascinated by vast expanses of unspoiled shoreline, by a feeling that places where the oceans and land meet have a special message for man -- Padre Island will always be memorable.

Over a hundred miles long, Padre is a splendid example of a barrier island formed by lateral currents and waves depositing billions of shell fish, the remains of other animals and eroded sediment from mainland Texas. Finally, about five thousand years ago, the island edged above the surface, the winds began building dunes, and vegetation began to establish a tenuous foothold with plants that are resistant to the scouring effect of wind-blown sand. They must grow faster than the sand can pile up around them or survive periods of inundation beneath this shifting surface, and they must resist the periodic washing by saltwater. The resultant vegetation -- including the picturesque, nodding sea oats and the purple-flowered railroad vine (beach morning glory) that stretches its runner for more than twenty-five feet over the sands -- are what binds these dunes and protects them against the strong winds and heavy seas of the Gulf, permitting the dunes to grow.

Padre, like all such barrier islands, is a living and dying piece of earth. In the natural sequence of events, this island will be pushed, during tens of thousands of years, by wind and waves toward the mainland, gradually becoming part of it -- just as another new barrier island may begin to form slowly somewhere offshore. For inevitably the time comes for every dune to become mobile when hurricane winds and tides break through and start moving it toward the mainland again. But the life cycle of Padre has been accelerated because of man. Regrettably, cattle grazing, dune buggies and motorcycles, by destroying vegetation, have contributed to the island's westward movement so that today in some locations Laguna Madre, the shallow body of water between the island and the mainland, is filling in at the rate of fifty feet per year.

Padre Island was discovered in 1519 by a Spanish fleet under Alfonso Alvarez de Piñeda when it was inhabited by the cannibilistic Karankawa Indians. First named *Las Islas Blancas* ("The White Islands"), because of its immense stretches of white rolling sands, like other barrier islands, it became known as a graveyard for ships. Probably the worst of naval disasters occurred here in 1553 when thirteen ships of a Spanish fleet were forced by a violent hurricane onto the sand bar known as Devil's Elbow. About three hundred persons survived the storms but only two of these escaped the animosity of the Indians.

The island acquired its present name shortly after 1800 when Padre Nicholas Balli and his nephew received a Spanish land grant that included the island. Their operations continued for about thirty years. John Singer, brother to sewing machine inventor Isaac Singer, was shipwrecked on the island and ranched on it for fourteen years. Patrick Dunn began ranching here in 1879 and his operation lasted until 1971 when most of the cattle were removed because grasslands had become depleted by overgrazing. Ruins of some of the buildings of the Dunn Ranch line camps can still be seen within the boundaries of the national seashore which was authorized in 1962 and dedicated by Mrs. Lyndon B. Johnson six years later.

The seashore includes 80.5 miles in the central portion of the island, with the northern and southern ends occupied by private land and county parks. Motels and restaurants nearest to the seashore are located in these areas. Camping is permitted along the Gulf beach but

A stretch of diamondlike sand sparkles in the morning sun on Padre Island, a barrier island off the tip of Texas in the Gulf of Mexico. The national seashore section of the island is an 80.5 mile expanse of unspoiled beaches.

there are no conveniences. Causeways at both ends provide vehicular access to the narrow island, which ranges in width from a few hundred yards to about three miles. Along the Gulf is a gently sloping beach of sand and, in places, broken shell that is ideal for swimming, surf fishing and other kinds of recreation. Next, paralleling the shore, is an alignment of dunes in various stages of stabilization that sometimes reach a height of forty feet. Behind these are smaller dunes and a few salt marshes and ponds and, finally, mud flats that merge into the waters of Laguna Madre.

Sport fishermen may go after a range of highly prized species -- weakfish, channel bass, croaker, redfish, red snapper, drum, pompano, sheepshead and shark. Occasionally porpoises can be seen leaping near the shore. Birds are plentiful, with 250 species having been recorded on small islands along the Intercoastal Waterway near Padre, including a dozen kinds of gulls and terns. The only white pelican rookery along the Gulf Coast or East Coast is located on a small island in Laguna Madre, but brown pelicans have become quite scarce during the past decade due to the effects of DDT. Other nesting birds include the great horned owl, burrowing owl, American avocet, marsh hawk, horned lark, Eastern and Western meadowlarks, bobwhite, black skimmer and several kinds of herons and egrets, including the reddish egret, an endangered species found only in Texas and Florida. Its name derives from its rusty-brown head and neck. Another distinguishing physical characteristic is its flesh-colored, black-tipped bill, but the most intriguing aspect of the reddish egret is the way it feeds in shallows by rapidly dashing about and making sudden turns and lurches, giving the appearance of a creature somewhat out of its head. An abundant variety of ducks, geese and sandhill cranes winter on Padre.

Sizable terrestrial animals are not as plentiful as on the mainland but the black-tailed jackrabbit and

The railroad vine, a kind of beach morning glory, has large purple flowers and runners that may extend 25 feet.

NPS

The Portuguese man-of-war is composed of an iridescent, crescent-shaped air sac that supports a colony of individual polyps whose filaments can reach 60 feet in length, paralyze fish and cause pain to humans who come in contact with their nettle cells.

coyote are commonly seen and occasionally white-tailed deer and javelina (collared peccary) swim over to the island from the mainland. However, most of Padre's animal population consists of small rodents, such as spotted ground squirrels, kangaroo rats and pocket gophers, and larger mammals such as raccoons, opossums and badgers.

Among the reptiles are turtles, lizards and a dozen different kinds of snakes, including the secretive and seldom-seen Western diamondback rattler and the curious hognose snake that is quite harmless though it hisses loudly, spreads a cobra-like hood and sometimes plays dead. At night scavenger ghost crabs dart back and forth in such numbers that they are almost impossible to avoid.

Padre Island's desolate, windswept beauty and its abundant marine and shore wildlife make it one of the most unusual and inviting national seashores. It has a spaciousness and wildness that will always distinguish it as an unforgettable pleasuring ground in America.

Pictured Rocks

National Lakeshore

Michigan

From the waters of Lake Superior, the largest fresh-water lake in the world, the afternoon sun brings out the deep colors of the rocky cliffs -- the reds, greens, browns and purples -- and the various shapes of the rocks are accentuated by long shadows. Inland the sun sparkles on the lakes and cascading streams, and the maples and birches ruffle in the breeze. The scent of pine drifts down the hillsides and, far away, a coyote howls. It is not hard to imagine a young Indian brave named Hiawatha paddling his birch-bark canoe on these lake waters. For this is the land of the Gitche-Gumee, the shining Big-Sea-Water, and nearby is the wigwam of Nokomis, who raised Hiawatha. It was at his wedding feast that Pau-Puk-Keemis danced on the beach and kicked up the sands that are called the Grand Sable Dunes.

Although Longfellow's epic poem is fiction, much of his setting was based upon the Pictured Rocks area of Michigan's Upper Peninsula. The Chippewa Indians resided here for many years, and French explorers and missionaries, including Pierre Radisson and Father Marquette, knew the area well.

The main single attraction are the Pictured Rocks themselves, fifteen miles of multicolored sandstone cliffs rising abruptly from the lake as much as two hundred feet. In the never-ending struggle against erosion, these rocks are fighting a losing battle, for the waves, rain and frost have carved arches, columns, promontories and thunder caves out of the cliffs. Ground-water, seeping to various sandstone levels and collecting minerals and chemicals on the way, drips down the sides of the eroded sculptures, depositing the staining chemicals. The names describe the formations: Miners Castle, Chapel Rock, Lovers Leap, Rainbow Cave and the Battleships. In the early 1900's Grand Portal, a magnificent series of several honeycombed arches jutting six hundred feet into the lake, collapsed, leaving lesser arches, amphitheaters and debris.

Just east of the Pictured Rocks along the shoreline are twelve miles of bluffs neither as steep nor as high and interspersed with many sand and pebble beaches.

Further east are the Grand Sable Banks and Dunes rising 350 feet above the lake. They were formed during the last stages of the Pleistocene Ice Age as sand and glacial silt were dropped to the bottom of an ancient lake made by the receding glaciers. A slight upthrust of the sandstone base pushed the sand several hundred feet up, and winds shaped it into dunes which are still active and moving inland toward the forests and streams.

Inland are many lakes, the most picturesque of which are Chapel and Beaver lakes. Streams connect them with Lake Superior, and along the Pictured Rocks shoreline, the water cascades over the palisades in spectacular fashion. Waterfalls are also numerous in the interior -- Munising Falls south of the Pictured Rocks drops fifty feet into a large natural amphitheater, and visitors can walk into a cavity behind the falls without getting wet.

A huge lumbering industry in the latter nineteenth century nearly exterminated the pine trees, but today the Pictured Rocks region has extensive second-growth forests, mostly mixed northern hardwoods of sugar and red maple, beech, birch and hemlock. There is one almost pure stand of beautiful white birch in the center beach area. A feeling of the "northwoods" is perpetuated with the addition of some quaking aspen, pine and mountain ash. In the bog areas are found white spruce, balsam fir, tamarack and arbor vitae. In spring yellow violets, trillium, Dutchman's breeches and orchids cover the forest floor and bogs, and in autumn the blueberry joins the trees in a spectacular array of color.

White-tailed deer are a common sight along the dirt roads, and black bear may occasionally be seen. Other mammals found here are the coyote, otter, fox, bobcat, muskrat, mink, porcupine, beaver and snowshoe hare, and the moose, lynx and wolf are sometimes present in small numbers. Game birds, such as grouse and woodcock, are plentiful, and a great variety of water and shorebirds -- bald eagles, ravens, herring gulls, and migratory Canada geese and loons -- may be observed.

In winter this area receives over one hundred inches of snow, an amount exceeded in the Upper Peninsula

Autumnal colors grace the white bark of a birch stand (left) in Pictured Rocks lakeshore on Michigan's Upper Peninsula. The lakeshore is the fictional home of Longfellow's Hiawatha and is an excellent example of northern Great Lakes woods.

Below: A wave crashes into Chapel Rock, clearly demonstrating how Lake Superior's waters were able to carve these magnificent Pictured Rocks. Many of the spectacular sandstone features can be seen only by private boats or on cruise tours.

only in the Huron Mountains one hundred miles west. Yet in comparison to the surrounding regions it remains fairly warm because of Lake Superior.

Pictured Rocks National Lakeshore, approved by Congress in 1966, protects thirty-five miles of Lake Superior shoreline from Grand Marais to Munising. It also includes many thousands of acres of forested slopes and inland waters. Some of the lakeshore is still privately owned, but there are dirt roads and trails to some of the scenic spots, and three primitive campgrounds. Developed campgrounds are located in nearby Hiawatha National Forest and Grand Sable State Forest. The best way to see the Pictured Rocks is from the lake, and tours are available in Munising during the summer. Future developments will include a scenic drive atop the lake cliffs and dunes, camp and picnic grounds and a beach, although Lake Superior waters are too chilly for any but the most hardy.

The fabled days of Hiawatha live on only in folklore, but the wilderness that he might have known remains essentially the same, preserved for all who want to enjoy the untamed beauty of the northern Great Lakes.

Point Reyes

California

Wind, waves and fog are the three elements which dominate the coast of the Point Reyes peninsula. The gusts, picking up force across thousands of miles of the Pacific Ocean, constantly lash this point of land jutting from the California shore. The winds push the water into powerful waves which batter the coast with spectacular force, creating tall, craggy palisades and smooth, sandy beaches. The monstrous breakers, whose wind-swept spray sometimes reaches a height of one hundred feet, are usually covered with a heavy sheet of fog stretching up to fifty miles out to sea.

The fog, which sometimes blocks out the sun for three or four weeks at a time, gives Point Reyes what may be the lowest midsummer temperature in the United States. During winter and spring, the fog is less common, and from the cliffs ships may be seen steaming toward San Francisco Bay, thirty-five miles south.

Inland on the peninsula both the terrain and the climate are different from the shore's. Sand dunes and rolling grassy hills enclose quiet lagoons, esteros and saltwater marshes; sharp ridges covered with evergreen forests surround freshwater lakes. The strong winds on the coast have become gentle breezes here, and due to the lack of fog, the temperatures are much higher. While residents of the hot, sun-baked San Joaquin Valley in central California enjoy the cool coast, visitors from the foggy San Francisco peninsula welcome the sunshine of the inland areas.

Point Reyes' only contact with the mainland is directly over the San Andreas Fault between Bolinas Bay on the south and Tomales Bay on the north. The fault, running northwest to southeast, is responsible not only for the long, thin bays, but also for the striking Inverness Ridge which parallels the fault on the peninsula. For the last eighty million years the peninsula has been moving slowly north along this fault, with an average rate of movement of about two inches a year. During the last recorded movement, the devastating San Francisco earthquake of 1906, however, the peninsula was shoved twenty feet out of line at Tomales Bay.

Because of this gradual movement, the rocks on the peninsula west of the fault are totally different in age and variety from those opposite, east of the fault on the mainland. The peninsula's rock is similar to that found

In Drakes Bay (below), Sir Francis Drake is alleged to have stopped in 1579 to repair his ship. This harbor of Point Reyes seashore is partly protected from the Pacific Ocean but is often shrouded in fog and wind-swept spray. Right: Inland, the peninsula is sunny and surprisingly calm.

Hyde

Surf fishing has become popular along the misty shores of Point Reyes' beaches.

many miles south near Bakersfield, California. Point Reyes is thus an isolated geological unit, and its conservationist friends now call it an "island in time."

The human history of this area is no less interesting. Coast Miwok Indians lived here in relatively large numbers for centuries, depending on the sea for food. Sir Francis Drake is thought to have repaired his ship, the *Golden Hinde*, at Drakes Bay in 1579 while on his voyage around the world. Drakes Bay is a partly protected harbor formed by the point's turning south. His men couldn't understand why this land at the thirty-eighth parallel, the same latitude as the Mediterranean, was cold in midsummer. Notes taken by Drake's chaplain, Francis Fletcher, mention "...thicke mists and most stynkinge fogges. Neither could we at any time, in whole fourteene days together, find the aire so cleare as to be able to take the height of sunne or starre."

Then the ship entered "a faire and good Baye, with a good wind to enter same." Seeing the Indians on top of the palisades, which reminded him of the chalk cliffs at Dover on the English Channel, Drake ordered a small fort to be built, but it was unnecessary, for the Miwoks were very friendly. While the ship was being repaired, Drake explored and found "hordes of Deere by 1,000 in a company, being large and fat of body." He called the land Nova Albion, claiming it for his Queen, Elizabeth I, and he "set up a monument of our being there . . . namely, a plate, nailed upon a greate and firme post, whereupon was engraven her Majesty's name . . . together with her Highness's picture and arms in a piece of sixpence current money."

This plate was found in 1936 near San Quentin, a few miles east of the coast on San Francisco Bay. But a San Franciscan resident claimed he first discovered it at Drakes Bay some years earlier, and, not knowing of its possible value, threw it away at San Quentin. Drakes Bay remains the spot where the *Golden Hinde* most likely anchored. Someday shifting sands may expose part of the fort which Drake built and give ample proof of his anchorage, which would make Point Reyes the site of an English landing that pre-dated the Pilgrims' landing at Plymouth by forty-one years!

In 1595 a Spanish ship, the *San Agustín*, loaded with treasures from the Orient, was blown ashore and wrecked near the mouth of Drakes Estero in Drakes Bay. Her captain, Sebastian Cermeño, decided not to take the treasure of Ming porcelain china with him when he returned to the Spanish outposts in Mexico. The Indians made good use of this china, for much of it has been unearthed at their village sites. Another Spanish expedition, led by Sebastian Vizcaino, stopped at Point Reyes in 1602 and gave the peninsula its present name, *Puerto de los Reyes*, "Port of the Kings." Later Spanish efforts to establish a permanent settlement here led to the discovery of San Francisco Bay in 1769. The bay quickly overshadowed Point Reyes as a settlement area and saved it from becoming commercialized. During the nineteenth century the peninsula was familiar to traders and whalers.

Point Reyes is a merging point of northern and southern California plant life. Stands of Douglas fir, normally found much farther north, are prevalent on the east slope of Inverness Ridge, while forests of Bishop pine, common in southern California, inhabit the northern part of the ridge. A stand of coast redwoods, fairly common in patches as far south as Monterey, adds variety to Point Reyes' landscape. On the brushy slopes near the bottom of Inverness Ridge are coast live oaks and California laurels. Much of the lowlands are covered with tall grass which is used for extensive cattle grazing. It is thought that these grasslands were originally covered with brush, which early cattle and dairy farmers cut down and planted over with grass.

Wildflowers bloom everywhere on the peninsula from February to July. Some of them, notably a species of lupine, a blue or yellow flower often tinged with lavender, are exclusive to the area. Two kinds of manzanita grow only here and on Mount Tamalpais, twenty miles southeast.

Because of the varied climate and flora, wildlife is also diversified, ranging from shorebirds to mammals found in the dense forests. Point Reyes has 338 species of birds and 72 species of mammals, including black-tailed deer, raccoons, foxes and rabbits. Herds of California sea lions thrive along the rocky coasts beneath the white palisades, sharing the area with large colonies of seabirds which congregate on the offshore rocks. A few colonies of aplodontia, or "mountain beaver," have managed to survive here in the thickets and brush of the lower ridges. This seldom seen animal is not a true beaver, but a rather cute rodent, thirteen to eighteen inches in length, which exists in small numbers along the north Pacific coast. The aplodontia has sharp claws, which it uses for burrowing, and a tail so small that it is not even visible. Preferring moist soil near marshes and forests, it is strictly nocturnal and is hunted by many predators.

President Kennedy signed the bill establishing Point Reyes National Seashore in 1962. It contains about 64,-000 acres, including tidelands and offshore waters up to one-quarter mile. Much of the land within the boundaries, however, is still privately owned and private property rights must be observed. A road leads from the headquarters, near Olema, where evidence of the San Andreas Fault may be seen, to the lighthouse at the tip of the point, which is not open to visitors. Various side roads lead to many beaches and Tomales Bay State Park, but only Drakes Beach with its visitor center is open for water sports. The Pacific beaches are a beachcomber's paradise and surf fishing is also popular.

There are nearly sixty miles of trails in the Bear Valley area which climb up and down the forested ridges and hug the coast. There are three developed "hike-in" campgrounds in Bear Valley, and numerous pocket beaches along Drakes Bay can be reached by the trails. Privately operated campgrounds and other accommodations may be found on the mainland, as well as public campgrounds in nearby Samuel P. Taylor and Mount Tamalpais State Parks.

Although the forests and open pastoral spaces convey a sense of tranquility to visitors, the main attractions at Point Reyes are the rough, craggy palisades and the sandy beaches which receive the full brunt of Pacific currents. The huge breakers continually batter this magnificent seascape, seemingly unmindful of the chilling fog which envelopes them. Point Reyes, for all who visit her precincts, is, in truth, an island in time where men and women may recharge "spiritual batteries" weakened by the ardors of civilization.

Sleek and golden, California sea lions populate the beaches along the peninsula. Adapted for almost total life at sea, the cows breed on offshore islands and produce one pup yearly to add to the bulls' noisy and voracious families.

ANCHOR
COMMEMORATING
THE LANDING OF
Francis Drake
AT DRAKE'S BAY JUNE 17,

PRIVATE PROPERTY
**NO
TRESPASSING**
FOR ANY REASON

Left: An anchor commemorates Drake's stay in this area once controlled by the friendly coastal Miwok Indians. Above: The bottom of Inverness Ridge, which follows the San Andreas Fault on the peninsula side, is covered with brush, ferns and live oaks. Right: Point Reyes' beach reaches out into the misty Pacific.

Hyde

Sleeping Bear Dunes

National Lakeshore

Michigan

A lonely road snakes its way through the wilderness moraines of the lakeshore area. Beech, oak, sugar maple and aspen supply these woods on the east shore of Lake Michigan with an array of color in autumn before shedding their leaves.

According to ancient Chippewa and Ottawa Indian legends, a black bear and her two cubs attempted to swim across Lake Michigan from the Wisconsin side. Nearing the Michigan shore the cubs became tired and lagged behind their mother, who climbed atop a bluff to watch and wait for her offspring. She is still there, the Sleeping Bear, a solitary sand dune covered with dark vegetation. The cubs still lag a few miles offshore, the forested North and South Manitou islands.

In fact, these massive sand dunes, glistening beaches, green forests, blue lakes and gently flowing streams are the result of glacial action. When the last stage of the Pleistocene Ice Age ended, the land was left in a jumble of glacial features. The basis of the Sleeping Bear region is the three-hundred-foot-high Manistee Moraine, which snakes along a few miles inland. Other moraines, called interlobate moraines, extend out from Manistee and are responsible for the various points jutting out into the lake. Erosion and lake deposits then worked on the shores, creating the beaches.

However, at Sleeping Bear Point the erosion carved steep bluffs some four hundred feet high. Continual battering of the eroded material by wind and waves formed sand particles which were blown up over the tops of the cliffs. At this point a decrease in wind caused them to drop and gradually cover the bluffs. Thus the Sleeping Bear Dunes differ from the Indiana Dunes three hundred miles south because they are not pure dunes, but covered cliffs.

Blowouts, breaks in the sand ridges where the sand has been blown away, are also present here. Many of the older dunes have been stabilized with vegetation, but the younger dunes, particularly the Sleeping Bear Dune which towers some 450 feet over Lake Michigan, are continuing to move inland, encroaching on the forests and glacial lakes.

Indians lived in the dunes area and on the Manitou Islands for many years, and Father Marquette visited the region during his explorations, preparing the way

Sparse grasses try to gain a foothold in the sand on the Sleeping Bear bluffs. Strong winds will carry the sand farther inland and the dunes will be reshaped.

for trappers and traders. But most of the land was sparsely settled by whites because it was not especially fertile. South Manitou Island has a fine harbor, however, providing protection against storms, and it became a regular stopping point for Great Lakes steamships. A large lumbering industry developed on the mainland, founding the communities of Empire, Glen Arbor and Glen Haven, outside of the lakeshore. Later, summer vacationers from Chicago, Milwaukee and Detroit began building cottages. Heavy industry, however, never took notice of Sleeping Bear, and most of the region remains in a relatively unspoiled state.

Many clear blue lakes, notably Crystal, Platt and Glen lakes, are surrounded by forests of beech and sugar maple. The more sandy areas support pine, oak and aspen. Excellent stands of white cedar exist on the Manitou Islands, and beach grass and cottonwoods grow on the younger dunes of the mainland.

Otter, badger, deer, beaver, bobcat and over two hun-

dred species of birds thrive here, and the two islands support large gull rookeries.

Sleeping Bear Dunes National Lakeshore was authorized in 1970 and contains about 71,000 acres, including sixty-four miles of mainland shoreline and the two offshore islands. Most of the lands are still privately owned, and no facilities have been developed yet within the lakeshore's boundaries. Planned developments include a thirty-mile scenic drive with overlooks, hiking trails, campgrounds, picnic areas, visitor centers and beach activity areas. The Manitou Islands will be kept as a wilderness with only primitive facilities.

From the top of Sleeping Bear Dune, Glen Lake sparkles in the middle of the maples, oaks and pines. The miles of curving white beach disappear in the distance, and to the west, Lake Michigan's horizon is indistinct in the bluish haze. Offshore the islands look like two small humps on the white, choppy waters. The mother bear and her cubs can now sleep on forever.

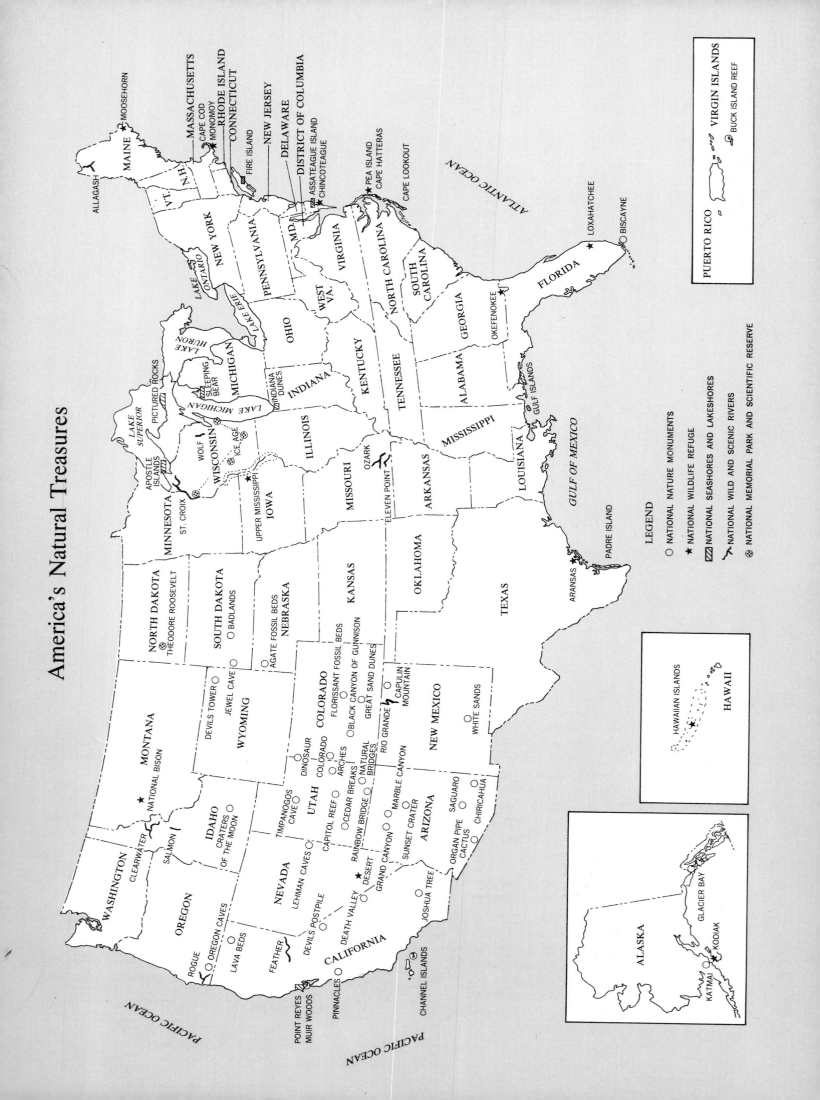

America's Natural Treasures

LEGEND

○ NATIONAL NATURE MONUMENTS
★ NATIONAL WILDLIFE REFUGE
▨ NATIONAL SEASHORES AND LAKESHORES
⋀ NATIONAL WILD AND SCENIC RIVERS
⊗ NATIONAL MEMORIAL PARK AND SCIENTIFIC RESERVE

PUERTO RICO   VIRGIN ISLANDS
⊙ BUCK ISLAND REEF

HAWAIIAN ISLANDS   HAWAII

ALASKA   GLACIER BAY
KATMAI   KODIAK